Lee Kofman is the Israeli- in Hebrew. Her short fiction, creative non-fiction and poetry in English has appeared around the world in *Best Australian Stories*, *Best Australian Essays*, *Griffith Review*, *Heat*, *Westerly*, *Creative Nonfiction* (US), *Brand* (UK) and *Malahat Review* (Canada) among many others. She is the recipient of numerous grants and awards for her writing, including an Australian Council grant and a Varuna Flagship Fellowship. She holds an MA in Creative Writing (University of Melbourne) and a PhD in Social Sciences (RMIT). Lee has been mentoring writers and teaching writing classes for over ten years. She also blogs about the writing process and her blog was a finalist for Best Australian Blogs 2014.

The Dangerous Bride

A Memoir of Love, Gods and Geography

LEE KOFMAN

MELBOURNE UNIVERSITY PRESS
An imprint of Melbourne University Publishing Limited
11–15 Argyle Place South, Carlton, Victoria 3053, Australia
mup-info@unimelb.edu.au
www.mup.com.au

First published 2014
Text © Lee Kofman, 2014
Design and typography © Melbourne University Publishing Limited, 2014

This book is copyright. Apart from any use permitted under the *Copyright Act 1968* and subsequent amendments, no part may be reproduced, stored in a retrieval system or transmitted by any means or process whatsoever without the prior written permission of the publishers.

Every attempt has been made to locate the copyright holders for material quoted in this book. Any person or organisation that may have been overlooked or misattributed may contact the publisher.

Text design and typesetting by Megan Ellis
Cover design by Nada Backovic
Printed in Australia by McPherson's Printing Group

National Library of Australia Cataloguing-in-Publication entry
Kofman, Lee, author.
The dangerous bride/Lee Kofman.

9780522866483 (paperback)
9780522866490 (ebook)

Includes index.
Kofman, Lee.
Kofman, Lee—Relations with men.
Open marriage.
Non-monogamous relationships.
Man–woman relationships.

306.8423

For all desirous people

CONTENTS

Author's note ix

1 A Tale of Wonderland (2005) 1
2 A Tale of *Modus Vivendi* (2007) 17
3 A Tale of Princesses and Charladies 39
4 A Tale of Ménage à Trois 63
5 A Tale of Adultery 89
6 A Tale of Candaulistic Couples 113
7 A Tale of Tragedy 139
8 A Tale of Domesticity, or—
    Who Really Killed Mayakovsky? 159
9 A Tale of Expanded Couples 179
10 A Tale of Pleasure Seekers 211
11 An Asymmetrical Tale 239
12 A Tale of Porous Couples 265

Interlude: InLoveLikeACat 283
Epilogue: A Tale of Elastic Love (2010–2012) 289
Bibliography 303
Acknowledgements 309

AUTHOR'S NOTE

This is a work that comes from my memory and, since any memory is fallible, this is my subjective take on the stories I tell, and has been shaped in retrospect. On several occasions, I've modified the chronology of events to ensure the narrative's flow. Most names, and some other identifying details, have been changed to protect people's privacy. Otherwise, I have tried to tell as truthful a story as I could.

'Of all forms of caution, caution in love is perhaps the most fatal to true happiness.'

Bertrand Russell

1

A Tale of Wonderland (2005)

'The unlived life, of which you can die.'
Rainer Maria Rilke

The night before I married Noah, in the oldest Australian synagogue in Ballarat, I kissed a girl dressed in a nurse's uniform. We were in a fetish club. The place, hidden within St Kilda's grunge, felt unapologetically decadent, unashamedly European, with its low ceilings, and décor featuring deeply cushioned velvet furniture, erotic books, rusty mirrors and paintings of nuns in various stages of undress. It was difficult to tell whether you were in a library-turned-bordello or vice versa. I, who had harboured a librarian and libertine duality, liked this ambiguity.

The girl was a willowy, pretty redhead with serpentine lips; her plastic uniform was dangerously short. Our kiss felt bubbly, but that may have been only the aftertaste of the two glasses of champagne I'd gulped earlier, for courage. For the first time in my three years with Noah, I was trying to live out the dream of love, entailing commitment but also sexual freedom, I'd cherished since adolescence. Right now, though, I wasn't being very successful at it. Our teeth clashed and she quickly pointed out it was *my* fault. I apologised, embarrassed, but tightened my grip on her slender back, again sinking my tongue into her otherness. I longed for the girl: not in a last-unmarried-night way, but as if to assure myself that my marriage was going to be a little wild, that it wouldn't rob me of the dreams of my youth. Paradoxically, the happier I felt with Noah, the more I wished for some debauchery in my life.

Several hours earlier, I'd been spending time with another woman. She was middle-aged, had abundant flesh, and wore a blonde, poodle-curled wig and a cotton dressing gown. Her breath smelled of onions and herring, as it always did during Shabbat, when the brushing of teeth is forbidden. That woman was my mother.

She'd recently spent twenty hours on a plane, stuffing her large, practical handbag with packets of sugar while battling the painful restlessness of her legs, which were embroidered with varicose veins, and her anxiety about transport-related catastrophes. She'd flown to Melbourne all the way from New York, leaving the Orthodox Jewish neighbourhood in Brooklyn to which my parents had moved from Israel, to witness her rebel of a daughter finally doing one thing in her life properly—getting married. Never a woman of leisure, my mother's mission now was to ensure that this proper thing would be done in a manner truly pleasing to God, and particularly that I wouldn't choose, as she said, 'a gay Chinese rabbi with a pierced tongue'.

My mother's activities had quickly taken over Noah's and my life. Our apartment, now strewn with prayer books and Shabbat candles, began to resemble the flat in Ashdod—an Israeli industrial port city situated about forty kilometres from Gaza's rockets—where, as an adolescent, I'd lived with my parents, following our first migration, from Russia. My parents, who once had drunk vodka straight from the bottle and read Chekhov with the same enthusiasm they'd later reserve for the Bible, turned religious when I was seven. I'd never got over that change in them and, at nineteen, fled from God and my parents to Tel Aviv—the city of libraries, cinematheques and parties—and, later, to Melbourne. But God had now chased me to the other side of the earth and, dismayed, I once again—for my mother's sake—pretended to be observing His policies. And, boy, did He stipulate in detail. Everything in our home, be it a glass of water or new clothes, was blessed; Shabbat ceremonies were performed; *mezuzahs* affixed on every doorway. To my added dismay, it soon became apparent that Noah—or 'the man of the house', as my mother took to calling him—was indecently happy in the company of his mother-in-law and her God, even if it meant he had to switch off football broadcasts on Friday nights.

I could understand Noah. He'd been brought up on the fringes of Jewishness, spending his early years in suburban public schools where his ethnic origins carried more weight for his bullies than they did for him. His parents even celebrated Christmas, although they did so by eating *lokshen kugel* and watching *Fiddler on the Roof*. In adulthood, Noah took to traversing the globe for business and for pleasure, courting *shiksas* (non-Jewish women), and becoming more at home with foreign customs than with his own. By the time we first crossed paths, by a winter fire at some party where he offered me a cigarette and I asked him for his phone number, Noah's spirit had already been forged differently from that of many other Australian Jews I'd met in my five years here, who seemed to be moving in a low orbit of their own, engrossed in intense family lives.

Noah was eight years older than me, but he had a palpable youthfulness, with his light step, smooth skin, and the trendy clothes he wore, with their many zips and pockets. He was a businessman who didn't take himself seriously and who, despite the pressures of work, never pretended to have outgrown the child he once was. I was taken with his sense of weightlessness, just as I was taken with his generous mouth, dark curls and wit. I looked at him and saw my future, where life would be our playground. But once we decided to get married, Noah was set on a proper Jewish wedding, with a *huppah* (the bridal canopy) and *hora* dances. I knew this was his chance to belong finally, but since the wedding preparations had begun, and particularly since my mother's arrival, I'd felt frightened of the shape my life was being moulded into. That fear from my childhood of being boxed in returned.

Much of my first eleven years was spent in the wilderness of Soviet hospitals, where people died frequently and openly, and where I, too, occasionally lingered on the verge of death, on account of my heart, which at my birth turned out to be faulty. This had made me come to fear any finality. As an adult,

I experimented with hair colours, fashions and countries. I tried my hand at being a journalist, a matchmaker, a caseworker with Jaffa's Arabs. I studied literature and social work, organised night-club parties and wrote fiction. Beginning anew so often wasn't easy, but I kept craving that feeling when you arrive somewhere foreign—whether cities, faculties or bars—that *everything* hadn't happened yet. I loved peeping through windows, stepping into doorways, shaking hands with strangers, being initiated into routines and politics that belonged to others. I developed a particular shy smile that I used to buy time while deciding which of my selves I'd put into action in each new place. Ironically, I felt particularly whole when I was a newcomer; it was when I felt utterly alive. With new lovers, I sought, alongside erotic titillation, that feeling of aliveness. I was greedy for my unlived life.

Yet, since my mid-twenties, I'd also yearned to wear a ring and use the words *my husband* (while pretending to take these words for granted). Possibly, and as much as I tried not to, I'd absorbed this yearning from my mother, who believed that for a woman to be fully realised, she must be in love. Yet, while my mother was vociferously proud of having found my father, I don't think he ever quelled her loneliness. Her energetic sadness became legendary in our family. 'Poor *Mamochka*,' my brothers and I would say, as she ran around cooking lumpy *kasha*, yelling, kissing us, praying, cleaning the wax out of our ears with her index finger. Perhaps she feared that if she stopped, she'd cease to exist.

I'd always struggled with wanting marriage, worrying that it indicated I was just like my mother; that wherever I went, loneliness laid its carpet under my feet too—even when I was loved. Still, I thought that, as a wife, you could belong to the country of one man. The trick was to find a man to whom I wanted to belong, particularly that he be someone not as aloof as my father. Not long after we met, Noah told me that if a car were about to run me over he'd shield me with his body, and I believed him. I was ready to be *his* wife.

But I didn't think that love, and marriage, had always to be bound with fidelity. This first occurred to me when I was seventeen, and still a virgin. It was 1990. The decade had just begun its electronic, hedonistic party and the spirit reached even Ashdod, which was populated by lifeguards, footballers, drug dealers, beauty queens, yeshiva students and the chronically unemployed, and where tradition oozed through every pavement crack. That year, *Henry & June* made a brief, yet dazzling, appearance at the local cinema, which otherwise specialised in re-runs of *Rambo* movies. That film introduced me to the possibility that a woman could have a husband *and* sexual freedom.

The film, wrapped in notoriety because of its subject matter—a three-way romantic entanglement between the writers Anaïs Nin and Henry Miller, and Miller's wife June—was the first movie in the world to be rated N-17 (between the R and X ratings). Even *Natural Born Killers*, that other controversial feature film of the 1990s, received a 'mere' R. Apparently, the censors considered couples who seduced other people more dangerous to the public than those who killed them. But I was more excited than scared to be seeing *Henry & June*, and took a bus to the cinema, which was tucked away on the main street among lottery kiosks and falafel joints where men with thick gold chains around their sun-darkened necks drank *arak*.

My mouth daubed with overbearingly purple lipstick and wearing oversized glasses, I managed to look old enough to be admitted into the screening or, rather, into the Paris of 1931, where twenty-nine-year-old Anaïs cruised the cobbled streets on the arm of her husband Hugo, the banker. I was immediately taken by Anaïs, who had everything that I could only wish for: a handsome man, silk camisoles, a luxurious home, literary friends. I, too, had writerly ambitions, hoping these would get me through the drudgery of my Ashdod-existence. I had copied a quote from Arthur Rimbaud into my diary:

> The poet makes himself a seer by a long, prodigious and rational disordering of all the senses. Every form of love, suffering, madness … he consumes all the poisons in him …

I was excited by Rimbaud's formula for the disordering of the senses as a fertiliser for creativity, and particularly that it included 'love'. I was unsure, though, how to engage in such disordered love until Anaïs showed me the way.

In the film, she is restless; preoccupied with forging her writing voice, and her new friends, the Millers—poor, seedy expatriates from Brooklyn. I understood her longings viscerally. I knew what she was feeling as we both watched June, the Galician-Jewish adventuress played by the stunning Uma Thurman, appear for the first time in both our lives, enveloped in a flimsy black frock, shadows hovering above her blonde splendour. Thurman's June is all voracious mouth, bare shoulders, jolly sadness. She is the June I'd later read about in accounts by her contemporaries and biographers. 'She wears the mask of death and her ghastly beauty makes them stare … When she talks to you, the ground slips under your feet,' is how the gossip columnist Wambly Bald described June when she arrived in Paris. He wasn't exaggerating. Even Picasso felt the ground shift at the sight of June, while a less-resilient admirer killed himself over her. June's charm was tough, made of black lipstick, plucked eyebrows and stained gowns slit up the side. She liked opium, gangsters, obscenity. 'I've done dangerous things, but I've done them superbly,' June tells Anaïs and, for a lingering moment, her vampire-sharp face fills the screen, delivering all the peril needed to set me on fire. Like Anaïs, I wanted to follow June, to cling to her. She was a disordering of the senses par excellence. But she was too unhinged to become my role model. Instead, she was the *objet d'art* Anaïs and I longed to create. We wanted to clasp the poison-consumers—to live and write outrageously through them.

On the screen, the tension was escalating. At a basement bar, the saxophone groaned, loosening my nervous system; a ravishing close-up showed Anaïs's feline eyes, smeared with green eye shadow, while June's crimson lips whispered into her ear: 'Take care of Henry for me. I'll be leaving in the morning.' The women kissed deeply and I clutched feverishly at the velvet rucksack I'd bought in Tel Aviv. Somehow, it all came together in that scene: the soirees abundant with cognac and clever conversation; the as-yet-unpublished masterpieces; the unorthodox romantic arrangements. The film, in line with Rimbaud, suggested that disordered love made you a better artist. And turned your life into a moveable feast. Yet, not just any type of disordered love would do for me, I decided. June, a failed actress, didn't seem happy as she moved restlessly between Henry and her other lovers. Anaïs's version of love seemed way preferable to June's, and definitely to that of my mother. Hers was a domesticated disorder—Anaïs had June to fondle and write about, and Henry to fuck. But in the end, she'd always retreat to Hugo, who was her beloved rock, waiting for her in their comfortable home. Such an existence never left you wanting. I walked, breathless, out of the cinema, into Ashdod's soundtrack of car horns and police sirens, convinced I'd found a pathway out of my life.

For the three days before our wedding, and in accordance with God's manual, Noah was banished from our home to his parents', to enhance the joy of our later reunion. It was left to us women—namely, Valerie, my *shiksa* friend and fellow poetry performer who organised my hens' party, my mother and myself—to farewell the expiring Shabbat with the *Havdala* ceremony, before Valerie and I left for the fetish club.

The start of *Havdala* depends on the appearance of the first three stars, which, in Jewish tradition, signifies the day's end. While Valerie and my mother—whose opposition to the *shiksas* in my life remained theoretical—were enjoying themselves on the balcony, squinting into the darkness to spot the stars, I retreated to change my clothes but, really, to demonstrate my resentment. This wasn't my usual exasperation with the Judaic tendency to complicate everything, even the notion of time. What was really getting under my skin was the pleasure Noah and our friends were deriving from my mother's Kabbalistic parables, her marvelling at wombats and the prices at Victoria Market, and that resonant laughter she used as abundantly as would a schoolgirl. Even more irritatingly, I, too, could see she was entertaining. But I know better than that, I reminded myself crossly while looking for a garment that would cure me of all the holiness that had flooded my life. Valerie, too, had realised what I needed when she suggested the fetish club. Now, as she was debating with my mother whether cinnamon or nutmeg was the better fragrance to use for *Havdala*, I drenched myself in Estée Lauder's Pleasure, inserted contact lenses in my large, myopic eyes, coloured my lips shiny gold, and stretched a one-sleeved dress over my body. I wanted to be unhinged, unbalanced, that night. In long-forgotten stilettos, I walked, or rather stumbled, out to mouth *Amen* to my mother's prayers. At least, I thought gleefully, I'll upset the holy air with my bare shoulder.

'Lubochka, you look very beautiful,' my mother said, to my disappointment. Occasionally, though, the first thirty, secular years of her life would raise their hydra heads alongside her pious wig-clad one. Since childhood, I'd wrestled with this confusion.

What makes fetish clubs, as opposed to striptease bars, unfit for hens' parties is their unpredictability. The real danger to marriage, according to common wisdom, lies not so much in debauchery as in the unexpected. Without the set three-course dinners and G-string-clad strippers accustomed to handling drunken brides, things risk getting out of hand, moving past sexual to *erotic*. The only rule at the fetish club was that you paid twelve dollars to become Alice, who, one unremarkable afternoon, fell into a hole that didn't behave like other holes. But I didn't stagger. As soon as I entered the club, my stilettoed feet automatically enacted the swaying walk of Salome.

My friends and I brought five personalities to filter through the place. Valerie flirted with the owner, who called himself 'Colonel'. Natasha, who never felt easy with the world, clutched her water bottle. Inga and Rachel created a two-person cocoon in which to discuss personal matters, leaving the outer world for later. And I, impatient, squeezed myself in at the bar, between a woman wearing only a midriff t-shirt and one who, dressed in a Queen Elizabeth-style suit and a fluffy wig, reminded me of my mother. The bartender, whose leather pants were cut to reveal an appetisingly taut behind, sank a strawberry into my champagne. The woman in the suit, who might have been a man, winked at me wetly. Nervous, I gulped my champagne and asked for another glass.

Alice, too, didn't hesitate when she was offered the potion.

What was I going to turn into?

I'd always removed myself to the edges of whatever groupings I came across. Among social workers, my then-colleagues, I automatically became a writer. In the company of writers, I'd wear the persona of social worker. The club, brimming recklessly with beauties clad in Adult World costumes, men in suits and cross-dressers, accentuated my prudishness. Now I wanted to be a good girl, who cringed when a naked, face-painted man blocked her way on the dance floor. With his tremendous afro wig and equally well-sized erection, the man seemed like a hybrid of the Mad Hatter and a noble savage. A trickster like everyone else there, from somewhere within his nakedness he produced a bottle of baby oil and enquired whether I'd anoint his back. I refused politely, unwilling to exchange my tedious goodness for something so slapstick. The noble savage didn't seem to mind, though, departing with the native greeting of 'No worries, love'.

Valerie, whose Colonel had had to resume his host's duties, summoned me into a side room, where we watched, through pink tulle curtains, the silhouette of a woman sprawling with a man's head buried between her thighs. 'Do you like to watch?' a tall, heavy-set man with a metallic suitcase on his lap asked casually, as if we were discussing horse races.

I liked the aura of polite debauchery that emanated from this man, and from the savage and everyone else I encountered there. In Israel, sex was never something that was reconciled with, accepted as a colleague of valued activities like moneymaking, familymaking, drugtaking; not even in the Tel Aviv of my youth, which literally reeked of sex. It was everywhere—in nightclub toilets, alleys, cars, university grounds, beaches, shared apartments. But, rather than being a pleasure, sex there was obscene, even mean. It was a battle—particularly if you were a young woman wanting to have sexual experiences and also be respected. Whereas in this club, while the emotions there were just as exquisitely heightened as they were in any places of pleasure, be they brothels or sports stadiums, the erotica felt *kind*. The lust was devoid of self- or other loathing. The patrons seemed to have suspended judgement in the face of wigs or baby oil. But while this atmosphere aroused me, the man with the suitcase wasn't to my taste. He was too bulky, and incongruous with his dark leather jacket, which, zipped high, transformed his benevolent looks, of freckled face, rimless spectacles and red goatee, into those of some refined movie villain.

I gave an embarrassed nod. Yes, I liked to watch. By now, though, the spectacle through the tulle had slid into monotony. More interestingly, the man introduced himself as a professional plumber and a semi-professional sadist. Like any decent tradesman, he didn't waste time, and opened his suitcase that showcased an assortment of whips, nipple clamps and other, less identifiable, instruments that could potentially suit either of his trades. Valerie, whose past was sexually rich, was losing interest. But I was keen to get as much out of my first-ever sadist as I could, even if he was freckled and wearing glasses. I tugged pleadingly at Valerie's arm and we followed the man to the club's torture dungeon, where a fleshy woman was elaborately tying a youth in red pants to something resembling a coathanger. I stared at the whip, sleek and dark like an eel, tucked into her belt. The sadist looked at me intently. Suddenly he plunged his sausage-thick fingers into my hair, massaging my scalp, then lifted my locks, baring the back of my neck to the air-conditioned coolness, and to the rhythmic music of the whip that, finally, after long preparations, was being put to work. 'You'd make a perfect slave,' he whispered into my naked neck.

The whisper, and the rough touch, drove me wild, bringing back some darkness from my past; something to do with J, the man I'd been living with when I'd first met Noah. Shivers knitted my spine while I was trying to decide whether the sadist's view of me was an insult or a compliment. A part of me was pining to succumb to his hands. The sadist must have noticed my confusion, shooting me a crookedly alluring smile. Tactful Valerie left us alone. My yearning to slide into the man's body, into his will, intensified. Yet something about the sadist's gaze thwarted my desire. He was looking *through* me, perhaps considering the contents of his suitcase and the tricks it could deliver. But I wanted to be the object of lust, not the means to it. I slipped past the sadist to the front parlour and it was there that I spotted the beautiful nurse. Oh well, I thought. The night was drawing to its end, so a girl would do …

Kissing the girl was more awkward than pleasurable, but that night it was what I wanted—the discomfort of flirting. I was in lust with the girl's foreignness, and with the woman I became when I kissed her: a stranger to myself. She was granting me my wish through her remoteness, and her unfamiliar sharp, slim tongue, which I, nervous as hell, now accidentally bit. Annoyed, she withdrew her orange lips but remained in my arms. I stared at the girl's elaborate chignon and the attractive roundness of her cleavage, inhaling her lavender scent. Her kisses, as most first kisses do, conjured up a loophole into a pure present. But, apparently, only for me. I soon realised the girl wasn't as interested as I was. To engage her, I tried more kisses, and even a conversation, discovering to my disappointment that behind her skin-tight uniform lay a corporate soul. She was an IT-something—a consultant, or some other title indicating a combination of money and tedium. Not wanting to dispel further the mystery of her dress, which I craved unbuttoning, I fell silent again, and into her.

Still seated on my lap, the girl let me slide my hand down her cleavage, feel the elasticity of her young breasts. Yet, her gaze, like the sadist's, was pinned beyond me, aimed at our one-man audience, whom she introduced as her husband. He was good-looking too, in that prosperous shaved-skull, gym-hardened way. As he looped his arms around us both, his minty breath tickling the hollow of my neck, I sensed his wife turn corpse-stiff. Clearly, my fun was over. I felt sad for the nurse, but also selfishly irritated in that familiar way, suspecting providence was once again conspiring with my mother, warning me on my last unmarried night that getting what I wanted was a doomed enterprise. A curvy brass clock of the kind you'd imagine would have been in de Sade's castle croaked six am. In a few hours, my *huppah* ceremony was to begin. I kissed the nurse one last time and left the world of wonders.

Outside, the springtime sky was already embroidered with pale sunshine. The early Sunday risers jogged past Valerie and me, throwing into relief our unhealthy partygirl look, of smudged mascara and crumpled dresses. My eyes ached pleasantly after the sleepless night, as though I were young again, back in Tel Aviv, which was rumoured never to sleep. In the fresh air, the champagne tide receded from my brain and I returned to my senses—they stank of optimism. Despite my lack of success that night, I felt great. The attempt was what counted.

'Are you going to tell Noah?' Valerie asked.

I hoped that if I did, Noah would be on my side. Since we'd met, there hadn't been much I'd been able to shock him with, not even when I'd told him I was living with J. Then, Noah accepted me as I came: dishevelled by the drama of my immigration and by J, elusive in what I wanted. I was a hard case but he waited around patiently, even walked away when I asked him to, when I feared J would harm him, or me, or because I couldn't handle any more love, which, in those days, seemed only to come hand in hand with war. By the time we moved in together, we'd already been through so much that nothing between us was ever taken for granted, except for the notion that we'd stick together.

Yet, we'd never made a clear pact about fidelity. After J returned to Israel and the threat of him lifted, lightness descended upon us—of a kind I'd never had with anyone else. Noah's apartment, where I'd already been living for several months in hiding, came alive. Friends came, bringing along their paramours to smoke joints on our balcony overlooking the city. We became good at throwing parties with wine casks and plates of whatever there was in the fridge, and at dancing with each other and with everyone else. In the mornings, we'd find people asleep in our spare bedroom, or on the living room carpet. Some nights, I fondled women in Noah's presence; once, we kissed a girl together. While I was studying and working hard to establish myself in Australia, my life still felt like a moveable feast where nothing was impossible. Or was it?

Sexually, I was more interested in men, but I suspected Noah might find affairs with them difficult to accept. I did occasionally skirt around the topic, trying to outline our boundaries. In those brief, disconcerting conversations, usually smoothed out by the darkness of our local beach and the beating wings of seagulls flying low, Noah would say, 'Do what you like, just don't tell me.' He didn't specify his own needs and I didn't ask, being perhaps too frightened of what I might find out.

'Did you really have to kiss her?' Noah sighed the day after our wedding, when I recounted the story of my hens' party to him. But his sigh felt like lip service to the previous day's celebration of tradition, rather than genuine disappointment. I spotted the familiar twinkle in his large, dark eyes.

The afternoon was unfolding marvellously. From our apartment, we could smell the salt of the ocean, hear the Tasmanian ferry's departing toots. Through the windows, the city buildings appeared wrapped, like gifts, in the sun's pink glow. We had a great time rummaging through the comforting symbols of domesticity always received for official unions: towels, vases, electric salt grinders, toasters resembling spaceships. We kissed and argued and answered congratulatory phone calls, putting the callers on speaker, as couples do.

The nurse was absorbed into our happiness—but then, she wasn't a man and a kiss wasn't intercourse. Wrapped cosily in the sunshine and Noah, I thought that if we were to live together unconventionally, it probably wouldn't always be this easy. But if I were to be happily married, I needed to know I was free to do as I liked. This seemed even more important than acting upon the permission. So, I was determined to discover if I could do non-monogamy in an ethical way, even if my first such attempt—with J—had turned out to be a disaster. I brushed that memory away.

2

A tale of *Modus Vivendi* (2007)

'Coupledom is a performance art.'
Adam Phillips

Ironically, by the time I decided to explore seriously whether non-monogamy could be an ethical ethos to live by and flew to a writers' residency in Perth to begin my quest, my marriage had started coming apart at the seams. As the plane hit the ground in possibly the most isolated city on earth, I thought hopefully that the distance and foreignness of this place might offer me some fresh perspective on what was happening at home. Encased in my Melburnian spring armour of long black t-shirt and pants, I disembarked into the western dust and heat, broke swiftly into a sweat, and was told my baggage was lost. My home life twisted its tail and slipped away at once, leaving me in the hum of the airport, shadowless.

Our troubles had nothing to do with infidelity. As far as I knew, the girl from the fetish club was our only extramarital venture in the past two years. But perhaps I'd been warned already on my wedding day, when I got my period, that our marriage wasn't going to go smoothly.

According to Judaism, menstrual blood is a manifestation of human uncleanliness. The Book of Leviticus warns that a menstruating woman contaminates whatever she touches—bread, a TV remote control, her husband. To protect men from impurity, religious couples avoid touching each other and sleep in separate beds for the week the woman is menstruating, and the following one too. The stakes of contamination are high: the polluted husband risks capital punishment (administered by the Heavens, rather than by its human servants), or some other disaster. It was from such catastrophes that my mother sought to protect me when she came to Australia for my wedding.

I told my mother and the *rebbetzin* in charge of *mikvah*, the ritual bath in which the bride, after her period has finished, purifies herself before the wedding, that my last menstruation had ended. I even assured them that, as custom required, I'd daily been checking myself for offending secretions by inserting white *bedikah* cloths into my vagina. But these were lies. I'd always resented the Bible dooming me to impurity for half my fertile life—two weeks out of each month. In defiance of this, I never bothered to keep track of my periods. Before my wedding, I just hoped for the best—that on the night of *mikvah*, I wouldn't be bleeding. And I wasn't. However—and I realise that if I were to include this in a fictional story, it would seem contrived—upon my return from the fetish club, a copper stain spread with gusto onto my panties.

To relieve the menstrual pain, I drank champagne straight from the bottle in the limousine carrying us to the Ballarat synagogue. And by the time Noah and I, overwhelmed by the wedding celebrations, stumbled into our bridal suite, the bleeding had metamorphosed into a Great Flood. Noah stared squeamishly (and not for religious reasons) at the red that coloured the sheets. Still, we embraced tightly and went to sleep. But even without consummating the marriage that night, we were, according to our shared tradition, headed towards the abyss.

As I grew older, it became apparent that I'd inherited something substantial from my mother, and not just her nose. It was magical thinking. Neither of us believed in coincidences or trusted the mundane to be what it seemed. To us, life has always been a mystery in need of decoding. So, the part of me that cannot run away from my upbringing is inclined to interpret the timing of my menstruation as an omen. The other part of me suspects the blood was a symptom; the lack of consummation was the disease. The longer our relationship continued, the more heavily the sex weighed on us. *Sexless* doesn't describe how we were together. Our bodies touched constantly; we'd built our love upon the sensuality of caresses, of a hand in another's hand. At night, we slept intertwined. When Noah touched me, I often shuddered. He loved it when I covered his wide, brown face with kisses, when I held him in my arms, but my touch didn't seem to affect his nerve ends the way his did mine. Rather than being sexless, I'd say we were fuckless. We made love perhaps once a month, occasionally more, but we hardly ever fucked.

Noah claimed to be happy, yet I found it difficult to believe he needed so little sexually. In every other way, he was a man of ardour. I loved his energy, his fierceness, the fact that his favourite mode of conversation was argument, whether about carbon reductions or the Magpies. I loved that his decision-making was quick and his humour dark. He drove like a daredevil, danced well, and generally moved with vitality. His love for me was vital too. You would call Noah passionate if you expanded the application of the word. He phoned to say he loved me during even his most chaotic working hours. He bought an overpriced, indecently red massage armchair just because I said I liked it. At weekends, he'd rise early to get coffee and croissants from the Starbucks downstairs while I slept. He bought me dresses that always fitted. Despite his lack of interest in poetry, Noah accompanied me whenever I did a public reading. 'Look at my wife,' he was in the habit of saying to anyone who cared to listen, 'Isn't she beautiful? I have no idea what's she doing with me.' Then his generous lips would pout in that particular way I loved, waiting for my kiss.

When we first met, I was struck by Noah's smell. Unlike the meaty smells of Israeli soldier men, his embodied the civilised man—a complex bouquet of fine cologne, chewing gum, Marlboros and fresh laundry. A long way into our togetherness, I'd sniff his clothes and wear his t-shirts whenever he was away travelling for work. As time passed, though, I stopped noticing his smell. Or maybe I willed myself to stop.

In our first years together, the strangeness of our passion that was passionless—or our non-passion that was so passionate—was less in the foreground for me. Shortly after Noah and I moved in together, my Australian residency was finalised, ending my years of not being able to study and working in odd underpaid jobs. I then plunged into chasing my version of the Australian dream, acquiring degrees, local professional work experience and, most importantly, becoming a writer in English. When my work began appearing in Australian and overseas journals, this counted for almost everything. Sex, I'd already exhausted with J; and then with him and Noah simultaneously and intermittently, during that year of madness when there were several other lovers too, when sex seemed like the most potent remedy. But once J returned to Israel, I redirected my libidinal energy into my work.

During my years with Noah, I'd sometimes forget I had a body or, rather, the kind of body that could be loved. At other times, I missed being grabbed, ravished. I had several secret crushes on the most improbable men: a chronically drunk poet with green fingernails; a much older novelist, who advised me on my writing; a much younger student at the social work faculty where I taught. I was disgusted with my desires, which were not even desires but compromises, as they were dependent on who I came across. I never acted on those desperate whims and remained technically monogamous. One night, I dreamed I was talking to one of the lecturers from my faculty, a lovely, but quite formidable and earnest lady, as social work educators tend to be. During our conversation, which was also earnest and formidable (having something to do with my academic future), I realised I was absent-mindedly wiping my face with a penis. It wasn't attached to anyone, but was a stand-alone fleshy, pulsating, firm entity, dripping sperm onto my face. I kept massaging the sperm, as though it were moisturiser, into my skin. The lecturer politely ignored my preoccupation, as people do when noticing someone picking their nose. As I recorded the dream in my journal, I knew things were getting complicated, since, rather than finding this funny, I felt nauseated and deeply ashamed of something I couldn't even name.

Eventually, sex came to colour much of our marriage. Out of sexual frustration, I began, at first jokingly, then compulsively, squeezing Noah's nose—allegedly, to clean his pores. This ritual, of course, didn't enhance my appeal in my husband's eyes. At times, I spoke to him abruptly, dismissively, even in front of our friends. We began fighting over things that previously hadn't mattered: the television not having been switched off, a joke that was too close to the bone.

'I find it difficult to reconcile love with sex,' Noah told me. 'You're too strong for me,' he also said.

The 'too' was particularly hard to take. I walked around feeling muscly, massive, looming. Too strong to be made love to, but just strong enough to be loved forever, as Noah promised. The scarred body I was packaged in following childhood surgeries meant I had always been alert to the possibility of sexual rejection, but the first time I encountered it was with my husband, the man who loved me so well in every other sense. This was difficult to handle, let alone understand.

We decided to see a sex therapist.

Our sex therapist, a star in his field, was optimistic. Armed with rimless spectacles and reddish hair, he strangely resembled the sadist from the fetish club. During the sessions, he liked sitting with his long legs wide apart and freezing his face in teeth-baring, lupine smiles that I found quite terrifying. He charged us a lot of money to point out what we already knew—that, actually, Noah and I rated much better than many other couples. We made each other laugh, we were affectionate, we never argued over who did the dishes. To let such a relationship go to waste would just be dumb. He said he'd cure us but, for the first few sessions, gave no indication what the cure might be.

When pressed for more information, the sex therapist lent us a book called *The Art of Sexual Ecstasy*, sub-titled *The Path of Sacred Sexuality for Western Lovers*. Although neither of us was interested in the kind of sexuality that, with its religious overtones, evoked my mother, to show our patient compliance, we got past the title page. Unfortunately, the next page, which contained only a dedication, 'To the Master within and without/ to the Goddess within and without/to Gaia, our planet, our mother', proved unsurpassable. Fearful of our sex therapist, but mostly in the hope of being cured, we agreed at least to meet a Tantra teacher he recommended, for a home consultation priced at several hundred dollars per hour.

The teacher was tall and lean; attractive in the manner of a young Germaine Greer. She folded her floor-length leather coat on our sofa and ordered Noah to take off his shirt. He looked at me, hesitant. I approved, although I felt uneasy watching this splendid woman trace with her pearly nails invisible hieroglyphs on my husband's back. I averted my gaze to the Chagall reproduction hanging above our couch. There, a bright-red woman wearing only a bridal veil was reclining on a daybed. Her voluptuous body was surrounded by Chagall's usual symbols, which belonged to that uncertain realm between the magical and the comical—clocks, roosters, donkeys, crooked Hasidic villages. Chagall was my kind of artist: a rebel haunted for life by the God of his childhood. His similarly rebellious lovers always courted danger, forsaking their own tribes for foreign horizons. This naked bride appeared dangerous, despite her languid posture—like a resting lioness. I remembered the night before my wedding when I, too, fancied myself to be sexily dangerous. What had happened since?

'Making love is like making art. It's all about the process,' the teacher whispered in a Dietrich-husky voice, summoning my attention to her demonstration of a tantric touch. 'You need to do this slowly.'

In principle, I agreed with her, although I also liked having urgent sex, when you tear through clothes, hair, flesh. But, by now, I hardly remembered what sex felt like—I mean, when it was really good, brimming with everything. What we really needed, I thought, was what Noah called the 'x factor'. Although he never admitted it, I suspected he never had that mysterious ingredient with me, whereas my sense of it with him was by now lost somewhere deep inside my body. Noah had become so familiar that I could no longer look into his eyes when we did make love without feeling I was committing incest. And I, apparently, intimidated him. Speed was the least of our problems, I was about to say. But, while I considered what effect my words might have on Noah, the teacher had already moved onto another topic: 'Tantra does miracles.' She left my husband alone and sank into the couch, making herself very comfortable. 'My *current* lover was a war prisoner. He was tortured. When we first met, he couldn't have long erections.' She pronounced the word *erections* with French flair, fluffing the 'r' as a peacock would fluff its tail.

'But Noah has erections,' I mumbled. Our inability to get it together wasn't physical; it was as though sex were a metaphor for something else. I just didn't know for what.

'Oh, does he?' I could see the teacher was disappointed she wouldn't get to tell the full story of her tortured lover. I also realised that it wasn't her beauty that made everything so difficult that night, but the fact that we needed another person to show us how to love each other. *That* felt like defeat.

The tantric arsenal, though, appeared inexhaustible. Once the question of erections was filed away, for the next hour or so we got stuck into studying how to arouse all our senses at once, because—the teacher promised—*that* was the sacred (and costly) path to sexual ecstasy.

After her departure, we attempted to implement what we had learned. I put on a black bra. Noah put on a Dead Can Dance

CD. As we fed each other grapes neither of us wanted, the vanilla-incense smoke made Noah have a coughing fit. When he finally recovered, he said, 'Let me Tantra you, baby ...' mimicking the teacher. I laughed till it hurt. I kissed his nose and eyes tenderly, and we went to sleep.

In the following session, upon our reporting of the Tantra experience, our sex therapist decreed that Noah's lengthy, and quite promiscuous, single life before we met was the cause of our problems and to be the target for intervention. I suspected this diagnosis to be somewhat coloured by the fact that the therapist, who had previously told me I was just like *him*—too brainy, over-intellectualising everything—might have wanted Noah all to himself. Nevertheless, I was relieved to withdraw from the sessions.

Now that our problem had transmogrified into Noah's and the sex therapist's problem, mystery surrounded it. The occasional notes my husband brought home reassured me that he was progressing well, whatever that meant. Soon, the sex therapist's satisfaction with Noah had escalated so that he suggested they start a business together, utilising his professional reputation and my husband's business talents. They'd open an online shop selling sex toys, which they'd import from Thailand, that were branded with the therapist's name. Or maybe it was the Philippines they were going to import them from. Whatever country it was, I finally put my foot down and our therapy came to a halt.

After the therapy phase ended and not long before I left for Perth, those rows that had been plaguing us for a while somehow dissipated. Around that time, I ran into a man from my gym, whom I hadn't seen for over a year. The last time I'd encountered him, he was newly married and seemingly happy. Now he told me about another life change: having a child.

'And how is your marriage going?' I asked with that casual familiarity—or merely absence of censorship—you can have with acquaintances who never enter your 'real' life.

'The marriage is fucked!' The man had such sweeping passion in his reply that we both blushed. To smooth things over, my gym buddy tried to disguise his unhappiness: 'It's not like we're arguing … it's just … the romance is gone, the sex gone. But I'm okay, you know. I have my work. I have the kid.'

The encounter made me think of an old friend who had spent long erotic afternoons with the man she later married and had children with. Several years earlier, I had stayed with them and been in awe of the glow that enveloped them on afternoons whenever they emerged from their bedroom. Lately, though, she'd been saying she felt restless in her now erotic-afternoon-less marriage and was fantasising about other men. Yet, she wasn't considering divorce. Then there were our other friends who in their first year together ravished each other, in public too. But as time went by, I saw them embrace less and less and knew they'd retreated into separate bedrooms. No separation loomed on their horizon either, though. Was I supposed to feel encouraged by this?

It wasn't just my friends I was contemplating. To gain some perspective about our situation, I consulted statistics, and found that sexless, but lasting, relationships were a fairly common phenomenon. They posed a challenge to the popular belief of my generation, entertained particularly in Hollywood films, women's magazines and television sitcoms, that our beloved is meant to satisfy all our needs. According to this model of the spouse as a universal remote control, Noah and I were doomed. But such expectations only set people up for disappointment, as, indeed, was the case if you considered the contemporary skyrocketing rate of divorces and break-ups of de facto relationships.

But there was another popular narrative about relationships, favoured more by therapists (and my friends) than by the entertainment industry. It suggested that the decline of excitement in a relationship is *inevitable* but also *natural* and, therefore, like giving birth without painkillers, good for you. According to this camp, couples could reasonably expect two, or three at the maximum, years of passion before moving to the next stage in the love cycle. 'You've got to make a transition to a stabler state,' an issue of *Time* dedicated to love urged its readers. The stabler state, known as 'companionate' or 'mature' love in therapeutic jargon, meant you'd rechannel your sexual energy into more honourable activities: child-rearing, community involvement, bushwalking. Perhaps for some, the narrative of companionate love works. Yet, the sheer extent of infidelity in these times must mean 'mature' relationships have their problems too. However varied and unreliable the statistics may be, they consistently show the numbers of cheaters to be high and to be getting progressively higher. Then there were the many statistically unaccounted for who kept (at least for now) their loins exclusively for their partners but consumed Internet pornography, or flirted in cyberspace.

I saw no answers for Noah and me. We obviously didn't satisfy all of each other's needs, but divorce wasn't an option I'd even consider. I couldn't comprehend a life without him. It was no accident that our wedding had a medieval banquet theme, as Noah was my shining knight, who had helped me to escape J. He was also the artery connecting me to the heart of my new country. I'd always prided myself on having an Australian husband, as though by marrying a local man, I'd truly put my imprint upon this land. Most importantly, he was my darling, the one into whom I curled night after night.

But I wasn't ready to settle for lousy sex or celibacy. Following that meeting with my gym buddy, and all the thinking I'd done since, I felt more hopeful about us. While I was doing all that research, it struck me that Noah and I didn't fit the 'companionate love' narrative either. True, we weren't passionate lovers, but we were romantic and still flirted with each other. Our marriage was infused with intimacy and physical affection. The fact that it had been sexually lacklustre from the beginning, rather than having undergone a decline, now filled me with hope that there were unused torrents of passion for us to uncover. I read David Schnarch's book *Passionate Marriage*, used as a bible by therapists internationally, and found myself agreeing with his central premise that passion between spouses can last if they work on it. But his working methods reminded me of those of our Tantra teacher. We didn't need better *techniques*; we needed to find our own way. But how?

I decided to look to famous dead people, whose romantic lives were usually written about more honestly than those of the living. One story that was particularly close to my heart was that of the English writer H. G. Wells and his second wife, Jane. She was the love of his life, and Wells was a man whose libido was as high as his moustache was lush. The author Katie Roiphe described him as emanating 'an unapologetic hedonism'. Unfortunately, Jane, a slim beauty who wore her luxurious blonde hair in a modest bun, seemed to have little interest in sex. In his memoirs, Wells described her as 'Dresden china', writing that she 'regarded my sexual imaginativeness as a sort of constitutional disease; she stood by me patiently waiting for this to subside'. He couldn't, as he liked, be rough or playful in bed with her.

To solve the 'sex problem', Jane gave Wells permission to have lovers, as long as he always told her everything—except for the telling, what Noah had offered me. She seemed to relish Wells's disclosures. She corresponded with some of his mistresses, even advising one, the writer Rebecca West, on household matters. Wells aptly termed their unorthodox marital contract *Modus Vivendi*: Latin for a treaty where parties agree to disagree in order to coexist.

It worked for this couple. Jane's central place in Wells's life remained non-negotiable for thirty-two years, until she died in his arms. Wells was known to emphasise to all, including his lovers, that Jane was the only woman he truly loved. She was a helpmate who raised their children and beautified his everyday life through her imaginative housekeeping—the splendour of her garden and parties, and so on. But this wasn't merely a *companionate* relationship. Jane was also Wells's sweetheart in a romantic sense. Occasionally, he was absent, spending time with his lovers, but when he was home, he brought Jane armfuls of flowers, drew cartoons about their marriage, cradled her in his arms. Even at the height of his passion for Rebecca West, he wrote from her bed to Jane: 'I love you very warmly. You are, in so many ways, bone of my bone, flesh of my flesh …' After Jane's death, he reflected in his memoir:

> We two contrived in the absence of a real passionate sexual fixation, a binding net of fantasy and affection that proved in the end as effective as the very closest sexual sympathy could have been in keeping us together.

It helped to know that a marriage lacking in sex could still be satisfactory and lasting, as long as it didn't sink into monogamy-induced celibacy. This was the kind of marriage Noah and I were already, more or less, headed towards. But I couldn't completely relate to Wells, or at least not to the public face of Wells. It disturbed me that whenever Noah and I did make love, it felt as if it were for my sake. I wanted to be with other people, but as an addition to, not to replace, sex with my husband.

At this time, Esther Perel's book *Mating in Captivity* came out. This was the first book about sexuality from a therapist's perspective that truly spoke to me. She didn't think that a graceful acceptance of passion's decline was healthy, and didn't suggest to reignite it with the kind of laborious sex I found in

Passionate Marriage, Tantra instructions and adult shops offering user-friendly S&M kits. Her recipe for remaining lovers for the long term was to expose the relationship to some danger: 'Excitement is interwoven with uncertainty and with our willingness to embrace the unknown … there is no such thing as "safe sex".' Perel's paradoxical suggestion, that to preserve love you had to be prepared to risk it, appealed to me. After all, most things I had ever truly cared about, like writing and my move to Australia, were bound up with risk.

Non-monogamy was on Perel's menu of risk-taking. One of the popular arguments for why non-monogamy cannot work, favoured by David Schnarch and another influential therapist, the British Andrew Marshall, among others, is that an interest in others always comes at our beloved's expense. Apparently, non-monogamists misplace their energies. But Perel's experience in her practice had showed her that couples who opened their gates were no less committed to each other than those who kept them closed:

> In fact, it is their desire to make the relationship stronger that leads them to explore other models of long-term love. Rather than expelling the third from the province of matrimony, they grant it a tourist visa.

In Perel's view, the entry of 'the third' can potentially *add* energy to some relationships, and can take several forms: as a substitute for sex between spouses, as in Wells's marriage; as a joint expedition into the wilderness (a threesome, for instance); as merely the threat of *possible* betrayal; or as a 'stabiliser', when lovers supplement something the spouses cannot give to each other, such as sheer novelty.

If, on the eve of our marriage, I had wanted non-monogamy for my self-expression, and because I feared finality of any kind, including sexual fidelity, the matter now felt even more urgent—as if our marital survival depended on it. I hoped Perel's method would help us to discover that elusive element that Tantra and mainstream therapists couldn't—some animalism between us. The time was ripe, I thought, to take risks. As I often did when I had a problem to solve, I conceived a book. I decided to find people who had tried non-monogamy, and ask them how such relationships worked and what price was paid. The writers' residency in Perth seemed like a great place to begin my quest.

One weekend, Noah and I came across a woman at a farmers' market selling the largest strawberries I'd ever seen. He said a fruit of this size had to be watery, tasteless. But I, covetous and impatient, grabbed one and bit into it. The strawberry was magnificently sweet. The woman explained her trick: she pruned all but one strawberry from each vine, so the plant's energy went into one fruit. That hit me exactly where I needed to be hit. I wrote in my journal: 'I'd like both my writing and my marriage to be like that strawberry. Writing and marriage. All the rest can be pruned.'

Once I made the decision, I pruned and pruned my constant busyness of writing, study, work, social occasions; all that marred our life together, by bringing out Noah's bitterness and possibly his lack of desire. At night, I switched off the computer and became a wife. We took to eating Magnums and watching the series *Carnivàle*, leaning into each other in the darkness that was dotted with the glow of candlelight and the TV screen. We followed the complicated manoeuvres of dwarves and clairvoyants, but mostly chatted, analysing the characters' desires and perhaps getting ready to discuss our own. I inhaled the man beside me, once again struck by his particular scent, remembering that he too contained all that wilderness that constitutes *other* people. Then the time for the residency came, too soon for my liking.

I wanted to enjoy my newfound marital peace some more, but instead packed a suitcase to go west.

I was about to spend four weeks in a place that served both as a writers' centre and a venue for writers' residencies. It was located on the outskirts of Perth, among the strangeness of mountains and creeks, vineyards and waterfalls, and away from trains, supermarkets, cafés, and other signs of life an urban princess like myself was accustomed to. In my eight years in Australia, I'd travelled in the country a lot, but had never ventured west. Still, I'd heard many stories about it: about the western primordial ripeness, vertiginous trees, volcanic depths, venomous stonefish and blue-ringed octopuses. I imagined the place to be so powerful, so imposing, that it could remould anything that came into it: insects, sun, rivers, tourists.

On my arrival, Perth was on fire. Heatwaves had left the people and flies as crunchy as dry leaves. The centre's volunteer told me on the drive from the airport that the place I'd be staying in used to belong to the long-dead novelist Katharine Susannah Prichard, and that her husband had shot himself in the house when he was forty-nine. The rest of the journey we spent discussing the volunteer's own family history, which was even more horrifying.

It was evening when I arrived at the Prichard house. The place was dusty and dark. The old furniture got in my way, to make sure I knew who was the boss. The man in charge of settling me in here conducted a tutorial on the activation of the alarm system, and I failed his test twice. He told me not to worry. My sole neighbour, a retired woman, patrolled the premises nightly with her dog. In case of danger, I could call her at any hour.

To occupy myself while I waited for the delivery of my lost-and-found suitcase, I read the guest book. The previous resident writers' entries mentioned nightly sounds of footsteps in the corridor, and of slamming doors and muffled voices, and visions of a man—presumably, the dead husband. There was even a detailed description of someone waking up to the sensation of invisible hands upon her body. This could perhaps explain the breathtaking elaborateness of the security system, which—I hoped—would be difficult to overcome not only for me but also for the ghost. I woke up many times that first night, but only to myself.

During the day, the house shook off its macabre history, and came alive with rabbits, lizards and writers slinking around its edges. Even the tradespeople who constantly came to fix, demolish or build something or other confessed to being novelists. Whenever I emerged from my room, I received gifts of self-published books. The only non-writer around, a handyman and practising Baha'i, also had reading materials for me—introductory brochures about his religion. In the mornings, elderly ladies and a handful of unemployed young men invaded the shared, and lockless, bathroom, often when I was in there. I had experience of writers' residencies, each with their own idiosyncrasies, but this one was particularly populous and chatty.

I missed Noah and our home, but my mood was improving. I was becoming an adaptable virus within the centre's evolved organism. When its activity overwhelmed me, I'd hide in my room, which was located near the main meeting space that was always being used by writing groups or committees planning more repairs, in turn bringing more men with their tools and unpublished manuscripts. But my writing desk faced a window onto the garden and the phosphoric-purple bougainvillea, which, in its flamboyant abundance, pushed the world out of my way and cleared space for my writing.

I was impatient to begin my interviews, but I wasn't sure how to find people to talk to. The American novelist Frederic Tuten suggested in an interview for *New York Magazine* that people can live non-monogamously, but should never speak about it in public. Ironically, Tuten's interviewer, Philip Weiss, chose to ignore his advice and, in the same article, admitted his own desire for extramarital sex, instantly fulfilling his subject's prediction. Readers responded with online condemnations, the kinder comments suggesting Weiss grow up and his wife divorce him, and others wishing upon him a range of misfortunes to put the biblical plagues to shame. Angelina Jolie didn't fare any better. Fans delighted in her confessions about incorporating knife-cutting into her bedroom repertoire as much as they did in hearing of her humanitarian work in Africa. But they were less amused by her publicly stated interest in opening up her relationship with Brad Pitt. In the ensuing outrage, Jolie was accused of driving Brad to alcoholism.

On a more modest scale, I had my own such experience. Not long before my wedding, when working for a community-based mental health service, I acquired the worst reputation of any of my then-colleagues. Such organisations tend to attract employees who live outside the mainstream, and who are therefore sympathetic to the plight of their clients, and who put up with largely symbolic salaries in return for limited restrictions regarding workplace etiquette. My manager liked discussing the size of her breasts, while my chronically underdressed co-workers, of all possible genders and sexual orientations, sported pierced eyebrows and tattooed bum cracks. Still, it was I, the unpierced and non-tattooed, the conventionally engaged-to-be-married one, who managed to upset our institution's elastic moral status quo.

This happened one night during after-work drinks, when we'd got to telling stories about our sex lives. Too drunk to think about my loyalty to Noah, and not wanting to lag behind the picaresque tales I'd just heard, I mumbled something about an 'agreement' we had. I used that word chiefly to keep things simple, but also because it sounded good. But perhaps it didn't. A sharp silence fell over our bubbly table. Everyone's eyes, strangely sober, became focused on me. 'What's the point of getting married then?' asked one woman, who had just told a graphic story about partaking in an orgy. 'If I ever get married, I know *I'll* be loyal …' she said, glaring at me. Soon after, the conversation turned to parenting.

I thought my colleague's response was typical of current social mores whereby (hopefully, wild) singledom and hermetically faithful coupledom are viewed as the only intimacy options. Statistics once again supported my gut feeling that in our hypersexual times we have become at once more promiscuous and more conservative. If in the 1970s, seventy per cent of Americans opposed extramarital ventures, when I went to Perth the number opposed to them had crept towards ninety per cent, and would keep growing in the years afterwards. Australians closely followed the US in expectations of intimacy. But I found it strange that, while *Dolly* magazine advised teenage girls how to perform fellatio with braces on their teeth, Sexpo exhibitions had become mainstream entertainment and cam sex was no longer a novelty, monogamy—whether serial or lifelong, passionate or sexless—was still considered to be the only realistic model for committed relationships. I thought the prevalence of infidelity meant that this attitude ruled out not so much other lovers, as honesty between spouses. People possibly cheated now more than ever while *trying*, or *pretending*, to be monogamous. So, why would non-monogamists step forward to reveal their secrets to me?

I asked the few people I had got to know in Perth if they could point me to someone to interview, but whenever I mentioned my book, eyebrows were raised, shoulders were shrugged, and amused smiles were produced like handkerchiefs out of old-fashioned pockets. The only woman who offered me a story had a straightforward infidelity narrative with a happy twist. She married her lover, and to him, she assured me, she was faithful.

The long-married Nina, a distant acquaintance based in Perth, wanted to know how I arrived at my subject—a fair-enough question, which, to my then highly strung mind, sounded like an accusation. But of what? Perhaps of the moral flaws usually attached to non-monogamy: shallowness, immaturity, selfishness, inability to commit to a duty. A friend in Melbourne had stared at me sternly when I'd told her what I planned to write about in Perth. 'Who has the time for such things?' she'd genuinely wondered. When couples she knew had spare time, they volunteered for their communities, she said.

To Nina, I mumbled something about using the topic of non-monogamy as a lens through which to see how people negotiate the common conflict between the desire for security and the desire for excitement. We always yearn for what lies beyond the fortresses we are in the habit of erecting, be these families, careers, homelands or fidelity, I said. Indeed, in my writing pursuits I've always been interested in the makeshift frontiers my generation has been mounting in the vacuum left to us by the rapidly collapsing grand narratives about gods and nations that once, more or less successfully, regulated the mess of the human condition.

Nowadays, we seem to be retreating behind smaller-scale bastions, be they corporations, alarmed fences or, I think, the idea of exclusive love, which may seem like a sound insurance policy against existential dread. This is a sentiment I fully share. With Noah, I felt I'd found a city of refuge. While both monogamy and non-monogamy can offer either the pleasures of intimacy or personal unhappiness, in theory, at least, it was monogamy's prerogative to soothe us by protecting us from the turbulence of new lovers. Besides, as a married friend once told me, 'In relationships we lay down a contract stipulating who we're going to be.' He meant that with our spouses, we can imagine ourselves as being consistent. The problem is, such a choice for salvation is only one side of that multidimensional coin called the human psyche, and the solace of exclusive love is lily-fragile. 'This contract,' the same friend added, 'is also bloody stifling.' I knew what he meant. It is precisely because the world that lies outside our fortresses is complex and dangerous that it is also so damn attractive.

My explanation to Nina was truthful, but I presented only the safest part of the truth to her. I was silent about my personal motivations for writing the book. So, how could I expect strangers to confide in me when I was so uneasy with my subject? While I waited in vain for interviewees to materialise, I began wandering into Perth's outskirts, falling for the landscape of endless rows of blackboys, the violent orange flashes of Christmas trees, the local flies that were as ubiquitous as dust.

Writers can be more perceptive than the most skilled explorers about places. Bypassing the surface, they go straight for the guts. During his brief visit to Perth in 1922, D. H. Lawrence was overtaken by an uncanny terror in the face of the giant, phosphoric 'unnatural West Australian moon' and, generally, what he called 'the spirit' of this 'raw loose' place. More than eighty years later, I could see what he meant. There was a touch of violence in the air. People I met crushed cockroaches with their bare palms and wiped them on car seats, on walls. This disgusted but also comforted me. After all, I too was capable of acting like this, but only in private. This public display of my secret digressions made me feel more normal. I was also struck by how everyone here, be they lawyers or elderly women, drove manual cars. As they navigated the hilly streets, their sharp and forceful, and at times erratic, hand movements lent complexity to their otherwise dignified appearances and low voices. This reminded me of Israel, where people either can't afford automatic cars or need the illusion of raw control that changing gears can offer. This desire for self-mastery that intensifies in dangerous and isolated places revealed to me some essence of Perth that was close to my heart. It also reminded me of that part of myself that had lain dormant since I'd settled down with Noah.

I wrote in my diary: 'I'm still not sure what I need and/or value more: the closeness of intimacy or the distance of Eros. These days my sexual appetite seems low.' But now, softened like butter by the heat, as I gazed at the purple debris of bougainvillea, I contemplated taking a lover. I couldn't decide whether this would count as a betrayal or was within the bounds of the vague permission Noah had given me. In any case, I stopped wearing my wedding ring.

3

A Tale of Princesses and Charladies

'Confusing monogamy with morality has done more to destroy the conscience of the human race than any other error.'
Bernard Shaw

To find lovers—for my book that is, I told myself—Nina suggested I place an ad in the local newspaper, but I found it difficult to describe what I was after. 'Non-monogamy' felt too definite. I wanted also to hear stories from people like me who skirted, confused, around the edges. I was interested in grey areas. 'Open' was the only other word I could think of but that, too, felt inadequate. I, for once, didn't want my marriage to become open like a window in summer, but neither did I want a closed-for-winter relationship. I wanted something in between, but I didn't know how to articulate it, let alone live it. In the absence of a more nuanced vocabulary, I placed the following ad:

A published writer would like to interview people who are/were in an open relationship, or a third party who is/was involved with a couple. Confidentiality guaranteed.

During the following week, I verged on paranoia, which was perhaps enhanced by the damp heat, that perverts might respond to my ad. I jumped whenever my mobile rang. But no one called about the ad. Instead, I got numerous invitations to be involved in the local literary life. I gave and attended readings, conducted a writing workshop, and met with local writers who—perhaps inspired by the perilous western geography—wrote predominantly about vampires and Henry the Eighth's beheaded wives. At one such event, I met a man, who, to my relief, wrote bloodless mystery tales.

The mystery writer had a longish blonde ponytail and tiny square glasses, and you could see the pallor of clouds imprinted on his translucent skin. I liked his quiet, gentle presence and how attentively he listened to everyone around him. His softly spoken English, remarkably clear of slang, brimmed with words like 'whippersnapper'. He even used a typewriter. Steeped in Conan Doyle and P. G. Wodehouse books, he seemed to belong to another era, one that had genuine gentlemen. In short, he seemed like a man who could do no harm to a lady. He appealed to that sensibility of mine I owe to having survived my childhood hospitalisations by reading European fairytales and classics. As a result, I grew up a romantic, a lover of tulle skirts and gypsy ballads, expecting men to open doors for me, to kiss my hands. Until I met Noah, I'd liked both courteous men and bad ones, but nothing in between. And now Noah wasn't here to remind me of how I'd changed.

The man offered to show me around Perth. I emailed a friend: 'I think he likes me ... I like him too, but he doesn't seem the type for a sexual adventure.' I was rushing to draw conclusions, perhaps because of the long oval of his face, the melancholy that was wrapped python-tight around him even when he laughed, and the shy but persistent way he watched me. He reminded me of my former boyfriend in Israel, the writer who wrote about places where drugs and girls were always for sale, but did so with a childlike, innocent enthusiasm, and loved me in a similar manner.

I wanted to see more of the mystery writer. I liked the person I was when I was with Noah, but I was also greedy for the other versions of myself. Under this man's gaze, I'd turn into the woman from my childhood books, grow lush with crinolines and summer parasols, blushes and a languid gait. Beyond that, I didn't think. The longer I stayed in Perth, the less real my home life seemed.

Summer was creeping up on us. The afternoon when I was supposed to have my tour of the city was too hot for such ventures. Instead, the man and I drank beer on Prichard's terrace, watching a lizard the size of a kitten trudge by. We talked about how, as children, we both kept re-reading Sherlock Holmes tales, how they made us believe that the power of intelligence could overcome the world's evils. I said that belief still persisted for me, despite all the contrary evidence I'd gathered. I said Sherlock

Holmes also inspired me to be an individual, an eccentric autodidact. The man nodded approvingly. We also talked about this elusive thing called a *writer's voice*, which I taught in writing classes but felt I'd lost. In teaching, as in writing, I often tailored the topics to my sorrows.

I write that 'we talked' but, in fact, it was I who did most of the talking. He listened. That dynamic seemed to suit us both. And whatever I said, I never mentioned a husband. And whatever joke I made, the man smiled. I came to Perth feeling sexless and voiceless, but by the time he drove away, I'd forgotten my troubles. Despite the rumours that Prichard's husband had a nocturnal habit of bothering writers staying in his house, that night it was a living man who came to haunt me in a dream.

Julia, the girlfriend of Tom, my friend from Melbourne who had recently moved to WA, called from their house in Geraldton. She asked how my writing was going.

This wasn't just a polite question. A visual artist, Julia knew how agonising 'creativity', nowadays offered in every community centre as a remedy for boredom, illness, domestic discord or any other existential crisis, could be. Still, I thought, if only I could paint … I envied the physicality of Julia's medium: the feel of brushstrokes, the painted canvas you could show instantly. Painting seemed to be a healthier occupation than writing. No wonder artists often outlived their writing contemporaries. Take the modernists. Dalí died in his mid eighties and Picasso persisted into his nineties, while Fitzgerald drank himself to death at forty-four and Hemingway called the shots (literally) at sixty-two. I didn't like my prospects.

I pushed away these morbid thoughts and told Julia I'd resume looking for interviewees in Melbourne; Perth was too conservative. She disagreed with my observation and told me about Fremantle's reputation for left-wing politics, arts and unconventional intimate behaviour. The latter is possibly the legacy of the Sannyasins, who practised the teachings of the infamous Indian mystic and Tantra teacher Rajneesh Osho. In the 1970s, a few hundred of them lived in Fremantle, becoming known for their vigorous sexual activities. Apparently, Osho recommended regular group sex as a pathway to what he called *superconsciousness*. It was this aspect of his teachings that so upset the locals that the Sannyasins eventually had to leave. Yet, Fremantle never managed to shake off its reputation as a place where anything goes; people who wanted 'anything' still flocked there from all over Australia.

'But I'm not writing about group sex,' I said defensively.

'I know. Listen, cheer up. I spoke to my friend Bianca. She has a story for you.'

'Really?' I couldn't believe my luck.

'Oh, yeah. She's very keen on your topic. For her, it's also a political matter.'

At that, my brain conjured an image of a Bianca armed with earnest spectacles and sensible shoes, looking like many of the women from social work departments where I taught, who were fond of taking definite stances on all sorts of matters. My joy was evaporating. Politically minded non-monogamy didn't interest me much. Like some left-wing activists, I, too, wished to challenge the link usually made between 'goodness' and 'fidelity'. But I wasn't planning to write a polemic against monogamy. I hoped instead to find stories nestled between doctrines, in a murkier realm.

Julia broke into my rumination: 'Kieran, Bianca's man, is a cross-dresser.' Now, *that* was murky.

As part of my research, I'd read about ideological non-monogamy, rooted in the revolutionary 1960s, when some leftist thinkers diagnosed monogamy as an extension of the patriarchal, capitalist and imperialist love of ownership. Fidelity was *wrong*. It had to be opposed, as part of a larger ambition to create a more just world.

The most sustained experimentation with such principled non-monogamy occurred within alternative communities sprinkled across the West. In some such communes, non-monogamy was a part of their overall anti-materialistic doctrine that advocated resource sharing. Others, like the Californian Sandstone Retreat, aimed specifically to help couples 'cure' their 'ownership problem'. The writer Gay Talese spent several months in Sandstone for his book *Thy Neighbor's Wife* that explored the effects of the sexual revolution on America. Talese's impression was that the estate's founder, John Williamson, was more interested in the wives of those at the retreat than in political theory. His consciousness-raising strategies focused chiefly on sex: spouses were prescribed such exercises as fucking others in each other's vicinity. No wonder most couples lasted in Sandstone for no longer than a few years. Those who didn't separate under the pressures of the commune, fled it.

Although the echoes of the sexual revolution sounded more faintly in Australia, some alternative communes existed here too. One of note clustered around the Melbourne-based theatre collective, Australian Performing Group, who wove Maoist politics into their art and operated out of a former pram factory in Carlton. Most artists lived nearby in share households. In those houses, everyone walked around naked, shat and showered side by side, fucked without locking the door. Moreover, that community developed an etiquette called 'The Carlton Letter', whereby if you wanted to sleep with someone's (consenting) partner, you left them a note asking permission. Refusal was considered impolite.

It was in that community that Helen Garner, a former member, set her novel *Monkey Grip*. Closely adapted from her diaries, the book tells the story of the addiction of Nora (a thinly disguised Garner) to loving Javo, a younger man who desires heroin more than he does her. Their already thorny affair is made more difficult by a culture where everyone 'thrashed about swapping and changing partners—like a very complicated dance to which the steps had not yet been choreographed'. *Monkey Grip* renders that 'complicated dance' as lonely and exhausting, unsustainable physically or emotionally. Not long before I came to Perth, I met the prototype of Angela, the novel's rock-singer character, who is portrayed as the most honest and outspoken commune member, during my stay at Varuna, a writers' retreat in Katoomba. One night, 'Angela' rock-n-rolled in, carrying a case of wine. 'I felt small and a bit shrivelled next to her,' Garner wrote, to illustrate the grandeur of Angela. And here she was, more than thirty years later and in her early sixties, but still loudly grand in her pink leggings, with a wineglass in her hand and emotions perched on the edge of her skin.

In Katoomba, we spent our time writing. But later, eager to talk about *Monkey Grip*, I visited Angela in her Melbourne studio stuffed with flowery china, fluffy cushions, and posters showing Angela's younger, slimmer self in all her musical glory. In the book, she was always the quickest to point out that compulsory liberty was an oxymoron. I was curious to know what the real Angela thought about this, and also where she'd bought the golden sneakers and striped pants she now wore.

'In the 1970s, we all moved out of home to have sex. I bought a double mattress at the Brotherhood of St Laurence, and that was my freedom,' Angela laughed, adding that she didn't think Garner had exaggerated anything. There was fun to be had, but eventually the freedom felt more like a pressure to be wilder than you wanted. Everyone was confused. Heterosexual women thought they should sleep with their female friends. Group sex was another thing people felt they *should* do. But, in Angela's experience, orgies frequently turned out to be more hilarious than erotic: 'It was so difficult to organise what goes where!'

She became more serious. 'See, it was never a conscious decision for most of us; it's just how we lived.'

'Couples too?'

'Monogamous couples were fucked!'

Historically speaking, the interchange between right and wrong, victims and perpetrators, bravery and cowardice, can be notoriously swift, depending on who is in power; just think of how many dictatorships were started by well-meaning revolutionaries. Naturally, in those leftist communes the monogamists became the real rebels. When Angela told me about a friend who wouldn't tolerate her husband's affairs, I could hear the admiration in her voice. As for Angela, she turned out to be more 'conventional'. For seven years, she had a love affair with a drummer, 'Willy', who was married to 'Paddy'. She also followed other passions along the way, just as Willy and Paddy did.

I asked Angela whether she'd been happy back then. She thought, then said slowly: 'I had times of great happiness with Willy, but it got more and more difficult. I felt quite territorial about him ... Really, I was most happy when my work made me happy.'

'Willy's determined constancy in loving both Angela and Paddy, while living with neither,' Garner wrote, 'was no less painful to her [Angela] for being ideologically impeccable.' Politically driven non-monogamy, just like the mainstream version of monogamy, doesn't lend itself to negotiation. Yet, love and Eros are antithetical to prescribed behaviour. *Angela wanted Willy all to herself.*

I suspect that the zeal with which non-monogamy was championed in those years produced the reverse result, and that the bittersweet experimentation, with all the hearts and families it broke, was partially responsible for the current tight embrace of monogamy. This sharp pendulum swing hasn't bypassed even the most committed non-monogamy champions. Two women I know, who during the 1970s belonged to anarchist and separatist lesbian subcultures respectively, told me the non-monogamous party in their circles was over. Co-dependency is the new black for lesbians, one said.

'All those fucking multiple relationships! I don't have any of them anymore,' Angela said with the directness I was used to in Israel and missed here. Like Garner, she eventually concluded that love, and motherhood, were incompatible with non-monogamy. For almost thirty years now, she'd lived in a monogamous relationship with Andrew, another musician with whom she had two children. Angela told me that when she left the commune to live with him, she lost her friends, but she was happy. Andrew, uncontaminated by political rage and in possession of a strong work ethic, was the sunshine that illuminated her life, she said, and her firm face with its bird-of-prey features softened under the memory's heat.

I asked her if *now* she was happy.

'I'm never happy in love,' Angela said, uncharacteristically quietly. 'You always get what you deserve. I pushed Andrew into living together, I pushed him into children … It's not one of those very affectionate relationships. Look, I've been tempted to have an affair on several occasions, but I won't do it. I respect him too much.'

In the photo glued above her desk, Andrew appeared very handsome, with large, wet-looking eyes and red wavy hair. When I expressed my admiration, Angela rolled her laughter like a joint. Apparently, the man in question was a French poet she'd recently met at some artistic retreat. 'I've had a crush on him,' she said. 'But it's platonic only.'

'We flirted and flirted in those weeks,' she said, returning to the subject just as I was leaving. 'Outrageously!'

The mystery writer asked me to go and see a French comedy film with him. By now he knew I was married and, in keeping with the propriety I suspected in him, his interest in me seemingly narrowed to literary matters. But my interest in him was only expanding. I said yes to the film. There was nothing else I could say. I needed sex badly now. Besides, I'd always had a weakness for men with long hair. Whenever we met to discuss his stories, my breathing would turn shallow and I'd become all body, a rolling Woodstock. Long after he'd leave, I'd keep shifting in my bed. I realised that if I didn't want this opportunity to slip away, as I'd let others slip away during my years with Noah, this time it was up to me to act.

On the train to Fremantle to meet Bianca and Kieran, I couldn't focus on planning my questions. Instead, I was devising a rather banal strategy for seduction—I'd make a move in the darkness of the cinema—but this was the one time in my life when I didn't give a damn about being original. As the train glided past the abundant blue-green West Australian waters, I felt guilty that I felt no guilt, only anxiety that my plan might not work and that the two days before we went to see the film would be unbearably long. When I finally broke free from the enclosure of my mind, I noticed that in this train, unlike in Melbourne, the crowd was thick with Indigenous people, and thin on suited ones. A young mother near me gripped her child's hand in a way that left me feeling uneasy. I heard police sirens weave themselves into the urban cacophony with a similar frequency to that heard in Israel and wondered what Fremantle would be like.

Instead of hippies and horny gurus, kiosks that looked like bars and bars that looked like kiosks populated the sand-dry streets of Fremantle. It could have been any cool Melbourne suburb but for the fact that everyone here smoked as if we were living in the era before healthism was invented. As I neared Bianca's building, tucked in among expensive boutiques, I re-imagined her as a classical femme fatale: tall, expensive, with cherry-dark lipstick. Would she seduce me, or scold me for my lack of political conviction? Both possibilities unnerved me. I wiped my forehead, tried to smooth my messy hair, then rang the doorbell.

'Kieran is singing with his band,' Bianca said. 'He'll join us later.' I felt relieved that my initiation into their life would be gradual. Although in Israel I'd worked as a journalist for some years, I'd never before interviewed strangers about their sex life. Not knowing what to do next, I leaned on the door, staring moronically at Bianca.

Small, skinny and blonde, she wore glasses and flat shoes, fitting uncannily well with my initial fantasy of her. Bianca's sharp little face had been dried up by the sun and she looked her age—mid-forties. Yet, the thin-lipped smile she offered me, serpentine in shape and impression, belied her tame appearance. I liked her for this incongruity.

We moved inside. A bit more relaxed now, I sat down on a little couch and looked around Bianca's apartment, which was as compact as its owner. Although Bianca utilised every available space, hanging the television on the wall, tucking boxes under the table, the flat felt lived-in rather than cluttered. Gaudy with yellow and blue glassware, and shaded with green curtains, it seemed like a place of pleasure.

Bianca reclined on the carpet near my feet and told me she lived here alone. She'd met Kieran six months ago, at a party. She felt lousy that night, something to do with a former lover who was dreadlocked and sexy, African–American and loud, very exciting, but very infuriating, and with a very, very big ego. Bianca kept smoothing her flowery skirt as she told me all that and I could see the hidden edge inside her now. The more Bianca spoke, the more I liked her. She struck me as someone who wasn't into small talk, or trying to impress. Rather, she was using conversation for her own curiosity, to make some sense of the world. Where did politics fit into all that?

'I was absolutely drunk, smashed … Kieran looked after me. He's a corrections officer and deals with people in meltdown all the time. He was empathic. He took me home. I woke up in the morning, when you usually go "Oh, crap, what am I doing with this person?", and instead it was "There is a real nice man in my bed".' Bianca laughed.

I was trying to delay the conversation I'd come here for. Partly, I was still (grandiosely) worried that Bianca might seduce me, and wanted to linger longer on more neutral territory. I also wanted to see to what extent her desire was reflected in the rest of her biography. To my mind, non-monogamous urges weren't only about sex, just as sex was almost never only about sex. Rather, our desires were symptomatic of human diversity in terms of personalities and life trajectories.

Iris Murdoch, the British novelist and philosopher, was a grand example of such interconnectedness. When she agreed to marry the writer John Bayley, she told him she couldn't commit to monogamy but her insistence on sexual freedom wasn't a reflection of how she felt about him. According to the accounts of Murdoch's biographers and of Bayley, their forty-year-long marriage, which continued until Murdoch's death, was a happy one. Murdoch's penchant for non-monogamy was a part of her lifelong rejection of whatever curtailed her autonomy, not a political construct. It seems to have been rooted in her character. 'Hers was in some sense a personality without frontiers,' Peter Conradi, Murdoch's friend and biographer, wrote. Her thinking, actions and emotional life were guided by her boundless curiosity and energy. Once she wrote to a friend that she wanted:

> To learn jujitsu, German, translate Sophocles, learn to draw decently, buy expensive and crazy presents for my friends, really go into the subject of comparative mythology, read

many very basic books about politics, learn about America, psychology, animals ...

And, for the most part, she did. In her lifetime, Murdoch wrote twenty-five novels and many philosophical works, and mastered several languages, including my difficult mother tongue. It was in that spirit of multitudes, I believe, that she once noted in her journal the 'impossibility of having only one man'.

Anaïs Nin, too, was, starting with her conception, destined for the difficulties and pleasures of parallel existences. She was a French–Cuban with a Danish heritage, and spoke Spanish, French and English. During her childhood and adolescence, her family kept moving throughout America and Europe, and, as an adult, Anaïs also wandered around the globe. She tested the limits of having only one life in other ways too: in her writing, switching between the genres of criticism, fiction and journalising, and dabbling in publishing and psychoanalysis. So, it is no surprise that during, and after, her affair with Henry Miller, Anaïs usually had several concurrent lovers. In her forties, she went so far as to become a bigamist. While still Hugo's wife, she married an American actor sixteen years her junior and for years ran two households. She once wrote in her journal: 'I have seen in each man [myself as] a different woman—and a different life.' With my own patchwork biography, I felt a kinship to Murdoch and Anaïs. But it wasn't about me now, I reminded myself, and asked Bianca about *her* life.

Bianca had grown up in the country. She said that those years, which she spent mostly hanging out in the ethereal, eerie realm between the ocean and skies, surfing, had taught her to dislike limits. Fluidity had marked her adult life too, as she kept moving between Melbourne and Perth; male and female lovers; and occupations often associated with times past, when people still handled objects for a living—working as a welder, then as a tram conductor. Lately, though, she'd taken on a job in arts administration and a mortgage, and, gradually, Bianca's appetite for an adventurous sex life had moderated too. Ironically, it was then that she met Kieran, whose history of desire was also complex.

'One morning, he said that sometime he'll probably have sex with a man, then I'll hate him and we'll be finished. But I said, "With me, you can be who you are." He was so surprised. Kieran told me then that he doesn't identify as bisexual: he can only have relationships with women, but he likes having sex with men too. Now, when he told me this, I actually relaxed,' Bianca laughed. 'And the same when he told me about cross-dressing. I realised we're more alike than I thought. Before, I was worried I might be too "out there" for him. He'd been married for years, with two children. Actually, his marriage broke down because he slept with a man … But I want him to embrace his sexuality guilt-free.'

'So, how do you manage this?'

'Well, for now, we're only talking about it …'

I tried to conceal my disappointment. Negotiations and action can easily go their separate ways. Stalin and Hitler made a pact before Germany marched its soldiers to the Russian borders; Arafat and Rabin shook hands during the Camp David talks, then the Palestinians withdrew. While I envied Bianca and Kieran's ability to talk with each other about such things, I thought that probably this interview wouldn't be useful for my book. Or for my marriage. Although I had resolved to leave my personal life outside of the interviews, it had pushed itself into Bianca's apartment as soon as I walked in.

I was too embarrassed to end the interview now and didn't want to hurt Bianca, so searched for something to ask her: 'Are you also interested in other people?'

'At the moment, it's more about Kieran's needs, because, quite frankly, we're just starting to explore each other.' My mind flicked back to the nurse and her eager husband in the fetish club. I felt somewhat protective towards Bianca.

'Have you ever had a *real* non-monogamous relationship?' I asked stupidly, just to keep the conversation going. My tongue was always like that: too quick and susceptible to generalisations. It was only when pinpointing words revolving in my mind onto paper or a computer screen that I slowed myself down and considered the options before choosing a position. But I couldn't conduct my entire life through writing.

'Ahh ... relationships.' Bianca suddenly looked embarrassed. 'I didn't really have that many.' She said this was partly because since the eighties she'd spent many years within the milieu of Fremantle. 'We were all very political there. We'd sit up half the night taking the world to pieces. Almost everybody I knew was in a relationship, but everyone was always going out with someone else as well. The way we lived was ... like *Monkey Grip*. Have you read the book?' I could see now what Julia was on about.

'How was this for you?'

Bianca smoothed her skirt again: 'I was always a feminist, making these claims of independence: "I can sleep with who I want." But let's lay it down as it is. It was also a lot of being scared of making waves and going along with male wishes. I think that had quite an effect on me ... it opened me up to being more flexible. But then, I didn't have many serious relationships. Mostly, I'd have friends who periodically were also my lovers.'

Bianca was usually the third party. At that time, her two most significant relationships, which lasted on and off (sometimes concurrently) for twelve years, had been with men who had girlfriends whom they later married and had children with.

'Did the girlfriends know about you?'

'Yes. They said they were cool with it, but I know it did hurt them.'

I was alert again. Bianca's story fitted with those of Helen Garner and Angela, and with accounts by men like Philip Roth and Norman Mailer, which all showed that during the sexual revolution's experimentation with non-monogamy, the men's wishes differed from the women's, and were fulfilled more often. Why did men have more fun? Was the popular explanation, particularly championed by evolutionary psychologists, that the current stress on fidelity is an agenda led by women, who now have more power, true? According to this thesis, even those women who stray do so not for pleasure but in a goal-oriented fashion: to solicit the best genes for their future offspring. But I didn't want offspring; at least, not now. Was I abnormal? Or was it something about how non-monogamy was practised in those circles that worked better for men than women? After all, research across various epochs and societies shows that when given the opportunity, women do willingly participate in more flexible intimate arrangements.

I recalled that I'd read *Monkey Grip* with as much irritation as pleasure; the gender relations depicted in the book drove me nuts. To paraphrase George Orwell, in the feminist-minded Carlton farm, the male animals were more equal—in love matters, anyway. The women seemed complicit in the situation, chasing the men, excusing their poor behaviour. One typically justified her inattentive lover by saying he was 'afraid of being emotionally pressured … because of course for centuries women have been the conscience of the world'. Nora, who bought Javo's meals, nursed him when he was sick, and chased him around town while he did very little in return, at least had the guts to admit that she came to feel 'like some kind of charlady'. Yet, she kept serving him. I didn't think such behaviour, and the way they no longer expected—the way women from previous generations did—to be courted and adored, was terribly progressive.

I think it is impossible to unpick what went on between the sexes in those circles without talking about what it means to be Woman and who owns the definition. Many influential feminists in the era of sexual revolution viewed what we call 'feminine' behaviour, particularly coquettishness, as collusion with patriarchy, and called upon their sisters to wipe out kohl, stop flicking their hair, and tuck themselves into jeans and boots to become men's comrades.

But things are never as simple as liberation theories would like them to be. While traditional femininity is in many ways bound with submission, it can also be a vehicle for power and pleasure. It was the latter that the second-wave feminists struggled to accommodate. Ironically, their ideology gave rise to another, and less fortunate, version of traditional femininity. Rather than capitalise on female erotic power, they played into male hands in some ways, since once women cleansed themselves of rouge, many also cleansed themselves of their sense of entitlement to male worship, and lost that age-old feminine puppeteer capacity to control suitors via the strings of their delicate shoulder straps. The creature that emerged from that generation's laboratory frequently turned out to be less a comrade than a self-effacing 'charlady', to use Garner's expression. 'Women are nicer than men, kinder, more open, less suspicious, more eager to love,' Nora said of the charladies of her commune. But whom did that niceness make happy?

'No one ever just threw himself at me,' Angela had told me. Nora noted that Javo had no reservations about courting another woman, who cared more for her haircut than for feminist dogma, while Nora was 'keeping the home fires burning after the princess has passed by'. Angela observed similarly in the novel: 'you spend years working on yourself to get rid of all that stupid eyelash-fluttering and giggling, and then ... you find out that guys still like women who do that sort of thing'. Despite their best intentions, men often fell for 'ideologically incorrect' women; charladies didn't turn them on. It seems that while women want roses, many men want to give them. Men want to adore, and they want the beauty and refinement we often associate with femininity, whether it's manifested in a sleek frock or a flirtatious smile. At least in my experience, men love princesses.

If desire between men and women feeds on differences, distance and power games—all that second-wave feminism tried to underplay—then it becomes clear that despite the amount of fucking that went on in that milieu, its ideology had a puritan, pleasure-denying streak. In Carlton and Fremantle, both sexes were locked in an unhappy cycle. Women who obeyed the prevailing doctrine had fewer chances to be loved passionately, the way that, for example, John Bayley loved Iris Murdoch. Bayley's love, Conradi wrote, both anchored and liberated Murdoch, becoming her 'base for operations' from which she explored the world. Such a secure base was also available to the men in those communes, most likely because their indifference further fired women's passions, and their insecurities, making them even more eager to please the men. This was why, I think, political non-monogamy didn't work, particularly for women; yet, men probably weren't the great winners either—at least, not in the long term. They must have enjoyed the female sexual availability, but some were also confused, dissatisfied with their lukewarm feelings.

In my generation, and younger ones, the 'charlady legacy' seemed to linger, albeit alongside the resurrection of one of the most restrictive princess-ish features—the imperative to look not just your best but perfect. My female contemporaries kept improving their bodies on a scale never seen before Botox and Cher were invented, but were still ambivalent about male gallantry. Many women I knew cringed if a man opened a door for them. If their date paid for their meal, they often worried they owed him a sexual favour. But why did so-called liberated women imagine a dinner to be an adequate price for their bodies, or, charlady-like, follow the current fashion of giving unreciprocated oral sex? I never understood such attitudes. Courtly, adoring male behaviour made me feel empowered rather than the reverse. A realisation was dawning on me that I needed my hypothetical future lovers to be gallant, romantic. I was drawn to the mystery writer's manners. But was it feasible to expect to be treated feelingly when *I* wasn't seeking love outside of Noah? And romance could lead to more complications. It was all so confusing.

I was getting increasingly distracted. Luckily, Bianca didn't seem to notice and was continuing her story. She said that, several years ago, she'd changed her 'butch look', growing her hair long, smudging her lips red, changing from baggy pants to skirts. She said: 'I feel now some backlash about the past. I'm not interested in opening up this whole gamut again where everything goes, because, quite frankly, it can be boring. The sex isn't as good. The engagement isn't as good.' Instead of 'this whole gamut', she and Kieran would proceed, carefully, with ongoing negotiation but without the mandatory honesty of political non-monogamy. For this reason, they already used condoms, just in case. Bianca thought talking would be important only if one of them developed feelings for someone else.

I wondered about Bianca's casual mentioning of the last point. I, for one, couldn't bear the idea of Noah getting attached to someone else (although I didn't entirely exclude this possibility for myself). I wondered whether Bianca loved Kieran, passionately, but didn't dare to ask. At least, it seemed they provided a secure base for each other. Kieran took care of Bianca and, recently, since his ex-wife and children moved to Indonesia, it had been Bianca's turn: 'He started dressing up more and showing me his wigs. I could see he needed a release, to be this other part of who he is, and I wanted to be there for him. Once he started talking about his children, that wasn't my world. But, hey, the Pride Parade was coming up! I suggested we march together dressed as Thelma and Louise. I thought it might be uncomfortable, but … just walking through the city together, hand in hand, him in his heels and all dragged up, was wonderful. Wonderful!'

I was quite disappointed when Kieran finally appeared. Perhaps I had expected too much from my first ever cross-dresser—some bold quirkiness, like I saw in the fetish club; some striking individuality. Perhaps the heat had melted him. Whatever it was, Kieran, small and thin like Bianca, seemed *undefined*, slippery. Even his clothes, bulky pants and a sepia buttoned shirt, resembled camouflage, blending him into the walls.

Outwardly, Kieran was all smooth surfaces: his face seemed untouched by his forty-seven years of age, his lips were generously wide. Yet, judging by how he measured his words as he spoke, diluting them with silences, impersonal pronouns and brisk, prickly laughs, he seemed rather furrowed inside: 'Being with one person is a lovely experience … and the chances are … you may not get everything you want forever with one person … Does it mean you have to throw away the baby with the bathwater every time you have some need?' He moved his already distant chair further away from us, looked at Bianca and shot out another jittery cackle: 'I feel like I've got someone here, with whom I can talk about this …'

I suddenly felt protective of Bianca; since Kieran's arrival, she'd mostly sat silently, smiling vaguely. 'How would you feel if Bianca had sex with someone else?' I asked primly.

'I can't promise I wouldn't be a bit challenged … But I'd like to believe that I'd be okay. Bianca could decide to tell me about it, or not, or somewhere in between …' Kieran gazed down at his knees, as though the rest of the answer lay there; I could barely hear his voice. 'But I'd rather that she did tell me, because I think our friendship would have more depth. I'd feel included and honoured. And I'd be most honoured if she invited me along.' He finally released a full ammunition of chortling.

Bianca offered to drive me back to the Prichard house. On our way to the mountains in her open-roofed sports car, I watched the heat beating the grey-and-white city into languid submission. The faint wind, a harbinger of the evening, soothed my skin. We tried to talk about lighter subjects now—films, books. Yet, the interview kept weaving itself around my inflated brain. It bothered me that in all of those five intense hours together, we'd never discussed love. Bianca talked about 'relationships', Kieran mentioned 'friendship'. But were they in love? More importantly, did he love her? I was projecting my own hunger here—there must have been something orphaned in me that meant I always needed to be carried on strong emotional currents. But, as a writer, I was supposed to investigate the full range of human emotions. I knew some people could be happy without romantic love. I hoped that as I continued to conduct interviews, I'd stop imposing my own desires on others. But, really, I hoped to find stories where freedom and love coexisted.

'Maybe Kieran will move to Indonesia next year, to be around his kids …' Bianca said as she dropped me at the house. 'And maybe I'll go with him,' she added quickly. I gave her a hug, hoping things would work out for her. With or without Kieran.

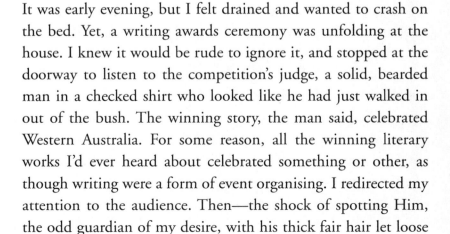

It was early evening, but I felt drained and wanted to crash on the bed. Yet, a writing awards ceremony was unfolding at the house. I knew it would be rude to ignore it, and stopped at the doorway to listen to the competition's judge, a solid, bearded man in a checked shirt who looked like he had just walked in out of the bush. The winning story, the man said, celebrated Western Australia. For some reason, all the winning literary works I'd ever heard about celebrated something or other, as though writing were a form of event organising. I redirected my attention to the audience. Then—the shock of spotting Him, the odd guardian of my desire, with his thick fair hair let loose today. And, from the way he returned my gaze, I knew why he had come. In an instant, I modified my seduction plan.

Once the speeches were over and the audience had rushed to munch on the crustless sandwiches, which, for some unfathomable-to-me reason, are popular in Australia, the mystery writer walked towards me. Through my haze, I watched his thin body, the bones of which seemed eager to flee the skin, wrestling a space for itself within the crowd, and thought of all those other sad, thin men who populated my Israeli photo albums, back when I'd sought the most refined of my countrymen but was unprepared for the winters that resided within them. I thought also of Noah, whose (small) excesses of flesh I found comforting, and who had so much life bouncing through his body. When we met, I hoped he'd extinguish the chill in me. I'd thought that was a new life, but here we go again. And again.

'I hate crustless sandwiches,' I said. 'Have you already had dinner?'

The only open local place we found was a bar that was rough at the edges with a flock of heavy-buttocked motorcycles parked at the gates. In its garden, illuminated with bleeding-out daylight and fairylights, among tables weighed with rows of empty beer glasses patterned with dried, frothy spiderwebs, amid Led Zepplin's hysterical guitars and the bitter smoke of hand-rolled tobacco, over the cooling nachos neither of us touched, I leaned towards him but maybe also into him. The stupid refrain 'it's now or never' wouldn't leave my head and, to exorcise it, and because of the pull of the desire aching at the bottom of my belly, I became the predator. But not really. By nature, by gut instinct, I was a princess. My mother had pointed this out to me many times since I was a child. So did my lovers. As a princess, I didn't have the interest, and I didn't have the courage, to face a rejection and so I summoned only those who I thought would obey. I told the man he reminded me of my former boyfriend, the writer. He said, 'What a coincidence.' I reminded him of his ex-girlfriend, the only woman he'd ever lived with: 'But she only stayed with me for two months. One week, I had a bad cold and didn't have the energy to talk to her. She moved out.'

I could have thought about how his version of their break-up was odd, but what good would come from that? Instead, I chose to focus on the similarities between these two gentlemanly, thin writers. In this place, never too far from snakes and always too far from cafés that served good coffee, comparisons comforted me. Although the Israeli writer had never made my body go mad, the way it was going now.

'My boyfriend was often sick.' I struggled with my breathing as I spoke. 'Not physically, but with sadness. He'd talk about the world's problems, but never about his own. Just before I left him, I found pills in his writing-desk drawer. He never told me he was taking them …'

The air grew heavy with cicadas. We loaded it up further, with more slices of our intimate histories, watching each other through the distorting binoculars of nostalgia, shaping some instant, excessive understanding, which was probably a misunderstanding. But questions of truth and artifice were rapidly losing their importance at the sight of his mouth so close to mine. I said, 'If you don't mind that I'm happily married, you can kiss me.'

The idiocy of my words, once released into the dusky, dusty air creaking with electric guitars, insects and motorcycles, acquired a life totally separate from mine. Once again, as at Bianca's place, and as in my marriage, spoken language failed me. I tidied up my life with Noah into 'happily married', and this man's feelings into 'you don't mind'. The mystery writer, who didn't seem foolish, although he did seem somewhat ethereal, probably knew there was no truth coming from my mouth. Despite that, and despite the chastity I suspected him of, he slowly, almost leisurely, placed my face into the cups of his hands. Starved for galvanic sensations, I sank into the hands, into the sizzling night, and, later, into bed in the house of squeaking floorboards, rampant flowers, ghosts and lizards.

The lemon slice of moon, the terribly fair body, the pleasant itch of a sleepless night in my eyes that made me feel I was young again, the blood pumping as loud as a motorcycle, the persistent mosquito song that didn't disturb us, the tenderness, the awkwardness that neither of us seemed to mind, the poetics of exhaustion. At dawn, he sneaked out just before our love den turned back into the writers' centre. Barefoot, like Cinderella before she became a princess, naked but for a blue satin dressing gown, I walked onto the already warm porch to listen to the birds. My body was skinless, acutely tuned into the air and sunshine, my hearing sharper than ever. There was a knock at the door. It was him again. I asked if he'd forgotten something.

'I did,' he said. 'To kiss you one more time.'

4

A Tale of Ménage à Trois

'Love is a crowded theatre.'
Camille Paglia

While I was still practising social work, I worked with an artist whose career had been disrupted by late-onset bipolar illness. Just as I decided to leave my job to focus on writing and academic work, this woman told me that she, too, was ready for a change. 'I'm going to paint a box black and lock my past in it,' she'd said. She meant that to recover, she needed to forget the high standard of living she'd had once, and also her more immediate, painful, past. Soon after, her life took a better turn: she finally found a job and didn't need our services any longer.

I wish I could be as sensible; at least about some of my past. But I've never had the heart to lock any of it away. This urge to document, to preserve, which is integral to writing, haunts me. Still, not all writers write about themselves as much as I do. Perhaps I'm so preoccupied with my life story because much of it is inaccessible nowadays. The Soviet Union, where my childhood took place, has vanished, becoming a country of those it once excoriated—businessmen, the unemployed, churchmen (although the *kegebeshniki*, KGB officers, are still there, still at the top of everything). Our house in Odessa, which belonged to my great-grandparents before the communists appropriated it, has been demolished, replaced by a glossy hairdressing salon. The story of the *refuseniks*, the Soviet Jewish dissidents, which is my family story, has been largely forgotten. The list of losses kept building as I, in search of adventure and a better life, kept moving. The main price I've paid for such a nomadic existence is that I've lost witnesses to my past selves. Being left with only a wobbly memory is another state of loneliness. So, I try to preserve.

J, too, is inaccessible nowadays, lost in the vastness of the globe and in his own restlessness. His back has always been a rucksack. Had I really shared my life with this man? Occasionally, I dreamed about him and woke up feeling trapped, short of breath. Then I'd be relieved to find myself in Noah's arms.

I'd been trying to write about J for years. I hoped writing would help me gain hold of that time with him and its logic, and prevent the alienation from my younger selves metastasising in me. I also hoped that once I'd pinned J down on paper, I'd stop him creeping into my mind. It didn't work like that. J always escaped from the pages back into my dreams. Yet, now that Perth was taking me over, blurring my immediate past and bringing out the distant one, I hoped that, at Prichard's desk, I'd finally make sense of it all and be able to leave J behind to be preserved. Or to rot.

I met J not long after I came to Australia, having left Israel because I'd grown tired of daily life there. I was twenty-six then, and living in Tel Aviv. By day, I was a reluctant social work student. At night, I earned money by organising dance parties, and also worked on my third fiction book. I was tired. Some say a change of geography doesn't solve anyone's problems, but they've probably never lived in a place where the sky is as low as a ceiling and the usual six degrees of separation diminish to one or two; where cars are parked on every sidewalk, and stray animals and drunk foreign workers lie in the gutters; where buildings climb on top of each other and people don't speak if they can shout instead. In Israel, we pushed constantly through each other—at the overcrowded bus stops and markets, in bank queues. We lived tentatively: from one newsflash to another; from one American dollar increase to another, because, although we earned shekels, rent had to be paid and loans had to be repaid at the foreign rate. No wonder we were always on guard, always waiting for the Messiah. What else could save us?

Eventually, I lost the stamina needed for trying daily to beat the infamous Tel Aviv traffic, pay bills and university fees, and avoid the news that was often hopeless and always full of danger, yet still follow security alerts about possible terror attacks. Several months before I left, hope made a brief appearance when Ehud Barak beat Netanyahu in the election. But this elation lasted barely until the next morning, when our new prime minister invited Shas, the ultra-orthodox party, to form a coalition. Still, the main reason I was desperate to get away wasn't political or economic.

Poets imagine love in the shape of a shrine, or a perfumed garden. But I, even before meeting J, envisaged love as akin to Israeli shopping centres—a place of pleasure where terrorism occasionally occurs. I felt this particularly thanks to the last boyfriend I had there. A social worker, he skipped over the conflict resolution theory in our training, and, instead, proceeded straight to international politics, attempting to kidnap me and keeping me in a park for hours, until at two am, I finally managed to run away. Cold with terror and breathless, I knocked on the door of the only nearby apartment in which the windows were still lit, and fell straight into the arms, and paws, of a startled cocaine dealer in mid-transaction and his two Rottweilers.

But even before that nocturnal marathon—with its eventual finishing line in Australia—the soldier-men of my country had lost their appeal. I felt worn out by their toughness, bravado and hypersexuality, which, understandably, came with their proximity to death, but often bordered on narcissism. When it came to love, instead of firearms and falafel, I now craved roses, fog, poetry and—as always—my dream inspired by *Henry & June*, which I felt an Israeli man would never share with me. Although Israel claimed to be a part of the West, it was, in many ways, still a faith-and-tribe-oriented society. I felt restless there. At night, I often wished to be somewhere I wasn't. Eventually, I developed a conviction that Israel was too small and incestuous for a romantic pilgrimage, and that to meet the right man, I had to get out.

Besides, my mother had told me not to come back.

'Until the Messiah arrives, there will be no peace in Israel. Make a new life for yourself, *dochenka*,' she said, tearily, the day before I departed. I doubted she meant the second part. But she patted my hair with a hand that smelled of herring: 'I know you won't come back. For generations women in our family have followed their husbands to remote places. Like I followed your father. You'll find your husband in Australia.'

I was appalled by her certainty, but also amazed. I'd never shared my romantic hopes with my mother. How did she guess what I couldn't admit even to my closest friends? And, as much as it irritated me, on crucial matters I always suspected my mother was right.

In Australia, I initially stayed in Sydney, with my father's sister and her family, but the city reminded me of Tel Aviv. It was expensive, fake, capricious. Then I visited Melbourne and found it was exactly what I needed—a complex city, with fresh greenness and ocean-ness, but also the chic of jazz clubs, bookshops and trams. It was all urban serenity, or serene urbanity, or whatever else my excitable younger version made of it. Soon after my visit, I moved there, to house-sit a place in Caulfield that belonged to my aunt's friend, Anna.

I'd always wanted to live alone, but Tel Aviv was wildly costly and, anyway, I always had a man in my life there. Now I relished the solitude in Anna's three-bedroom house, which was luxurious, at least by Israeli standards. It was a substantial place, like where the families in the American sitcoms I used to watch—*The Cosby Show, Who's The Boss?, Family Ties*—lived. I loved the chocolate-brown floorboards; the wooden table with a surface fit for banging with your fist while arguing a case; the many books; the large windows framed by heavy, creamy curtains, overlooking a garden overgrown with tomatoes, mint and roses. I felt as cosy as a hobbit there and, away from routines, discovered the simple pleasures one finds in slowly paced spaces: long baths, walks in the garden, painting my toenails pink.

My first Melbourne summer was running its course, still with plenty of sunshine but already mellower and a little windy. I began venturing beyond the house. I visited museums and bookshops, but mainly preferred the streets, which were all lavender and birds and sunglasses, and fire jugglers fooling around on public lawns. Overtaken by wonder, I vigorously, like a young horse, clacked my platform shoes upon the wide, friendly sidewalks. The public transport that operated during Shabbat, the cheap sushi, the absence of cockroaches—all these luxuries the locals took for granted filled me with joy. I was amazed at how in Melbourne even police cars drove by quietly. After a while, whenever their sirens did sound, I no longer thought about bombs. I was also taken by the Australians, who, I thought, had an angelic, soft look about them. I marvelled at how strangers would often smile at me. Even the so-called 'white trash', whom I saw at train stations, lacked the nervous energy of Israelis and said 'Sorry' if they got in my way. I relaxed. I lost my need to tower above the world and slipped out of my platform shoes, losing at least ten centimetres. I felt humbled by my rediscovered natural height. My tan faded. I stopped colouring my hair blonde and let it grow dark and messy, no longer tamed by fashion. I didn't lipstick my smiles anymore, and tried smiling only when I really meant it. One day, I glanced in the mirror and noticed the return of that melancholy in my eyes, evident in my Russian childhood photos, which the Israeli sun had bleached out of me. In Australia, another country built on a desert, my past had caught up with me. The irony of geography …

Australia felt like a cushion on which to rest my head and I began dreaming about having a different life here: solid, like Anna's house; joyful, like the inner-city streets. Still, my exhilaration was embroidered with edginess. In a month, I had to give the house back to Anna. I had few savings. All I had was a huge suitcase I could barely lift, stuffed with books, dresses and my novel-in-progress. I didn't know yet whether I'd be able to stay permanently in Australia, so every lovely alley I discovered, every person I met—in short, every beginning—also signified a possible ending. Whenever somebody asked me if I was here on holidays, I felt a painful pang.

With no work permit, little English and my money running out, I rejoiced when a job offer came my way. My prospective employer, Boris, knew about my financial struggles. We worked together at the only job I'd managed to find and that earned me five dollars per hour—at a Russian video library in East St Kilda. This was the Australia I knew best then: a migrant-land, where the shops sold Siberian pickles, and every bench and corner was decorated with Russian pensioners topped with baseball caps and spitting cornflower seeds onto the sidewalk.

Boris, who barely reached my chin and had small, button-like facial features—and small, button-like grandchildren—summoned me to discuss his work proposition before his morning shift began. We sat at the table in the middle of the library, where, usually, customers lounged with shopping bags at their feet, reading newspapers or scanning the rising caviar prices. I was still getting used to this place, which was really a cross between a neighbourhood house and a crazy supermarket that sold everything from smoked salmon to South American soap operas dubbed into Russian. I was paid peanuts, but at least I got a priceless trip back in time, surrounded by films from my childhood. Now I watched them again, all too ready to shake off my Israeli self.

'Ho, mama, mama, mama! I love a gypsy man!' a red-mulletted singer of indeterminate gender was screaming from the television hanging above us. I hoped Boris's offer would help me to delay my moving in with a man from Moscow on whom—perhaps as part of my Russian renaissance—I'd recently developed a crush. I liked the Russian way he courted me: with red roses and recitations of Pushkin. I particularly liked his stories about his youth, during Glasnost and Perestroika, which I'd missed out on, since we'd left the Soviet Union in 1985, just before Gorbachev began his reforms. The man, an engineer, claimed he'd done business with the mafia in those days. In my eyes, this only added to his appeal.

Although, as a newcomer, I now had an opportunity to cleanse my life of bad habits, my housekeeping wasn't perfect. I was finally living as a writer in the purest sense—alone and working diligently on a novel that, unsurprisingly, was about a search for love—but dangerous men still trailed me and I wasn't doing much to discourage them. A drug-soaked arts student and a gambling surgeon had pursued me in Sydney. And I didn't trust the peace pendant my Russian suitor wore around his neck. I could smell his dubious past in the overflowing ashtrays strewn all over his apartment. I didn't want to move in with him so quickly, but couldn't manage any rent on my current pay. Meanwhile, the man in question had already bought me a pillow.

As a prelude to our conversation, Boris sliced some cake his wife had baked. Since I'd begun working in the library, I'd realised that even the minutest Russian social interactions involved food. Here, customers routinely offered me candies and home-pickled herring as a token of their affections.

'I'm unwell,' Boris told me. I felt concerned both about his health and my own future. If he was ill, he wouldn't be thinking about my work prospects.

'My doctor said I lack protein. And one of the best protein sources I know of …' He paused to wipe cake crumbs from his tiny mouth. 'Dear Lee, I'd pay well. If I can go down on you once a week … Don't misunderstand me, please. It's only for medical purposes …'

A few days later, I moved in with the Russian engineer. But first I met J.

'I can prove to you that God exists, and also that he doesn't,' J told me, perching uncomfortably on the couch. I could see he was trying hard to impress me and had no idea he'd just touched on the topic I detested most. At least J didn't discriminate between theologies, as he occasionally visited temples as well as synagogues. Perhaps his god—or, rather, gods—was more of a relaxing hobby than, as it was in my family, a vocation. Even so, I kept looking impatiently at my wristwatch.

I wasn't impressed by the suit J turned up in either. It seemed to belong to someone else, with longer legs and broader shoulders. Besides, what man turns up to a blind date dressed in a suit? Later, we'd argue over that suit. J asserted that in Australia you couldn't overdress for a night out. I'd argue back that this was just another of his misconceptions about this country: that Australia, like Israel, was built by pioneers who didn't appreciate excess. Eventually, I won and J entrusted to me his clothing choices. But not much else.

For now, despite the suit, I could see that J was quite beautiful, in the kind of casual, tough way Israeli men manage best—the dark hair; brilliantly blue eyes; the swagger in his pumped-up arms, which showed themselves when he took off his jacket. He was embroidered with muscle and nerve. But there was something feminine about J too, particularly his delicate nose and red lips that would have been more fitting for a glamour girl. His nervousness made him beautiful too. As J would recount later, Anna's daughter—who had introduced us, with the hope of saving me from the Russian man—had told him I was a writer. So, now he moved apprehensively in territory that to him was foreign, in a house of books, with a woman of books. J was trying so hard that night that the version of him I met seemed almost tame.

Before too long, I ushered J out. I was sure he was a mistake. I was trying to shape myself anew, with a man who offered me the mother tongue I'd rejected years ago when my family moved to Israel, and that I now wanted back. I was moving in with a man who, to my delight, didn't care about God (although, like all the dangerous men I'd known, cared about something he vaguely called 'spirituality').

'I'm actually moving in with someone,' I told J at the front door, flushing with embarrassment. To my surprise, he didn't seem perplexed or angry. He didn't even ask why, then, I'd agreed to see him in the first place. Instead, he asked:

'With that Russian fellow you mentioned before?'

I nodded.

J seemed concerned in that friendly, involved way Israelis quickly develop with each other: 'I hope it'll work out, but isn't this a quick decision?'

He was advising me while I was rejecting him. This was complex; at odds with my previous romantic experiences.

J gave me a business card that indicated he was one of those men who play *Monopoly* for a living: 'Call me any time if you need something. We Israelis should look after each other here.' I liked the sound of his warm, deep voice, perfect for radio broadcasting, and appreciated his offer, even if his point about communal concern rang strangely. From what I'd gathered, J was a loner. In his four years in Australia, he'd made more money than friends. I liked loners.

'Thanks,' I said awkwardly. J brushed my cheek with his lips and walked away, with his suit trailing behind him like a dark cloud.

I've always thought of myself as a feminist. As a child, I preferred Scandinavian mythology to other folktales because its women, such as the Valkyries who rule the battlefields, are more active. In the fairytales I used to invent back then, my princesses rescued the princes. But in games, my girlfriends and I enacted more conventional narratives, and I liked playing the role of the princess in trouble. I enjoyed wearing my mother's lipstick and being kidnapped by monsters, then being rescued by a handsome royal who, I imagined, would carry me away with the train of my dress floating through the air like a promise.

At twenty-six, I still fantasised about rescuing men—now, mostly from their loveless existences—but being rescued still felt sexier. I lasted a month in the Russian man's flat, which was choked with cigarette smoke. Then I called J. I told him I didn't know what to do next. I'd overestimated my talent for survival; I was running out of money. I was thinking about going back to Sydney, to the family I hardly knew, or even to Israel.

'Don't worry,' J told me. 'You can stay with me, think things over. I have spare bedrooms. When should I come and get you?'

Just like that. *When should I come and get you?* As decisive as a fairytale prince who would always help a princess in trouble, and just when I'd decided princes didn't exist in Israel. But perhaps they'd all left for Australia?

J came to pick me up in a black Toyota and lifted my suitcase with one hand. In the day's brilliant light, I noticed a little curved scar near his ear. I slid down into the passenger seat. J shut the door. I kept sliding and sliding, down and down, as though there were no bottom to his car.

We took off.

J lived away from the kind of Melbourne I had got accustomed to. His house was in Bundoora—in suburbia, which makes do without boutiques selling vintage wares and delis offering goat cheese. We drove there through a tapestry of fences and low red roofs, with children on bicycles, lemon trees, parks with toylike bridges, a cemetery. I liked what I saw and began fantasising about birdsong in the morning, about hanging out in a local pub.

If in Israel I'd often felt claustrophobic, Australia's vastness made me crave the comfort of smallness. J's house, though, was neither small nor comforting. It was a bargain he'd bought in order to resell. The place felt like an underground train station, with its bare walls and echoing emptiness occasionally disrupted by old, hard furniture. The narrow corridor, punctuated by numerous doors, reminded me of Bluebeard's castle. At least there are no dead wives here, I thought hopefully. For me and my suitcase, I chose the bedroom furthest from J's. He smiled at my choice, with the uncertainty of someone who was more accustomed to chuckling. I felt my stomach turn. But, at twenty-six, I wasn't friends with my intuition. Drunk on the scent of jasmine in the muggy autumn air, I suggested an evening walk to the local cemetery.

For our walk, I arranged my long hair in a schoolgirl's pigtails. Perhaps I meant it as a warning to J, who was ten years older, to forgo romance. It was a sultry night, though, with a buttery moon, and the stars yolk-yellow and swollen, as in Van Gogh's *Cafe Terrace at Night*. Despite my lack of interest in J, I was preoccupied with my desirability in his eyes. I wanted to confirm my worth through charming a man I didn't want. I wanted to conquer, particularly as no other victories were on my horizon.

I'd always been drawn to cemeteries, I told J as we walked among the graves. The proximity of death rendered my own life precious, and living more urgent. I said I had felt a similar exhilaration during the Gulf War, as I huddled in a sealed room, and years later, when a terrorist blew himself up near my apartment, shattering my bedroom window. In response, J told me about Esther.

What I saw as a subversive game—jumping the fence of a nocturnal cemetery—for J, apparently, conjured raw feelings. The memory of Esther was evoked here, among the eerie beauty of the tombs. She had been dead for some years now, having been killed in a hiking accident in the Australian outback.

'She wasn't much older than you when she died,' J said.

I stared at him through the tulle of darkness, with a budding yearning. This story showed him to be deeper than I had thought, made of genuine adult fabric sewn with intimate knowledge of death. And I had a weakness for people who had been touched by tragedy, particularly men as handsome as he and particularly when I was as unsteady as I was that night. My own life, which I'd so far thought of as quite unusual, now seemed pulp fiction compared with J's classic novel of endurance. Handsome, wealthy, brooding and with a dead woman in his past, J, I hopefully deduced, was Mr Rochester incarnate. But I was no Jane Eyre; I found dead women attractive. I could write about them.

'That was the price I paid for this migration,' J said, ending our silence, his nervous energy bubbling through the soupy air. 'She was my soulmate. It was *our* dream to start a new life here ... Since she died, I've lived here alone. Like a dog.'

I noticed how J stumbled over each word. Clearly, this wasn't one of those rehearsed narratives that I, the professional storyteller, carried around, ready to use. For J, the telling was an effort, which meant his clichés sounded fresh, important.

'So why didn't you go back to Israel?' I asked somewhat impersonally, like the curious journalist I'd once been. Oddly, although J now appealed to me, I felt no jealousy towards the 'soulmate' he'd just thrown into the air between us.

'I felt like I owed her this, to stay ... Like her death would be a total waste if I went back. Do you think that's odd?'

No; I understood him. For me, too, going back—whether to Ashdod, to a former lover or, now, to Israel—would have felt like a defeat. I thought that in life, as in chess, only powerful figures could afford zigzagging. Most of us were pawns—to get ahead, we had to keep moving forward. J, Esther and I must have envisioned Australia as the eighth rank, where you could become anything, even a queen. *J, Esther and I …* In hindsight, the idea of the three of us had already formed before there was a two of us.

'Look, it was my idea, that hiking. I could have prepared better, done research. I was careless. But, I tell you, I didn't know …' The blue flame of his eyes fixed upon me as if I had the power to offer him absolution. And, I admit, I liked the power I imagined he offered me.

By now, the graveyard stars were in full bloom. For no apparent reason, I told J that two years after Van Gogh painted *his* stars in *Cafe Terrace at Night*, finally developing the bright palette he would become known for (albeit posthumously), he shot himself. In Australia, I had time to indulge in self-education, hoping this activity would help me develop my own, writer's, palette. For now, though, all I seemed to achieve was a head full of obscure facts. Yet, J seemed interested. In Van Gogh, too. We kept strolling through the cemetery until our hands gravitated towards each other.

The first touch and its electricity.

'Why won't you sleep with me?' J asked the next evening on his return from some obscure activity he called 'work'. He wore tracksuit pants and smelled of paint. His face was flushed with the late orange sun. I wasn't used to men like him, who worked with their bodies. Perhaps it was better this way. The social worker I'd been involved with proved he was mad when he'd tried to kidnap me. The writer was well-versed in antiquity, but couldn't face a bank queue or living in this world in any other practical way.

'You said you were cold last night. With me, you'll be warm. I won't touch you if you don't want me to.'

J, already showered, and steaming with soap and health, seemed breathtaking in his simplicity. Even his smile appeared simpler now.

'Or maybe I'll just lick your feet.' He kept the ocean of his wry eyes on mine, shattering my fantasy. 'But that would be all, I promise. I'll lick them clean.'

Boris came to mind. What was it about me that pulled the strings of men's tongues in Australia? Or was it Australia that loosened up the tongues, and sexual repertoires, of its male new arrivals? Or perhaps loose men were targeting this country as their refuge? I was too new an arrival myself to draw conclusions. Instead, I got into J's bed, which was just a mattress on the floor, and stayed there, on and off, for the next two years.

It had happened again. I'd crossed to the other side of the earth, only to find myself in bed with an Israeli man. Researchers say travellers and migrants are susceptible to reckless infatuations. But I also blame my ears, which are even lustier than my skin. It's my mother's fault. A gifted storyteller, she breastfed me on retellings of opera librettos and popular Soviet films, and the stories from her childhood. Her tales, seasoned with humour and artfully chosen details, were among my first sensual pleasures. Perhaps *she* should have become the writer. Perhaps, for all my rebelliousness, I remained unweaned. Whatever the truth, if there is one to be found, I fell for J's tale. When I climbed into his bed, I was looking for his lost love between the sheets.

In the first week in Bundoora, I begged J for their story. Obligingly, he adjusted his weight on the lumpy mattress, and leaned against the wall. His teeth shone in the shadows, like animal bones.

Once they got here, he told me, they bought a van at a bargain price, setting out to explore Australia and to decide where to settle.

My view of Australia then was light-hearted. Even the countryside I'd seen seemed benign, tame, made of manicured lakes, penguins you lined up to watch from a distance, two-dollar-entry museums dedicated to any trifle. It hadn't yet occurred to me that snakes, spiders, sharks—all these creatures with names that hiss—lurked here too. I was lulled by the ubiquitous signage telling me to watch out for koalas, where to unleash my hypothetical dog, which way to turn the door knob. I felt relieved by the pettiness of these concerns. But J had missed having action and was drawn to the parts of Australia that were still beyond the law. He and Esther behaved like clichéd tourists, he said, deciding to take on the outback. They felt invincible—out of ignorance, or maybe arrogance, which often go hand in hand.

J sounded self-critical, yet, by now, I'd noticed the excessive confidence with which he navigated the Toyota: one hand loose on the wheel, treating traffic rules as mere recommendations. His car, a well-trained animal, was always ahead of us, getting us everywhere on time, even when we left home late. I wasn't sure J had the wisdom of hindsight, but I said nothing. Being a writer, I never let the truth get in the way of a good story.

He should have known better, J said. Being a dedicated traveller, by then, he was conversant with the risky parts of the world. But J remained cavalier, assuming that once he left Israel, his life would roll on smoothly, as the van did for some hundreds of kilometres through the outback, with its blue flowers and dragonflies, all that blazing jewellery of summer meant to mask the deadliness of dirt roads and rocks; or, perhaps, to redeem them? After all, the Australian outback was an Antipodean version of the alluring siren with an appetite for foreigners. But how were they to know? On a steep path, amid that sultry party of buzzing, crawling flora and fauna, Esther, who also didn't like rules and so didn't wear proper hiking shoes, slipped and flew off the rock.

In the army, they teach you that preventable dangers, although less common, are often the most lethal. But who would think in those terms among the flowers and the sunshine?

Esther died instantly.

J plunged after her and got a cut near his ear.

I leaned into his chest, trying to imagine what it had been like for him to check on Esther. The worst was the uncertainty, he said. He didn't know whether he'd discover suffering he wouldn't be able to relieve, or the even more unthinkable—the bizarreness of a familiar body turned into a dead one. He bent over Esther, wishing for the cicadas to grow quiet so he could hear her heartbeat. Hope outlasts facts, we all know that.

That moment, when J realised she was dead, must have seeped into his skin. I already knew about their bond; or, at least, J's version of it. He described the two of them as a self-contained unit operating against the world, which had proved to be hostile since they were children. Esther was estranged from her religious parents; and during J's teenage years, his mother moved away to be with her lover, leaving him with his father, who was better at handling money than people. When Esther and he met, they clung to each other. Then she slipped off the rock.

J showed me the photo of Esther at the morgue, where she lay with her hands crossed non-Jewishly over her chest, a rose from J twined in her fingers. I'd have liked to describe her using the vocabulary of *Song of Songs*; to say she was 'all fair'. This would have been a boost for my vanity, as, unable any longer to separate myself from the story, I felt J's choice in women reflected on me. But Esther didn't look good there, or in the photos from their travels around Australia. In the pictures in those battered, small albums, her dark hair was carelessly gathered on her nape, her strong jaw and aquiline nose were rendered sharply, her curves were obscured by bulky pants, her dark skin was already greying with death. I wondered what had happened during those days, because in other photos, from Israel, Esther was beautiful, her long curls flying above her head like protective birds. Or, at least, kind of beautiful, eighties style: dressed in clothes with padded shoulders, and with feral smiles loaded with lip gloss and showing large, pristine teeth.

J described Esther as his mate. But this wasn't what I saw in the photos. To me, she smacked of a fecund, primal femininity incompatible with camaraderie. Her looks made me think of excessive love of children, large dark areolas, generosity with the wrong men. I wondered what she'd have said about the disparity between J's and my visions of her. Was I minimising my rival? Who was Esther? I felt burdened by her mystery, particularly given that to solve it could also mean finding out what the future held for me. I wished I could sink into the well of J's soul to find Esther at its bottom. But I suspected that even if I could, she wouldn't have talked to me. She wouldn't have liked me. I'd have been too Russian for her: pale, bookish, a dreamer. Whereas I, now that I'd seen Esther's photos and she'd become real to me, was developing a relationship with her.

Finally, the tale took its toll and J had tears in his eyes. A social worker by training, a tragedy junkie by vocation, I was never afraid of others' unhappiness. In my element now, I kissed J's eyes, drinking in his sorrow, held him tight among the shadows that kept creeping up on us like spiders. I was full of pity for him; yet, I must also have gorged on that pity. J's tragedy drew me into something larger than I'd ever known. But Esther was the heroine. J was the hero. If I wanted a part, it would have to be that of the chorus: I'd document their story and offer commentary. I felt purposeful, inspired. I forgot my own troubles. Even before I got to my notebooks, I was writing their tale.

I wasn't the first woman to begin a ménage à trois with the ghost of my lover's lover, whether dead or absent in some other way. In artistic circles, such arrangements can even be conducive to creation. Like my mother, I am suspicious of coincidences, and several weeks before I met J, I had found Deirdre Bair's biography of Anaïs Nin in a second-hand bookshop in Flinders Street. And, like many bookish people, I often live out what I read.

The film *Henry & June* ends with June leaving for New York, and the only thing the final credits tell us about her subsequent fate is most improbable: 'June became a social worker.' Bair writes that after she was gone, Henry and Anaïs's relationship grew stronger. Much productive activity ensued in Henry's apartment, paid for with Anaïs's money: meals were cooked, bedsheets and pencils rustled. Sometimes when they made love, they spoke of June to enhance their pleasure, but they didn't depend on her to maintain the passion. Miller's letters to Nin are full of fire: 'I love your loins, the golden pallor, the slope of your buttocks, the warmth inside you, the juices of you … came away with pieces of you sticking to me.' What June really amplified for the couple was their work: she remained their muse for the ten years their affair lasted. Henry and Anaïs dwelled jointly and separately on her every gesture, frock and scheme. Anaïs presented Henry with an analysis of June's role in his life and it was more astute than his. Miller used Anaïs's ideas in *Tropic of Cancer* without asking her permission. But it wasn't just Anaïs he robbed when composing that book. After years of trial and error in forging his writing voice, Miller finally found it; or, rather, pulled it out of June's throat. Once he bestowed on his protagonist the volcanic quality of her monologues, the character finally came alive.

Although Henry's theft upset Anaïs, it didn't seriously damage their affair or Anaïs's writing. June was fascinating enough to inspire many more works. According to Bair, 'for almost twenty years June remained fixed in Anaïs Nin's imagination', appearing in *House of Incest* and *Henry and June.* Miller, too, kept producing June novels—*Tropic of Capricorn* and *The Rosy Crucifixion* trilogy. Ultimately, it was the muse who would lose the most.

During their marriage, and despite June's many affairs with other people, she adored Henry. Despite her bravado, June carried in her marrow a pious, migrant childhood, which, combined with her doubt about her acting talent, gnawed at her for life. She saw Henry as her anchor; her meaning; and her 'genius', as she called him. Showing herself to be far more perceptive than Miller gave her credit for, June recognised his talent long before anyone else did, and supported him for years so that he could write; mostly through gold-digging, which strained her already edgy nerves. But when the genius finally produced his masterpiece, June found herself, to her horror, depicted as a heartless liar, the tormentor of Henry's prototype. 'He has to whip himself by hatred in order to create,' June told Anaïs, begging her to convince Henry to revise the book. 'He stole my soul.' But Anaïs wouldn't interfere. After all, she, too, wanted June's soul. Later, her works also immortalised June only as the con woman, the seductress.

The completion of *Tropic of Cancer* precipitated another ending. June must have realised then that in this threesome, her lovers preferred her to be absent, most likely because the presence of grand personalities in the flesh wreaks havoc incompatible with the discipline that writing requires. June, defeated and penniless, left her marriage and Paris. The next, and final, time she'd see her genius would be in 1961, when most of the books she had inspired had been published, turning Miller and Nin into celebrities. That day, Henry, mortified, witnessed his splendid muse's transformation into a poor, lonely hunchbacked woman with a shortened leg and a sick heart. An expert in the art of being cunning, June proved to be not as calculating as the couple who, for years, had picked apart her flaws. 'However bad things are for me,' June once told Anaïs, 'I always find someone to buy me champagne.' But in 1961, she appeared champagne-less.

Iris Murdoch also profited from a ménage à trois involving an absent lover. Before she married John Bayley, she was involved in a tempestuous three-year affair with Austrian–Jewish writers Elias Canetti and his lover Friedl Benedikt. This unhappy liaison was further complicated by the existence of Veza, Canetti's wife, and his other mistresses, and by Iris's lovers. But mostly it was complicated by Canetti's personality.

Murdoch called Canetti, a short man with a gigantic forehead and an equally sized ego, a 'demon-angel'. Later, she'd reason she had needed to experience being miserable in love, but this need was atypical of her usual disposition. I suspect this urge was bound up with the place and time of the affair, which unfolded in the England of the early fifties, just after the Holocaust had stretched our understanding of human nature and when Europe was coming to terms with itself. Murdoch, guilt-ridden by Britain's initial inaction in the war, had a series of crushes on the Jewish survivors who flooded England at the time, and she mistook Canetti for one. When he kissed her, violently, roughly, she must have submitted her lips with the martyr's sense of purpose. When he pulled at her hair or publicly ignored her, she must have felt she deserved it. But Iris was knocking on the wrong door. Canetti had escaped the Holocaust in time, unscathed, and, with London's intellectuals and women fussing over him, was anything but grief-stricken.

There were other reasons for their mutual attraction. Canetti must have recognised that under Murdoch's veneer of being a moral philosopher interested in goodness and sainthood, lurked something of his own manipulative nature. Both were nosy, obsessively analysing their friends' behaviour and utilising the insights gained for their own ends, such as writing. Canetti wooed Iris with tales of Friedl, who fell in love with him when she was very young, after reading his novel *Auto-da-Fé*. At twenty-three, she followed him and Veza to London. Friedl explained that decision to her parents in a letter strewn with romantic fatalism: 'My life and his are bound together forever, he taught me to write and to live.' Canetti, though, far from feeling bound to anyone, divided his life between her, Veza and other women. In her despair, Friedl, usually obedient (once, she aborted a child following Canetti's order to do so), began stalking Canetti. For hours, she'd wait for him on the streets, repeatedly tidying her hair in case he appeared. Friedl's love for Canetti, according to Murdoch's biographer Peter Conradi, was 'quasi-religious'. But Canetti, by the time he met Iris, had tired of Friedl's physical presence and bade her farewell.

At the start, Canetti and Iris had another candidate for the absent-third-party role—another Jewish refugee, Franz Baermann Steiner, the brilliant poet who had lost his family and health to Hitler. Shortly after proposing to Iris, Franz, unwittingly, introduced her to his friend Canetti. Several months later, he tactfully got out of their way, when his heart failed him at forty-three. So, why was it Friedl who became the leading topic of conversations and correspondence between Iris and Canetti? It seems to me that tragedy alone—even at its grandest, such as a premature death—won't suffice to make a lover into a muse. The absent third party must be also wild, enigmatic, sexually magnetic—like June. Like Friedl. Like, I'd learn later, Esther.

Chaotic but charming, Friedl knew how to drive men wild. A Hungarian painter, in his rage over her preference for Canetti, tore her dress into ribbons and slashed his own paintings. A more tender suitor promised her an island. But it was the ugly Canetti whom Friedl craved. Still, as masochistic as she was, I wouldn't summarise her simply as Canetti's victim. She took her revenge in her novels, where Canetti appears as The Monster—the rapist, the liar, the slave-collector. Yet, she wasn't as strong as Iris either. In the year Canetti rejected her, Friedl fell ill with Hodgkin's lymphoma, but also with a broken heart, and died quickly, aged thirty-six. Afterwards, Canetti and Iris made a pilgrimage to locations in Hampstead that were meaningful to Friedl. In the gardens of St John's College, they made daylight love on a bench and Iris carved 'Friedl' on the seat. Later, Canetti would use Friedl's story in his memoirs, but it was Iris's fiction that she'd inspire the most.

American spouses Michael and Barbara Foster and their lover Letha Hadady wrote in their study of threesomes, *Three in Love*, that it is common for artists to feast on a third. They described Anaïs and Henry as cannibals who 'devoured June down to her last gesture. While they disgorged their creations, the woman, left to fend for herself in the real world, became a shadow.' In another time and place, Iris's friend Carol Stewart made a similar observation: 'Murdoch ate people up.' And in J's bedroom, I was salivating, sharpening my teeth, so that I could drag Esther from the pedestal that belongs to the dead, especially when their corpses are as young and alluring as hers. June and Friedl, I thought, conquered many men but couldn't keep the one they loved. And how did Esther fare?

Jam-dense wind snuck in through a window that had been left ajar; my locks stirred like Medusa's snakes. Was I really dangerous, or in danger? The truth must be somewhere in between.

At the Moomba festival, the fireworks painted the Yarra candy-red. Melbourne was a foreign city and, for me, the red river, the fairy floss sold at stalls, the night that flowed with Kylie Minogue's music and the wind, were all charged with rampant emotions. I felt happy and wanted to do silly things. I convinced

J to take a roller-coaster ride, even though he didn't seem like a man who had ever been a child. When we were up in the sky, pulsing with fireworks, J felt sick. I said I'd stop the ride for him. He laughed kindly, in a way I couldn't have imagined him doing, and held my hand tighter. I didn't know then that troubles were J's happiness, that stopping the ride was the last thing he'd want me to do. For now, I mainly noticed J's tender spots. His tragedy rendered him vulnerable, and this filled me with optimism. Whenever I fancied a man, I'd search for his vulnerabilities. If he revealed them to me, I'd know I'd be loved.

J announced his love for me a week after I moved into his house. When he, whose body seemed permanently contracted, with the muscles rolling under his sleeves like snooker balls, said in our shared language, *Ani ohev otah*, he appeared to be liquid. I was surprised by J's speed. But his liquidity, the echoing house, the slowly chilling city, my insecurities but also my confidence that I was loveable—all these made me believe him. Still, I already suspected his love wouldn't make me happy. Wouldn't make him happy either. But I let these thoughts float away through the window into the yellow autumn. J looked at me, awaiting my response. I touched him. He felt like a lion—dangerous but tameable. This turned me on. I wanted to test my taming skills.

I was making another hopeful beginning. It was always I who moved into a man's place; like a dog, I marked J's territory as mine too. I moved our mattress into the living room, which overlooked the grassy backyard, and spread the things I considered essential to the making of a home: books, candles, and a chessboard from a two-dollar-shop. J approved everything, even though he preferred possessions that could be deposited in a bank.

One night, sprawled on the mattress, we watched a documentary about a phenomenon that had puzzled scientists for over a century. Every year at the end of monsoon season, when it was particularly misty, migratory birds of various species flocked to a village in North Cachar in India. Apparently, this isolated land strip of just 1.5 kilometres is the only known place on earth where birds go to commit suicide.

We watched on television the fog spread its net through the moonless night. The birds, dazzled, dishevelled, dove like shot-down jets, head-first, from the sky into the trees, painting the foliage crimson. The film made visible what I'd long suspected—that self-destruction was frequently bound up with beauty. I wondered whether it was the place that drove them to their death, or whether the suicidal urge originated with the birds. I thought, what if my own poorly planned arrival in Australia were only the continuation of all the other risks I'd taken in Israel, the financial and intimate ones, and the risk of not being who I really was—a bit Israeli, a bit Russian, a bit of a dreamer. And what if, because of who I was, Australia became risky too? What if the places we go to are merely spatial representations of our internal minefields?

'When these birds begin their migration, do you think they know they'll die?' I asked J. He shrugged, uninterested in such speculations, and said he'd like to see the village for himself. It suddenly struck me that he hadn't included me in his plan. That hurt. But, at least, that felt like I thought love should feel.

5

A Tale of Adultery

'Adultery is a most conventional way to rise above the conventional.'
Vladimir Nabokov

Once the electricity of desire for the mystery writer hit me, I was hooked. What I thought would be a one-off act turned into a series of encores, Warhol-like repetitions of arms, legs, lips, nights. My lover's bristles peeled the skin off my chin, and I carried my wounded face around like a medal. Yet, the electricity wasn't at the high voltage I'd hoped it would be. My lover seemed content in his role, but also eager to do coupley things—drink Johnnie Walker in a bar, walk around Kings Park hand in hand, kiss in the cinema. I liked all that, but whenever I had things my way, we did what I most liked doing with men, what Noah wasn't interested in: we led a languorous, moist boudoir existence, where shadows and bare skin ruled, where we lived through our oozing, smelly, sticky flesh even when we weren't making love.

I emailed to a friend: 'Funnily, being with him feels almost like being with Noah: so much intimacy, embraces, kisses, laughter. Still, he's new to me. He makes me feel alive.' I should have added something about the strands of his sun-coloured hair shadowing his face, driving me wild. And about how every time I saw him, the sheer pleasure of our secret was so sharp that something inside me snapped. The resemblance of his behaviour to Noah's only enhanced his appeal: my lover appeared deliciously foreign, yet not dangerous. Whenever darkness spread its satin bedclothes over the Prichard house, I listened for his knock, then turned off my mobile phone. I responded to Noah's messages in the mornings. He enquired about my nocturnal pastimes, but not insistently, which I took as permission.

The inky harbour, dappled with lights from faraway places, lay underneath us, shaggy and lazy like an expansive animal. Fremantle dribbled its hot, viscous honey over our heads. I peeped through oblong, narrow windows into the former lunatic asylum that had been built by convicts and now pretended to be an arts centre, searching for history. In Australia, the sense of history was more fragile than in the places I came from.

Here, I missed the mystery of ruins. I didn't trust nostalgia, but neither did I believe things from the past went away. Sadness, like evil, seemed to seep from one generation to another—in my family too—and it felt safer to know where the past lurked. I kept peering through the windows. It was too dark to see much, yet I began imagining bare corridors, under the gothic ceilings, and the lonely shuffling of past inmates. My lover asked if I was okay. I said I was thinking of my father, who—prone to occasional bouts of depression—as a young man did a stint in a Soviet psychiatric facility. That hospital lacked the beauty of this place, but had a similar function: as a depository for social ills—prostitutes, alcoholics, freethinkers, eccentrics. My father fitted the latter two categories. Luckily, they kept him there only for a period of weeks.

My lover listened intently. Like me, he was from here but not exactly. His early years were spent in London, while it was still swinging. He was a man shaped by an intensity he didn't embody, now living in a country that didn't embody it either. For him, too, the past wouldn't go away. Perhaps that was why he travelled so frequently and loved it when I talked to him of remote places that, at least for us here, were safely dangerous.

'Are you really okay?' my lover asked. I nodded. With his arms looped around my shoulders, I felt utterly okay. And utterly confused.

Like Scheherazade, I'd often seduced men with my words. I emailed my lover the most erotic story I'd written in English. It began: 'With Paul sex has become vicious altruism: Come on, I'll give you what you want ... This is what he teaches her: the availability of humiliation; the intolerable easiness of pleasure.' With some variations, 'she' was me. Paul was J. By the end of the story, she leaves him. She'd have it easier than I did, though, without the threats of deportation, the months of hiding, the coughing fits I'd experience after our fights.

However, rather than relishing the story's abundant sex—man-on-man felatio, orgies, and the pedestrian-in-comparison crime and punishment stuff—my lover focused on the damsel's distress. He emailed me to say that as he read my story he felt a strong desire to reach out and rescue the female character, which he guessed was more or less me, from that relationship. The email ended with his apologies for these feelings; he was concerned I may interpret them as a sign that he was a chauvinist and be disappointed in him.

Oh, but how could he have possibly disappointed me …? At the word 'rescue', my ears pricked, my dress plumped up with crinolines, a tiny golden crown budded through my tangled hair. I took to staring dreamily at my lover's business card displayed prominently on my writing desk. It said 'senior financial advisor', a profession that usually made me think of misplaced life priorities. Now, prongs of excitement went through me whenever the words 'financial' or 'advisor' were used in conversation or on advertisement billboards. I particularly admired the adjective 'senior', re-reading it on my lover's email signature accompanying his electronic kisses. A senior financial advisor took an interest in me. I emailed back:

> This isn't a macho response, but a manly one. Remember I told you that as a young girl I identified with fairytale princesses? I'm sure many women fantasise about being rescued, but don't admit it. I do.

No longer able to focus on my own writing, during the day I was editing a local writer's manuscript in which the protagonists fought each other with radioactive swords and other weapons that sounded like a cross between medieval arms and modern kitchen appliances. The characters were so busy fighting that they had no time for inner lives. In want of human contact that didn't involve exchanges of blows or bodily secretions, I went to visit Nina, that same acquaintance who had prompted my reflection on the frontiers of monogamy, and who—to finance her law studies—did secretarial work in an office nearby. Her husband was a cousin of the Melbourne-based friend who had kindly asked them to look after me during my stay in Perth.

Nina, in her mid-forties, a suburban mother of two teenagers, and with her creamy blouses, grey skirts and shopping bags, differed from my Melburnian friends, who usually lived in the inner city, owned poetry books and old record players, travelled to countries only they knew about, had more cats than children, and refrained from eating meat but kept smoking, despite our health-conscious times. But Nina had quickly grown on me. I loved people like her, who were dark, rich and bitter, like good coffee. Nina's curiosity, aversion to euphemisms, and irreverent humour cohabited uneasily with some deep-seated fragility. I suspected that that insecurity, which bent each sharp statement Nina made into a question, had to do with her unhappy childhood in a poor neighbourhood in Toronto with countless siblings and little parental attention. Nina had settled here more than twenty years ago after meeting her Australian husband. But she'd never adjusted to the relocation, to all the distance that now lay between her and her difficult clan. Despite having her husband, children and friends around, Nina was prone to bouts of loneliness.

The afternoon stared us down defiantly. The air conditioner in the now-empty little office where Nina worked wasn't functioning properly. Still, I was eager to talk—about husbands. Nowadays, every marriage became a secret I wanted to crack, as if by doing so, my own would be revealed to me. In Perth, whenever my mind escaped the protective haze of flesh and science fiction manuscripts, I thought of Noah. Our phone conversations left me feeling uneasy. The distance seeped into them, diluting our exchanges to affectionate commonplaces. I didn't think this was happening just because I had a lover. During our other separations—Noah's travel for work, my writing residencies—our phone conversations had also turned anaemic. Noah was a talker, but an argumentative, reactive one. In any debate, he'd play the devil's advocate role until eventually revealing his own position. I loved his willingness to consider things from several points of view. Whereas I liked to be right, Noah listened. He was also entertaining, spotting the hilarious in everything—breakfast cereals, cockroaches, national disasters. For his wit, and his natural warmth, people gravitated towards my husband when they were in trouble. He laughed them out of sorrow at break-ups and illnesses. But Noah had no flair for plot or detail. He wasn't a storyteller. I knew that during my absences he partied deep into the night, but he said nothing concrete about that.

In Perth, I had the rare luxury of time for reflection. I began realising that for years I'd been simplifying my husband, photoshopping his surfaces to manage his otherness. My version of Noah had become teddy-bearish, that he was the always sacrificing, accommodating man—a man whom I adored, but also took for granted. I'd begun patronising Noah and developed a series of cute nicknames for him: *sweety, baby, angel.* I meant all of them affectionately, but in overusing these nicknames I was robbing him of his wildness.

In our first years together, Noah would repeatedly ask me to go dancing, join him on his business trips, hang out with him in cafés at weekends. But I rarely had time for him. Instead, I gave him liberally what I wanted for myself—freedom. I thought that was the happy modern relationship: a parallel existence, with occasional restorative intersections of love and warmth. Unwittingly, I made myself into the kind of wife not to have fun with. I gave my husband freedom and eventually he took it. Some dawns, he returned home exhausted from nightclubs, his breath suffused with gin and tonic. Several times, I found left open on our computer web pages in which pretty women copulated with mechanical cocks or brothels in exotic locations were advertised. I dismissed these as trivial at the time, but now I wondered whether he had wanted to get caught.

I began worrying about that other life Noah had, wondering whether he took liberties when I wasn't around. I wasn't overly jealous; the scenarios that could have plausibly happened, like the brothel visits, I could tolerate. Fleeting adventures didn't concern me much. But I was afraid we were drifting apart, that the unsaid things would grow bougainvillea-wild between us until we'd lose sight of each other. I did want him to tell. I said this to Noah during those few uneasy conversations we'd had over the years about introducing some sexual freedom into our relationship, giving him my, unasked for, permission. But he always denied there was anything to tell.

I decided that on my return to Melbourne, I'd slow down again, the way I did just before I left, and spend more time with Noah. I also decided to override his condition regarding not telling. I didn't plan to reveal everything—not the fire that ate at me now, the loss of appetite, the lush harem that my headspace had become. But I wanted him to know that my body had come alive again—to make him suffer a little for all that lovemaking he'd denied me, but more to let him know I was ready to play again—with him too. Or, mostly with him. The telling would also mean—at least, in my mind—that what I did wasn't adultery. The distinction mattered deeply to me.

Requited love was such a great but complex project, I was thinking now, in Nina's stuffy office. Our marriage had become an intersection of all three temporalities. It required perpetual attention be paid to the future, but the past, too, lurked around always, folding into our present embraces all the other embraces and hurts we'd ever shared, waiting to take over whenever vigilance lapsed. If I wanted to fix things, there was so much to consider. I asked Nina what it was like, being married for more than twenty years.

There were things about Nina's marriage I already knew. I knew her husband was once her great love, but that by now his status had shifted to that of a dear relative, someone whose absence would cause her acute discomfort, but whose presence didn't relieve her emotional yearnings in a sustained way. In short, she was in what was considered a 'normal marriage', similar to what many other love-based relationships I knew of turned into, and that I had no talent at surviving. Nina's version looked pretty good, though. When I went to visit, the garden overflowed with petunias and butterflies; the grey hills swelled grandly beyond the windows; the living room brimmed with the chatter of their children, who still nestled, like puppies, into their parents; and the house smelled of Nina's husband's spicy cooking. I could also see the marital tepidity wasn't mutual. Nina—with her fiercely dark eyes that defied her soft, round appearance, and her wavy thick hair—was still Juliet to her husband's plump, shortish Romeo. The way he looked at her reminded me of Noah.

'My husband grips me in ways that hurt.' Nina answered my question with a ferocity that shook me. 'He doesn't enfold me. He catches me, he grabs me. He sucks on my nipple like a child. When he kisses me, there is this urgency that makes me think, Well, if you let me meet you in the middle, I'd feel like it. But you're taking the life out of me!'

I stared speechlessly at Nina and at the shopping bag, with the spring onions sticking out of it, nestled at her feet. Maybe it was the heat. To my shame, as well as empathy, I felt envy, wishing Noah had been that urgent with me. 'So, why did you marry him?' I eventually asked, as though everyone but Nina made wise romantic choices.

She didn't seem to mind my question, saying that she was young when they met: 'I naively thought that with marriage comes safety. But my husband wouldn't know how to protect me.

He's so loving, but he wouldn't notice if I burst into flames!' She said that her understanding of this solidified during the agony of her first labour, when he'd failed to protect her from having visitors in the birth room. Since then, his touch had irritated Nina. 'But,' she swivelled in her chair, shaking herself, like a kaleidoscope, into a more presentable picture, 'if I say to him, "I need to talk to you," he always listens and, to me, this is worth everything, even if I miss out on being held.' Nina laid her sharp eyes on me. 'Enough about me. What's happening with you?'

'Ah, the usual. I can't find anyone to interview,' I mumbled, even though my lover's story kicked and screamed inside me. I wasn't sure what aroused me more, being with him or talking about him. I'd always loved re-experiencing my erotic ventures through storytelling. But as much as I liked Nina, and despite her sudden confession, she was still the priestess of family life, stoic in the face of marital disappointments in a way I couldn't be. I didn't think she'd approve if I told her about him.

'I don't think it's the book that's making you look so distracted,' Nina said. 'What's going on between you and that blonde man?'

'Ah ...'

'I knew it! I know this stuff, Lee, when I see it. You look great together, by the way.'

I must have appeared shocked, because Nina reached across her desk to squeeze my hand. Then she said abruptly: 'I'll give you an interview. See, it's a win-win situation. You have a book to write and I need to get this off my chest.'

I had thought the West Australian suburbs, with their hills and large backyards, were free of existential angst, but perhaps all you need to do to find interviewees anywhere is tell the truth about yourself.

'It feels to me like I have to play at being this middle-aged, happy family woman.' Nina's voice turned mud-heavy: 'Allow people to have the idea that I'm a beige-brown woman who would never consider anything outside the mainstream.' I looked sideways.

Seven years into Nina's marriage, when she was thirty-four years old, the age I was when I went to Perth, and already had two small children, she and her husband had a threesome. This happened not long after Nina's father-in-law died, when they were living in a bleak mining town. Her husband, she said, had let the sorrow eat at him, retreating into himself. Frustrated at her inability to help him, and lonely, Nina had, to distract herself, joined a regional choir. She went away to a nearby town to do a singing workshop and met there another amateur singer, who was a builder in his other life. The man was fifteen years older than her, tall and slim, with greying hair and large hands. Nina, impressed by his size and calmness, saw shelter in him.

The builder knew she was married, but still invited her out for dinner, at which the steak was overdone, the waitress ignored them and the place stank of tomato sauce, but, unlike Nina's husband, this man saw the hilarity of it all. They laughed all through the meal; the better she felt in his company, the more terrified she grew. At night, she dreamed of him.

In life, irony seems to be in even greater supply than it is in art: it was Nina's husband's arrival the next day, on a work trip, that set things in motion. In the windowless motel room, among the shit-coloured curtains and Nescafé sachets, Nina's husband, thrilled to see her, grabbed eagerly at her flesh. That familiar irritating gesture was the catalyst for her to act out her desire. Concealing her frustration, she reminded her husband of the fantasy they occasionally entertained—to invite a stranger into their bed. She made her case as playfully as she could manage that today was the day. The town was foreign to them, and she knew of a suitable candidate. If her husband didn't mind, she'd go fetch him.

The hot shadows in the office loosened Nina into her more primal, darker version. Her eyes and lips glistened. 'See, for me, it was a pretext to see him again. It had nothing to do with the threesome.' Her voice turned hoarse. 'I still resent my husband for not standing up to me. That typified our relationship: I made a stupid decision, which I knew would damage our marriage, and he just went along.'

'So, you wanted him to say no?'

'I would now. Then I'd have fought him, because I was obsessed.'

The builder's large body filled the doorway of his house. Nina told him why she'd come and he simply followed her lead. Like my lover did, when I asked him to kiss me. Like men do. In the motel room, the three of them sat around a scratched Formica table, chattering nervously. Nina kept drinking champagne, to calm herself. The husband, the only one who seemed to know what he wanted that night, placed a hand on her knee, suggesting they move to the bed.

The husband beamed while Nina was undressing. She told me she felt like he was proudly showing her off to the stranger. But she was embarrassed. To forget her nudity, Nina focused on the builder's gaze. He kissed her—her face, breasts and, most of all, her lips. His kisses were slow, deep, balanced with passion and tenderness—just what she had always wanted. That was all he did that night while she and her husband made love on the bumpy mattress. 'But kissing is more intimate than sex,' Nina said.

The night passed uncomfortably, with all three of them shifting restlessly, but the morning's sunshine washed away everything—fatigue, life histories, too much champagne. The man slid awkwardly into Nina. He proved not to be as skilled in the art of eliciting female orgasm as her husband was, but she didn't mind. Her husband, oblivious to the emotions underlying the sex, delighted in Nina's pleasure.

'Later, all this turned into a disaster,' she said shakily. 'But that morning was wonderful. I was the linchpin between the men, their sole focus. They adored me openly, like parents would a child. I put on the smoothest stockings and high heels. I felt beautiful. During breakfast, I made them laugh. It was all so civilised. My husband and I actually felt close after we dropped the man home. But then I couldn't get him out of my mind. I was completely in love with him. See, as a woman, if you make love with someone, you end up falling for him.'

I did not want to believe her.

That night, during the casino's all-you-can-eat dinnertime orgy, Nina's husband watched her fork freeze halfway to her lips. She burst into tears and he finally understood what was at stake. 'This must finish,' he told her, 'or I'm leaving.' His voice wasn't angry but muted, blue. Terrified at the prospect of losing her husband and worried about the children, Nina promised to sever all ties with the builder and that this was the last time they'd ever mention the 'incident' to each other. Yet, once another opportunity arose to go to the town where the builder lived, she took it.

Nina had always thought she didn't enjoy sex because something was wrong with her, but in the builder's arms, she was wild. It wasn't his technique that did it: 'The way he used his hands comforted me. I felt held by him. I went for it, fully and completely, and my husband was so absorbed in his work, he didn't even notice I was having an affair.'

'Were you looking for someone *instead* of your husband?' I interrupted.

'Probably. And you?'

For three years, Nina shuttled between the two towns, between pleasure and sorrow, between wanting to leave and stay in her marriage, until she fell pregnant to the builder. She said it was an incredible strain keeping the pregnancy secret in their small community and from her husband, but she managed this until she had an abortion. That termination, though, extinguished not just the foetus but also her feelings for the builder. No matter how her lover held her, on the surgery table Nina felt alone and came to realise this man wasn't her panacea. When she left him, he wept. She, too, wept in subsequent years—over what had become of her marriage. The affair, she told me, had destroyed an innocence she used to associate with her husband.

I watched Nina slumped, pale, in her chair. My writing project seemed to have its own plans, expanding rapidly beyond the scope I'd initially envisaged. Somehow it hadn't yet occurred to me that in writing about non-monogamy, I couldn't escape pondering the very nature of love—why people came together, why they stayed; or didn't.

Now she spoke slowly, with deliberation: 'Sometimes, after the affair ended, I thought about leaving. But I *chose* to love my husband. Real love isn't connected to emotions. It's a decision. And there isn't any room for anybody else if you do this properly. But it frustrates me that for a marriage to survive, it has to be exclusive. That you have to … turn off that alluring side of yourself.'

It was past hometime for Nina, and my lover would arrive soon. But I kept lingering at the doorstep of the office, unsure about leaving her alone with her story and whether I could walk away steadily. She gathered her shopping bags, smoothed her tailored skirt and hair; our gazes interlocked. She said: 'Soon my children will move out. I'm worried I'll be so bored I'll again do something that will precipitate a crisis. But then I think it's a joke, because who would look at me? That's what it's like when you don't feel alive … My husband says one day I'll realise he's a fool and leave him, but I'm equally insecure. He doesn't know it, but I'm not going anywhere.'

I should beware of stories, written or told. Once I come across them, they insert themselves into my life. My husband arrived in town on a brief work trip. In the early evening, I watched him park a rented scarlet car outside the Prichard house and bounce towards me in his three-quarter-length pants, his maple-coloured face tipped up towards the sky, his smile kissable. I watched my gorgeous boy-man and knew I wasn't going to tell him. Not yet, not until the fire in me had gone and I could carefully wrap up the sharp edges of my story. For now, I promised myself to give us a chance: not to call Noah 'angel', not to squeeze his nose. I yearned to feel his warm skin.

'What happened to your chin?' he asked at once. 'Did you kiss someone?' He was smiling, though, and this, too, I took as permission for what I was doing. I threw my arms around him: 'You're silly.'

The house was uncharacteristically empty. I led Noah into my writing cell turned love den, where my lover and I, unnerved by the newness of each other, spent unslept nights. For the first time, I felt Noah to be an intruder. This hurt. I hoped wildly that after all that time apart, he would now push me onto the bed with a passion strong enough to exorcise my pain, and possibly my lover. Instead, he scrutinised the room, his protective arm around my shoulder. In the remaining daylight, under my husband's critical gaze, the place turned into a pumpkin. I noticed again that the mattress was lumpy, the carpet worn out, the flowery curtains musty. 'Let's get out of here,' Noah said, falling back into his usual role of my knight. 'I booked us a B&B.' Once again, I picked up my huge suitcase—the same one that, eight years ago, I'd carried to Australia all the way from Tel Aviv—to follow a man.

The B&B merrily brimmed with plastic koalas, boomerangs, local maps and photos of beach huts. We fled the Australiana into a steak restaurant, which was invaded by blonde men who kept coming and going, coming and going, as though there were no end of them. I instinctively covered my chin with my hand. Noah noticed the gesture but, rather than saying something, pointed at another blonde man in a t-shirt printed with Che Guevara's portrait. 'Che Guevara should be renamed Cli-che Guevara,' he said. I smiled. Noah knew how much the popular adoration of murderers upset me. In one Melburnian bar, a mural of Stalin, responsible for about twenty million deaths, took up an entire wall. But to hell with that! I was actually feeling cheerful now, for we were talking easily again. I blew him a kiss.

Back in our room, under the crisp sheets, Noah placed his hand between my thighs listlessly, as if out of obligation. I shuddered, fearing one day I'd come to resent his touch the way Nina did her husband's. I closed my eyes in an attempt to create some erotic distance between us. But the less regularly we had sex, the more incestuous it felt when we attempted it. Noah would often smile at me in a friendly, brotherly way, shattering the tension, and I lacked the patience to wait for its return. My spinning thoughts dissipated gradually into the fog of flesh till I fell asleep—and into Noah.

In the morning we drove to Geraldton, to visit Tom and his girlfriend Julia. Tom was my first made-in-Australia friend. I'd met him two years after my arrival in migrant-land, just when I'd started doubting authentic Australians existed. But even Tom, born here to Anglo-Saxon parents, wasn't very convincing as a representative of Oz. He did like football but spoke excellent, self-taught, Russian and hung out with a pack of Russian migrants we both knew, who were fond of electronic music, and magic mushrooms they'd expertly gather in Victorian forests. Shortly after we met, I asked Tom, an editor, to edit my attempts at writing in English, and got lucky. He loved words as much as I did, and was the only person I knew who—well versed in the migrant idiosyncratic use of English—understood that when I wrote about 'the man with asparagus', I actually meant someone who had Asperger's syndrome. Over the years, I came to depend on Tom for my self-reinvention in Australia as a writer in English. Now that he had moved to Geraldton, I missed his company. With both Noah and me in WA, he offered to throw a party if we drove to his place. Leaving Perth seemed like a great idea. I thought Noah and I had a better chance of reconnecting away from places I associated with my lover, and within the familiarity of friends. Before arriving at Tom and Julia's, we cruised around Geraldton, taking in its pebbled buildings, the flat white-sanded beach, the gorgeous little bridges and the grand turrets of St Francis Xavier Cathedral. Like many regional towns in Australia, Geraldton appeared to possess more churches than residents. Still, some freethinkers surely lived in this town, or Tom wouldn't have settled here.

Tom had a flair for throwing parties. Tonight his house was full of all the right ingredients for a soiree: wine, drums, dope, an impressive record collection. We ate home-cooked curries in the company of Geraldton personalities: actors, musicians, pub owners, environmentalists—the kind of people Tom gathered around him wherever he lived. Seated on Noah's lap, I told a couple with dreadlocks about the first, and last, dinner Noah had made for me. We'd just started seeing each other again, after I'd finally fled J. Noah said he'd cook for me, warning me not to eat that day, since the feast he planned was fit for kings. I arrived at his place, hungry, to discover the feast was a bowl of chopped raw vegetables with no dressing and three beef skewers, two of which Noah at once ate. Since then, I'd been the designated family chef.

'All true,' Noah nodded earnestly, to the couple's delight.

'I like how you guys laugh together,' the dreadlocked wife said. 'You look so in love. Have you only just met?'

People often said such things about us. If only they knew how complicated our love had become …

At the front of the house, where the air was sweet with frangipani, darbukas and guitars joined forces. We sat under a tree, listening to Tom sing in Russian the bard Vladimir Visotsky, as famous for his music as for his critiques of the Soviet regime. Few of his songs were officially released, but many people, including me, grew up on his music, which was distributed illegally around the country. In hindsight, repression and Samizdat were the best things to have happened to Russian art, while the rusting of the Iron Curtain was probably the worst. In recent years, Russian artists had taken up money as their cause. Music, literature and cinema had grown progressively shallower, echoing Western bestsellers. Now I was getting goose bumps at the sounds that had fired my childhood, spent in underground circles—those of Jewish dissidents, where I first learned about the thrills of risk-taking. But then anxiety kicked in. I worried that, in my absence, my lover might decide he'd had enough of my marital complications. I went inside to check my emails.

To my relief, a new story from my lover was waiting in the inbox. This time, it was a fairytale, about a princess kidnapped by a Black Prince and held in his castle of shadows and dust. Despite his poor public profile, the Black Prince was gentle with the princess. He lavished delicacies and other comforts upon her. Still, all the princess wanted was to return to her bright palace. When the Black Prince understood that, he, to princess's surprise, let her go. To her even greater surprise, once she was free she realised she missed his company and headed back to his castle. Upon her return, the place brightened up and the royal lovers lived happily ever after. Whereas upon my return, the tale's author was asking me out for a dinner by the beach.

I stumbled out of the study, unfocused. Or, rather, focused on a new mission. I felt needed, as I did when J had told me of his tragedy. I had the power to brighten someone's palace. Or was I reading too much into the story? Nearby, I overheard a woman with a military crop and the scratchy voice of a heavy smoker say, 'Every time I drink gin, I burst into tears.' I found it difficult to picture this woman as prone to tears. Nothing was as it seemed, it seemed. Noah, as always, surrounded by people, holding court, waved at me from a distance. The tale still drumming in my head, I waved back with a big, grubby smile.

On Noah's last night in Western Australia, the ocean rolled noisily, heavily, beyond the window of our hotel. My husband snuggled into me. I couldn't sleep. The story of Nina came at me like tsunami waves, flooding me with sadness. I felt touched and unnerved by it, but it wasn't the kind of story I was hoping to find. I didn't think Nina was non-monogamous at heart; it wasn't a desire for multitudes that had made her reach out to a stranger. Besides, her non-monogamous stint had fast turned into adultery. Apparently, the borders between non-monogamy and adultery could be more slippery than I had realised. If I wasn't careful, I could join the ranks of the adulterers. And if my suspicions about Noah contained some truth, did this make him unfaithful? And why did it matter to me so much?

I wasn't like the American writer Louise DeSalvo, who, in her memoir *Adultery*, described with an admirable lack of judgement the impact of her husband's affair on their marriage. She was upfront about her hurt, but rather than condemning her husband, she attempted to understand him. DeSalvo came to see adultery in positive terms, too: as an expression of autonomy, openness to change and adventurousness. She also framed adultery as a challenge to the social status quo. I could see her point. Under repressive regimes, adultery can become a revolutionary activity. In some Muslim countries where infidelity is criminalised and may attract a death sentence, illicit lovers turn into unfortunate heroes fighting the battles of human rights. So it was in the Soviet Union, where communal interests were consistently privileged over individual ones. This, I think, is partly why many Soviet citizens cheated on their spouses with the kind of dedication the State had hoped would be shown to collective activities. For many, those rendezvous were the closest they got to experiencing personal liberty, and were perhaps the only revolts they dared engage in.

I find it harder, though, to attribute qualities of rebellion to adultery in democratic countries, as I doubt the extent of the challenge that cheating poses to such societies (as opposed to affected spouses, of course). Adultery appears to me as the other side of the monogamy coin, reinforcing fidelity instead of undermining it. If stories of adultery are bound up with deception, with sneaking around the borders, then the existence of borders is crucial to them. Often borders themselves are at the heart of desire. Casanova's preference for marital bedrooms as the location for his rendezvous comes to mind. He seemed to be aroused more by the danger of his actions than by the ladies. If Casanova had lived through the sexual revolution, his famous potency might have dwindled.

Besides, the faithful need the adulterers just as much as the latter need moral codes in order to transgress them. Societies tend to develop stronger collective identities in the face of existential threats. German invasion, for example, was one of the best things to happen to Stalin. Despite his Terror, in the face of a foreign enemy Stalin's rule was legitimised again. Similarly, seeing relationships of others corroded by adultery can provide just enough of a threat to glue couples together more strongly. And there is also something titillating about the lurking threat of adultery. Hypothetical rivals can spice up marital monotony. Otherwise, why are sexual fantasies about being cuckolded so popular among married men? If the threat of infidelity didn't exist, surely therapists would have invented it.

Such speculations may explain why adultery has been one of the most popular artistic themes, whether in the Middle Ages' courtly poetry about love between knights and married ladies, or in the entire canon of French cinema. And where would the novel be today if Anna Karenina and Madame Bovary had remained faithful to their husbands? More recently, confessional blogs about illicit liaisons have proliferated as widely as their readers. Such narratives are indispensable: they provide us with voyeuristic pleasures but, at the same time, don't confuse us. After all, in these stories it is easy to tell the good and bad guys apart. The language, too, is familiar—sin, weakness, pleasure set like shiny jewels within the dull frame of guilt. All this we tend to condemn, but also understand. Although, lately, this division has become more complicated. Up until recently, in popular films and literature, and often in real life, cheated-upon spouses have tended to react to unfaithfulness with automatic fury, immediately jettisoning their 'bad' partners. Yet, in the last few years, probably because the sheer extent of infidelity has made it less viable to end every 'slippage' with divorce, there seems to have been a paradigm shift. The shift, as per usual, is bound up with linguistics. Slowly, but steadily, public oracles have begun talking about *understanding* infidelity. Andrew Marshall, the British marital therapist, insists on substituting the damning term 'adulterer' with the more neutral (and euphemistic) the 'discovered'. Others, like Kate Figes, the author of *Couples*, talk about 'surviving' affairs, as though infidelity is akin to a terrorist attack or natural disaster.

The infidelity narrative is gradually metamorphosing from being about transgression into being about adversity or a curable pathology. As such, it is rebranded with redemption. A small but robust sub-industry of relationship counsellors has recently emerged to help couples in the aftermath of adultery. These therapists share an assumption consistent with our zeitgeist, being steeped in positive psychology and commerce (both of which are capable of finding benefits in anything), that it is possible to capitalise on infidelity. Discovery of an affair, they tell us, should not mean the end of a relationship, but may even be the beginning of a better one. The promised prize for the 'survivors' is a more satisfying and, of course, monogamous relationship. In this vein, the reformed cheater and memoirist Julie Powell claims that she and her husband became closer. Louise DeSalvo writes similarly that her husband's betrayal taught her to be more autonomous, turning their marriage into a more egalitarian—and monogamous—union. Flaubert's writing always tackled his era's hypocrisies and taboos. When *Madame Bovary* was published, it caused much controversy due to its non-judgemental depiction of female infidelity. However, I imagine that if Flaubert had lived now, Emma would not have cheated on Monsieur Bovary but invited him to join in with her lovers. And I, the offspring of dissidents and a lover of Flaubert, was also interested in challenging the status quo.

The night kept advancing and my sleep kept retreating. It was time to admit my plan to conduct an objective study was slipping further away. Who was I kidding? I'd never really intended to write a book of *any* stories I'd come across. I didn't want to hear heart-wrenching violins—like those evinced by Nina, Angela and, possibly, Bianca—but victorious trumpets celebrating non-monogamy, because … I hoped I wasn't a violin. Even if my current infatuation could be a symptom of unhappiness, I hoped my marriage was curable. True, I'd recently imagined slipping into a conversation the words 'my husband, the senior financial advisor'. But it was the novelty and improbability of saying it that delighted me. I needed to meet people whose makeup was non-monogamous to see if I were different from them or not. But I was starting to doubt such people existed.

Shortly after Noah's scarlet car disappeared around the corner, I waited for my lover in a café adjacent to Perth's Art Gallery, whose collection, I, too absorbed in my personal dramas, would never get to see. The shrimp-pink sun was slowly descending upon the city. The waiters, uniformed in starched white, paid me no attention; the floors were so rigorously polished, my eyes hurt.

My lover was late. He didn't believe in mobile phones, which meant every meeting was framed with delicious anxiety we'd miss each other. I wondered whether, if the communication between us failed, he'd pursue me. Every man I'd ever been involved with had pursued me at some stage (Noah waited almost a year while I battled J). Even the more aggressive chasers among them didn't evoke bitterness in me, perhaps because I believed I was worth chasing and feared the possibility of not being pursued. Can you love from such a position? I wasn't sure, but at least I finally managed to kill a fly that, in the absence of other stimulation in this sterile place, had been persistently hovering over me. I smashed it with my bare hand, like a local, and it was then, when I had the fat insect smeared on my palm, that my lover finally appeared. I wiped my hand discreetly.

From a distance, and with the distance of the past few days between us, the man appealed to me less than he did when we pressed into each other, or when I daydreamed about him. If forced to be objective about him—something I'd tried to avoid—there was a lifelessness in my pale lover that made him opaque to me in a way no other lover had been. But that opaqueness was also a convenient surface on which to write whatever I fancied.

My lover took me in his arms, apologetic, fatherly, just as I liked him to be. As did Noah, he exhibited a rare combination of nurturing and playfulness. Yet, with my lover I had to work harder to bring out his childish side. I had to dishevel him, disrupt him with jokes, kisses, tickles. Whenever he laughed, I pinned his smiles on my dress like medals. But at the pricey restaurant by the beach, where we held hands and played at being despairing lovers in the face of my imminent departure, neither of us laughed.

Later, in Prichard's bedroom, the moon turned thin, like my lover. I couldn't see his eyes, couldn't make out his face. I recalled the fairytale he'd written. If I were the princess, I'd not have liked the ending. I wouldn't have wanted the palace to become bright. I was wedded to darkness.

'Was that a story about having a choice, or about depression?' I said, inserting a hoarse whisper between our bodies.

He ignored my question, instead saying that the night before, he had dreamed about us.

'I came into your room. You were a princess.'

'Like in your fairytale?'

'Yes. But you were naked. You ordered me to undress and forbade me to touch you.'

'And did you listen?'

'Of course. I did as you told me …'

'I like hearing that.'

'What would you order me to do now?'

I said nothing. Instead, I wrote my own tale on his body, shedding years like snakeskin, catapulting myself back to who I was when I had first come to this quivering, naked country, back to the days when I had desired everything.

6

A Tale of Candaulistic Couples

'Sexuality is a murky realm of contradiction and ambiguity.'
Camille Paglia

I'd have liked to, but cannot, blame Esther for chasing me into the present. *I* was the ghost provocateur. I had brought to the Prichard house a yellow dress that once belonged to Esther. I wasn't sure why I brought it along—it was unbearably short and tight; its hue was too bright. The other dresses I inherited from Esther were predators too: sleek and breathtakingly bold. I wonder whether they expressed Esther as she was or as she wanted to be. Or perhaps as J wanted her to be? I wonder also what they say about me, since I've kept them all, even though they have started coming apart at the seams.

Soon after I settled in at J's house, he offered me a tattered backpack containing Esther's clothes. I took it without hesitation. I could say this was because I didn't yet have a work permit, and since my arrival in Australia, had taken whatever people I met offered me, slipping into others' choices with creepy ease. And I particularly needed Esther's warm clothes. When I'd packed, I'd imagined Australia as it appeared in films—a summer country. Now the days were getting colder. Then, there was also my old desire, to live as many lives as possible. I rummaged through the backpack's contents.

'What you don't want, throw away,' J said.

I stopped at once and looked him in the eye to see if he meant it. I knew that since Esther's death, he'd moved around a lot, never burdening himself with possessions; yet, he'd kept her bag. Now I'd come along, and he'd handed it to me. He wouldn't interfere with my choice of clothes, wouldn't keep what I didn't want. J was handing me his heart in that backpack, I decided. How could I not take it?

I tried on Esther's dresses, choosing one for the night. To relieve our aloneness, we were about to go to a dance party at a local Tabaret. Before we met, J's life had been more crowded, mostly with energetic, always scheming, overweight women with grand tresses and tempers. I was unsure which of them

J had slept with, but they all seemed to resent me for being his lover. J's workers, young Israeli tourists, hovered around too, and so did a few professional hangers-on: a male stripper who kept planning some elaborate drug deal, an Israeli hairdresser who was married to an Australian callgirl, an oncologist who never seemed to work. I didn't like those people, and J rejected the few Russian friends I had made, as he did most people who were not deferential to him. So we lived like a two-person island, spending many evenings watching thrillers featuring con men— an activity J seemed to be treating as professional development. On other nights, we went to the local pub, which served cheap, gigantic steaks, to practise our English and snooker with the regulars, who were mostly truck drivers.

For now, I found this life, like anything that involved mixing with the locals, exciting. But J felt differently. From the start, his boredom hung heavily over us, like a wet towel; he seemed to hate having steady earth under his feet. Sometimes I lectured him about developing his inner world, but J had his own methods to break the routine. Like on the night he set off to steal for his renovations wood, which he could have easily afforded, from a building site. He came home empty-handed; apparently, the security guard had noticed him. J had dropped the loot and, to avoid identification, left his car hidden nearby. He'd walked several kilometres home. 'It wasn't a big deal, I needed the exercise,' J said on his return, looking tired but content. It dawned on me then that, in order to feel alive, he needed trouble. But tonight, it was just a party that he wished for.

Finally, I settled on a blue turtleneck dress. It just fitted me, strangling my throat, stretching tight across my breasts and pelvic bones, ending just below my pubic hair and drawing out my hips excessively. Already, I began making comparisons: I wanted to know whether Esther's hips were narrower than mine or whether she didn't mind the discomfort as long as she looked good. I adjusted the woollen fabric and tossed my hair—long like hers, but not as curly. I turned around, a hand upon my overemphasised hip.

'You look stunning,' J said, without the usual lust but with gratitude. Or so I thought.

'Like Esther?'

'She was the prettiest girlfriend I had in Israel. You're my prettiest one in Australia.'

I decided to take this as a compliment. Meanwhile, the dress took over, making me feel dangerous and also an imposter. To recover myself, I walked—or maybe sashayed, as though I were on a catwalk—towards J. But was this really to recover myself, or to return Esther to him? I was no longer certain of my motives.

The party was tucked behind gaming machines, in a windowless room crowded with other wog-looking misfits. The men wore mullet haircuts and excessive facial hair, the women were wrapped in animal prints. Kylie's 'Spinning Around', our then-favourite song, was playing. J threw his arms around me, or, rather, around the thick blue fabric. I'd read that when people lose their limbs, the brain sometimes remaps the neural pathways of the missing body parts onto existing ones, enhancing their sensation. In one known case, a man from Arkansas began experiencing amplified orgasms after his leg was amputated. Perhaps brain remapping can also happen when you lose a lover? I wondered whether this embrace was meant for both Esther and me. If so, I hoped the two of us would suffice, would finally fix J in one place.

Esther, J had told me, was a seductive dancer. At nightclubs, men hung around her in packs. But on that account, I, the Tel Aviv girl, wasn't intimidated. Under the quaint disco ball, among the sweat and smoke of gamblers and foreigners, I placed a languid hand on J's shoulder, looped my stilettoed leg around his. I pulled him towards me. I pushed him back. He obeyed me with skill, tuned into my every move, and, since I trusted him to follow me, I felt free to improvise.

The dimensions. The hair. The language of the body. Ménages à trois with absent lovers thrive on optical illusions. Anaïs was not just interested in June for artistic inspiration. Even before June's departure, she took to wearing her tiger's eye bracelet. Later, she grew bolder in her attempts to reshape herself into the kind of femme fatale she fancied June to be, developing that 'dangerous, rebellious, perverse side', as she wrote in her diary. Anaïs plucked her eyebrows thin as lemon zest, had a nose job, practised a ravishing June gaze. For the next two decades, she'd continuously compare herself with June, who, when it came to a genuine comparison, was conveniently absent.

When it came to appropriating the absent lover's physique, Iris Murdoch had it easier than Anaïs did. I couldn't find any photos of Friedl, but Canetti and Murdoch claimed she resembled the pale, broad-boned, blonde Iris. Yet, Iris, unlike Anaïs, didn't want to *become* her prey. Even at the height of her obsession, she was analytical enough to see her lot was better than Friedl's. Rather than be Friedl, Iris wanted to *wear* Friedl in Canetti's company. 'How strangely little I resent C's identifying me with Friedl,' she noted in her diary. 'I continue her for him, through me he enjoys her again.' Perhaps this complacence, even desire, was rooted in Iris's secret aspirations to sainthood. But while it is easier to understand the motives of Iris, whose external modesty concealed grand ambitions, it is harder to explain why Canetti, who tired of Friedl at least two years before she died, wanted to resurrect her. I suspect he secretly blamed himself for Friedl's death. Not long before she died, she directly addressed him in her diary: 'I have lived in your light, but could not find my own.' Guilt-ridden people can be particularly tender about their past lovers, and Iris, with a self-aggrandisement similar to mine, fancied herself as Canetti's consolation. She, of course, fancied this as long as Friedl was absent and she had the stage in the theatre of his life all to herself.

Anaïs tried to be June; Iris played at being Friedl. But probably neither felt the need to, or believed she could, outdo the one she'd substituted. I did. I went for it that night, like Salome must have done. Enveloped in Esther's bordello glamour, I shook my hair, my limbs, my heart. J followed. I could see us in the mirror—we were fire. I wanted to think it was I who shaped that dance, but it might have been the dress—the real femme fatale; the archetype that fitted any country, decade, dance floor. I'd be wearing it again two years down the track, when I met Noah, with J lurking around, monitoring us from afar.

'That Henry and I can sit and talk about our love of June, about her grandiose moments, is to me the greatest of victories,' Anaïs wrote. But ménages à trois involving absent lovers aren't exempt from jealousy, and underneath her exalted ink, more pedestrian feelings lurked. While Henry wrote *Tropic of Capricorn*, a novel that was also a bitter love poem for June, jealousy nibbled at Anaïs. And Iris, who once, in a fit of generosity, offered to transfuse her blood into Friedl's drying-out veins, shook off her saintly halo when Canetti left for Paris to sit by Friedl's sickbed, and now wished death on her rival. I had to find out who Esther was, so that I could identify and display her weaknesses parallel to my advantages. Anaïs and Iris had known their rivals, but the only materials I had to work with were photos and J's version of events.

To J's credit, he lent me a hand. 'She was nowhere near as smart as you are,' he told me as we ate breakfast at the kitchen table that doubled as my writing desk. 'I wish she'd been stronger and hadn't done everything I asked her to. If she'd been more like you, we might have been happier.'

If she'd been more like you ... I added J's words to my comparative study. Only once I had finished gorging on the bones of the dead did it occur to me *we might have been happier* was a curious departure from his usual soulmate narrative.

'What did you ask her to do?'

'It wasn't just me, you know. We both loved sex,' J said, somewhat apologetically, while placing generous scoops of caviar and tsatsiki onto his slice of raisin bread until it resembled a wedding cake. I liked this abundance and did the same with my own slice.

'She loved the power she had over men. Guys salivated over her.'

I didn't like the last bit. I wanted a straight answer, not a love song for Esther. J didn't notice my frown.

'Usually we'd get a guy, because with women, she could get jealous. We'd lick his cock together. Very thoroughly, very clean, we'd lick it,' J said, his voice now racing with childlike enthusiasm. He got up to pull a bunch of young carrots out of the fridge.

The mention of a 'guy' didn't take me by surprise. I already knew J's sexuality was tangled, even paradoxical, in many ways. He was an avid pornographer and a romantic: his few possessions included an assortment of dildos and George Michael ballads. J exuded a meaty, satyr-like sexuality. Yet, while he was capable of intimacy only with women, he sometimes also liked being a nymph—giving men fellatio or letting them fuck him. Far from being off-putting, J's desires were an endless source of curiosity for me, who'd lost my virginity at twenty and had more steady boyfriends than sexual positions on my résumé. Now I had found my mentor. I loved how sex with J was unpredictable and versatile, not the timed athletic contest I'd previously thought it was. Our lovemaking had a more natural flow, without precise start and end points; it was a part of our everyday, an accompaniment to other activities, such as car rides or watching TV. Whatever we did, J's hands found their way under my clothes.

I loved how badly he wanted me no matter the time of day or place, and regardless of my monthly bleeding, and that he always whistled at me with appreciation when I changed clothes, even when I put on his baggy tracksuits. I even liked that in his sleep he held me so tightly I couldn't breathe. Voyeur that I was, I found in J my exhibitionist, my risk-taker, my June. I did feel some jealousy about his occasional visits to men's saunas and Grey Street girls, but was prepared to pay this price to hear his stories later. Yet, I was possessive of *our* space. There, I wanted to be the centre of J's attention. The 'together' was a new thing. It made me feel uneasy.

'We were a good team,' J said, part self-mockingly, part nostalgically, then, holding the carrots by their green tails, sank his strong teeth into all of them at once.

They were a good team … Ladies and gentlemen, forget the absent lovers, at least for now. I have a saucier tale to spin for you.

Rimbaud thought that in order to write, we first have to live dangerously. But this can also work the other way around. Several times, what I imagined in fiction later manifested in my life. I first wrote about J and Esther before I knew they existed, when I still lived in Tel Aviv and worked on a novella telling the story of Yoav, a recently decommissioned combat soldier. J appears as the Danish tourist who enters briefly, but dramatically, in both the novella and Yoav's virginal anus. This happens during Yoav's traditional Israeli holiday in Sinai, where he encounters Nicole, Esther's prototype. To his astonishment, glamorous Nicole invites him to her *husha* (Bedouin hut). Yoav is so stunned by her attention that during their fucking session, he drops the alertness that is habitual from his training. It is then that the Danish tourist joins in and forces himself upon Yoav.

This sexual humiliation is the peak event in a succession of misfortunes Yoav endures before becoming a more mature and nuanced man. For me, the story was about the pain I saw as being necessary to grow as a person. The sexual game of the couple, although vicious, has for Yoav an educational value that, I considered, outweighed anything the Israeli army offered its young soldiers. Hiding behind Yoav's gender, I was writing about my own army years, which I thought a waste of time. As for the Danish tourist, he had to be a foreigner, because, at that time, although I wanted to live out my dream as inspired by *Henry & June*, I'd never yet met a non-monogamous couple, not even in Tel Aviv. What I found in that city was a sharp, lewd, ecstasy-loaded scene reserved for single or adulterous people, not couples. Now, with J, I thought I possibly had my chance.

To find out more about J and Esther, I waited until our next daytrip, to a little secluded beach, where I hoped J would be in a relaxed, storytelling mood. He owned a beach house there, which he had renovated with the intention of selling it for a profit, as per his usual way of earning money through making things appear better than they really were. 'Australia is heaven for Israelis,' J told me every time he closed a deal in his favour. 'Australians are stupid. They let opportunities go. But we don't.' But I was a different kind of Israeli; my existence complicated J's anthropological thesis. So he called me a dreamer.

The beach was marvellous—wild and overtaken by rotting weeds and swarms of pelicans, whom I adored for the splendid ugliness of their long, cancerous throats, and for their self-destructive stabbing of their chests with their beaks. We sat on the freshly painted veranda of J's house and I read to him an excerpt from my novel-in-progress, in which an ageing plumber arrives at a singles' agency, looking for love. J, who mostly read books to help his self find peace or make it rich, was nevertheless enjoying my writing, particularly the description of the plumber's bargaining over the agency fee. The air was chilly, but the champagne I drank straight from the bottle while listening to J's compliments was rather warm. Since I'd arrived in Australia, J was my only reader. Pleased, I thanked him and offered the bottle. J took a swig, hesitantly. Another of his paradoxes was that he was extraordinarily healthy in his habits. I smoked and drank;

he liked orange juice. I ate meat; he preferred vegetarian dishes. In a similar vein, although he let men fuck him for the thrill of humiliation, they had to be youthful, smooth, gentle boys. As pervasive as J's self-destruction was, it was never executed with true abandon.

It was my turn to hear a story, I told J as I lit a joint a Russian friend had given me. I asked when Esther and he had started looking for other people. Soon after they'd met, he said, when she moved into his two-bedroom apartment situated in a typical Tel Avivian art deco building, teeming with high ceilings, cockroaches, decay and sadness.

Here, the memory of J's tale is fleshed out through my imagination. The narrative is his, but the detail is mine, for the purposes of our joint entertainment. But the emotional truth I saved. Not long after the twentyish Esther, then a nurse, packed her cosmetics, stuffed animals and dresses, and moved into J's apartment, a former, and still infatuated, boyfriend contacted her. Esther had known him when she still lived in the provincial town of her childhood. He was a handsome, wholesome man, what Israelis call 'the salt of the earth'—physically strong and psychologically honourable. But, emotionally speaking, the boyfriend was of a soft ilk that couldn't satisfy Esther. She needed J, whom she considered a tower she could look up to. She told J about the phone call, and J, at once, devised a scheme. Esther's extended family was large and messy, patchworked with divorces, stepchildren and half-siblings, and dispersed across the country. Even a sharper ex-boyfriend would have been confused by her familial constellation. J proposed she invite him over and introduce J as her older brother, and Esther, he said, was game.

It was late evening when the man arrived in their living room, tall and lanky, in a well-fitting navy officer's uniform. Esther took his hand and led him in. J left the summer-sticky leather couch to the 'love birds', as he referred to them in his affectionate, brotherly manner. He sat opposite, in a wicker armchair popular with

Israelis; anything that put them in mind of the 1960s always was, being antidotes to their present, ambushed by enemy states and unremitting inflation. Esther and the boyfriend drank vodka. The 'brother' sipped on orange juice. While the men conversed awkwardly, she slunk around the smitten officer like a kitten. I wonder whether he found it odd that the older brother, whose skin was fairer than his sister's, was so indifferent, and polite in the face of their caresses, more interested in his newspaper. They left him and headed towards the shrine of the boyfriend's desire, the second bedroom, which, Esther told him, was hers.

Seagulls, low in the sky, flew by. I noticed a forthcoming storm, even through the haze of alcohol and marijuana that overtook me. The purple sky appeared dishevelled and murky, wobbly. The way it couldn't stand still increased my nausea. I rarely smoked joints, but marijuana and champagne were the main methods of self-destruction I could show off to J, so I seized the opportunity that now seized me by the stomach.

'What happened next?' I asked.

'Earlier, I'd drilled a hole in the wall between the bedrooms. I watched Esther fuck him and m-a-s-t-u-r-b-a-t-e-d.' J smiled that elusive, buttery smile I knew all too well.

The former boyfriend was never invited back. The nature of those games, Esther and J agreed, should be fleeting, to maximise diversity and to avoid attachment. There could be only one genuine bond in their lives—between the two of them. Esther could do what she wanted, but she didn't allow J out of her sight when he fucked other people, J told me, somewhat proudly. Together, they gathered their amusements in bars, on beaches, streets—anywhere they could. When, later, they bought an apartment in a newly built tower of the type that had overtaken Tel Aviv since the 1990s, J drilled another hole.

He left the story there, suspended in the previous millennium, as, in the new one, I finally vomited violet champagne onto his newly built terrace.

Some non-monogamous relationships are driven by the kind of shared sexuality that is often judged as perverse or loveless and has some combination of voyeuristic and exhibitionistic bents. Being a voyeur myself, I had no moral grounds for judging J. Yet, my voyeurism was less to do with sexual arousal and more with leading multiple existences. When I watched others have sex, the emotion that would overtake me resembled what I'd feel when watching David Lynch films: awe. I then felt admitted into uncanny spaces existing beyond red velvet curtains, somewhere wild and mysterious, where jazz, magic and apparitions ruled. So, whatever voyeuristic opportunities came my way, I took them, like I did when I was eighteen and already lived in Tel Aviv. For some months, I rented a room from the same ageing plumber who would later appear in my novel. The man had a big mattress in his living room on which he enjoyed orgies with bisexual women. I, a virgin then, was allowed to watch.

Still, J's story profoundly disturbed me. The image of him masturbating behind the wall kept revolving in my head; my coughing fits began. I was conflicted about the shadows hanging over J's life. My own shadowy self was finding its expression through J, just as in my youth, when I was a reporter and hung around junkies, runaway kids, women living on the edge, being shielded with the excuse of writing. But I didn't live with them, didn't kiss them. Now I was pondering—was J a man in distress after losing his beloved, as I had first thought, or a heartless pimp?

A biopsy of the two marriages of Gala—originally a school teacher from Kazan, the obscure city of Tatars—who became famous as a surrealists' muse, sheds light on how integral voyeurism and exhibitionism can be to love. Possibly, Gala's two husbands, the French poet Paul Éluard and the Spanish artist

Salvador Dalí, shared not only a wife and membership of the surrealist movement. Both, I believe, were also prone to a type of voyeurism bound up with romantic love: *candaulism*, a man's desire to expose a woman he loves to a male gaze and/or watch her fuck other men. Psychologists hypothesise that male identification with the beloved's body underlies such a wish; the men experience their women's pleasure as their own. And Gala, narcissistic, sexually confident and voracious—in short, an exhibitionist par excellence—was a candaulist's paradise.

Neither photos of Gala nor her many depictions by Dalí reveal the secret of her allure. All show a woman with broad shoulders and a severe, masculine face (although her perky breasts are appealing). What the images fail to convey, but the record of Gala's romantic success supports, is that whatever she lacked in looks, she made up for in the force of her character. Louise Staus-Ernst, the wife of Max Ernst, another of Gala's surrealist lovers, likened her to a panther. Dalí affectionately called her 'lionette'. Gala was 'smoky, sexy, mystical, superstitious, famous for accurate tarot card readings and for her laserlike gaze', as Francine Prose described her in her study of muses, exuding charisma and full of the so-called 'feminine mystique'.

At twenty-one, Gala followed her first husband, Éluard, to Paris. There, with his knowledge, she bedded the city's most distinguished artists. Her lovers included Picasso, Breton, de Chirico and Aragon. Plenty of evidence exists that the permissive Éluard, who proudly showcased Gala's nude photos to his friends, loved his wife. His poetry and letters, and the accounts of his contemporaries, all point towards the conclusion that Gala was his greatest passion. Even when, after twelve years of marriage, Gala left him, Paul would continue to be her troubadour. Éluard wrote after her departure, in one of his many poems about her, that as he was no longer seen by Gala, his face ceased to exist. Even after remarrying, for years he sent Gala love letters that often involved his candaulistic fantasies: 'I saw you … completely naked and your legs spread and possessed by two men, in the mouth and in the sex.' He also imagined being watched while making love with Gala. But Éluard's letters also trace his gradual, painful realisation that he was losing her. 'I see you everywhere, in everything … I love you to death …' he wrote to her years after their separation. 'You are the embodiment of love to me …' Until his death, Éluard said that to have been loved by Gala was an honour.

Candaulistic love doesn't rule out jealousy Éluard's poetry about Gala is suffused with torment, yet without hateful or vengeful innuendo. Rather, he likens his wife to a bird—admirable, yet exasperating, in her freedom. His distress peaked in the last years of their marriage, when Gala had her most enduring extramarital affair—with Max Ernst, the only painter I know of who managed to capture her magnetism, through a striking close-up portrayal of her barrel-deep dark eyes. Initially, Éluard encouraged—or, at least tolerated—Gala's involvement with Ernst, who was also his friend and artistic collaborator. When, in 1922, both families spent a summer vacation together, Louise was dismayed at how Max and Gala openly enjoyed each other, but Paul observed them with pleasure. Ernst often joined the couple on their travels, and at times lived in their house, the walls of which he painted with nightmarish creatures. Sometimes, all three shared a bed. Yet, gradually, this claustrophobic relationship strained Éluard's tolerance. His voyeuristic enjoyment became punctuated by jealous fits; his poetry was filled with mist and birds of prey. After one quarrel over Gala, when Ernst lost control and hit Éluard, Gala decided to end the affair, for the sake of her marriage. Ironically, shortly after that she met Dalí, for whom she'd leave Éluard and their daughter, Cécile, for good.

The loony, brilliant Dalí first crossed his future wife's path during the summer of 1929. Gala, then thirty-five, arrived at the Spanish village Cadaqués for a vacation in the company of surrealists. Dalí was ten years her junior and still a virgin (at least in regards to women). He'd heard much about Gala's charms. To impress her, he shaved his armpits until they bled and added blue dye to the dried blood; wore a pearl necklace; put a red geranium in his hair; then joined Gala at the beach, where he hovered over her continuously, bursting into occasional hysterical laughter. Despite Dalí's peculiar style of courting, Gala—the amateur psychic and professional muse—knew a genius when she saw one. 'My boy,' she told him the next evening, with her typical Russian fatalism, 'let us never be separated.'

Superficially, the neurotic Spaniard and the Russian lionette, as Dalí called her, appear to be the greatest mismatch in the history of love. But, perhaps, as Prose argues, they were made for each other:

> They belonged to the same species. Both were … self-mythologising and gifted with a talent for intuiting the spirit of the age and calculating the precise chemistry of outrageousness and titillation that would grab and hold the popular imagination.

Gala was both a mystic and a realist—a shrewd businesswoman and a genius in public relations. Once she took Dalí under her protective paw, his success was set in motion. And Dalí, who often acted madder than he really was, knew what he owed Gala, and even took to signing his paintings '*Dalí-Gala*'. But their relationship was not all business. Dalí preferred masturbation to sex, and was averse to breasts and vaginas. Even with his beloved Gala, the only woman he allowed to touch him, he didn't practise much penetration. Yet, their marriage was sexual. At least for the first twenty of their fifty-three years together, Dalí and Gala touched each other abundantly, giggling and necking in private and public. In photos, they often not only embrace or hold hands, but literally burrow into each other.

Dalí sang her praises in his memoir: 'I name my wife: Gala, Galushka, Gradiva; Oliva, for the oval shape of her face and the colour of her skin …'. He adored her teeth and buttocks. Dalí's nude paintings of Gala are considered to be some of the most affectionate known depictions of a middle-aged female body.

Then, of course, there was the candaulism that was their sex life. Dalí, ridden with countless phobias, had suffered from troubled sexuality, and Gala became the link between him and the world of carnal pleasures. Under her tutelage, he grew to be a dedicated voyeur. In his later years, when Gala would go mad due to ageing and her lost sex appeal, and things between them deteriorated, Dalí would preside at a distance over orgies he'd paid for. But he followed the spectacle half-heartedly. It was always Gala whom his gaze, and heart, desired. Until his death, he would pine for her, and for those happier days when, through her, he enjoyed the handsome young men they both liked. Dalí so admired Gala's sexual vitality, he even accepted her having rendezvous with Éluard; once, she, the keen performer, fucked him in front of Dalí. Let us now leave the Grand Muse there, at that moment where she basks in the simultaneous love of her two husbands, the years of bitterness still far away.

Problems can flare even when candaulists meet their match. But what if they fall for someone who isn't, as probably happened in Nina's marriage? It is likely that Nina mistook her husband's sexual preference for betrayal. I wanted to know how Esther felt that first time, knowing J was watching her through the hole, or in later years, when their games became the centrepiece of their affair.

And, generally, who was Esther?

This impulse I have, to cleanse contradictions from life, is an affliction for a writer. It is time to admit the dresses weren't all I found in Esther's bag. There was also a bulky blue coat that didn't seem fitting for a woman of her passions, but hinted at possible qualities, like basic decency, and even modesty, which, in my angst, I didn't want Esther to possess. J told me she bought this coat during their travels around Australia. Perhaps something happened between them during those weeks and the purchase was meant to curtail her seductiveness, as a punishment for J? Or maybe she just wanted to disappear?

I kept the coat, and also the oversized jumper, the type that women wear for comfort; but not the puffy silk blouse that was also bought during that time, the kind that flatters only anorexics, the kind only women who are lacking in taste wear. I had thought Esther was more self-aware about appearance. But maybe she was losing her judgement. J had said that sometime before they took off to the outback, Esther grew tired. But he insisted on ticking off the touristic attractions, kilometres, towns. She followed him—in her tight blue dress and big blue coat. Some say blue is the colour of depression. But saying this, too, is an easy way to summarise and discredit a rival. What if she followed J in Friedl-fashion, a blue hurricane, sweeping along men and anything else she could, including herself? And why do I, in my retelling of their story, make *her* follow him, casting her in the victim's role? Perhaps because J told me she was a follower. And because he was the one to survive, and I the one to inherit her place. But I also wanted her in this obedient role, so that I could be her opposite—the lion tamer. So that I could look down on her. So that I wasn't her. So that I stayed alive …

Oh, Esther, the nurse, the ravishing dancer who danced with everyone she fancied, or J fancied, the provincial girl from a town even smaller than Ashdod. But who was she really, beyond those labels? The truth is, Esther's complexity terrified me once I had opened the bag and realised her wardrobe could easily be divided between several different women. Perhaps she and I were actually somewhat alike. What if she—who, like me, came from poverty and tradition, from a life of duties and prohibitions—also wanted all she could eat after escaping the world she was from? That night when I opened the bag, I did consider that J had more insight than I'd previously thought in singling me out as his next love, then suppressed the thought.

Yet, in years to come, I'd try to fictionalise this woman I'd never met, hoping thus to add her missing dimensions, and maybe even give Esther a happier ending. Instead, I got writer's block. It took me a long time to admit the futility of resuscitating Esther with my writing. Despite my best intentions, I've always been a self-centred chorus. I realise now what I really sought to write about, in order to understand it (I always write to understand), was *my* obsession with Esther. I also wanted to think that if there had been no Esther, J and I might have parted quickly, before our emotional tentacles locked onto each other. But this was another simplification. Curiosity might kill felines, but it definitely prolonged the life of our affair. I could never let a good character go. Gradually, my preoccupation with Esther extended to J. After that day on the beach, I began entertaining escape scenarios, but also observing J with greater care. Always the good student, I took notes:

> J, who has a talent for moneymaking and for looking powerful. J, the businessman, who is also into the business of falling in love with me. J, the wealthy man in borrowed clothes, in borrowed houses, where everything can always go for the right price.

J was, I began realising, more than a character, he was a novel—an overbearing, maddening novel, impossible to complete or discard. This was particularly so now that, after living under his protective wing for several months, I stopped believing I could do Australia on my own.

That winter, a fog descended on Melbourne, bathing the city in Chekhovian melancholy. I wrote in my diary: 'The men I choose are never capable of consoling me. To control my moods, I need to charge my batteries through solitude, learning, reading, writing.'

My mind became my salvation, just as it used to be in my childhood, when I'd lay for weeks, sometimes months, in overcrowded Soviet hospitals, with lice in my hair, an unemptied potty under my bum and book after book in my hands. Now I was rapidly reverting to my younger self, with my brain in overdrive. On days when I didn't work in the video library, I read the Russian translation of Sartre's trilogy *Roads to Freedom* and an English-language biography of Anaïs Nin, and worked, in Hebrew, on my novel. I thought racing off in three linguistic directions at once would invigorate my thinking and subsequent writing. Yet, the Hebrew words kept flaking off me like dandruff, while the world of the novel that I had once known so well—Tel Aviv's streets and joints—felt unreal now. This sent me into panic: I'd always been a writer grounded in a sense of place. As much as my novel was about love, it was also my love poem to Tel Aviv. I waged writerly battles at J's kitchen table until I learned to capitalise on the geographical distance, instead of mourning it. The gulf between me and my beloved city made it strange to me again, as it had seemed when I first arrived there from Ashdod, so I wrote about Tel Aviv as if it were a myth:

> The neck of Allenby Street was intertwined with phosphoric swollen veins, and was strained and sore. The energy there had a beat I'd never known. It was as if I dived into the painting *The Last Day of Pompeii*.

The ring of J's mobile phone interfered with the beat of antiquity. Back from work, he stared at the kitchen table, which was overtaken with my books, dictionaries and manuscript pages. J didn't like mess; to him, any misplaced plate was a provocation, possibly because his brain was already so crowded that any external mess was more than he could bear. Now he looked at the table but said nothing. The wintry sunshine coated him tentatively, the rays bouncing off his sparkling sunglasses, and illuminating his strong jaw and blindingly white teeth, his washed out t-shirt stained with paint. He looked beautiful. A phrase of Sartre's I'd just read, *the sunshine streamed in like silk*, mixed in my mind with the phosphoric lights of Tel Aviv. Bursting with feeling, I forgot about his messy clothes and rushed to embrace J.

J, who had taught me that intimacy meant there was no clear boundary between you and your lover's body, that you could intrude on each other anytime, moved aside sharply, looking annoyed: 'Can't you see I'm dirty? Don't touch me.'

'Just one kiss …'

'Let me have a shower first.'

With Sartre's silky sunshine still streaming in my head, I stared at J, confused. He pulled a stack of dollars out of his pocket: 'Look, clean money! What do I need the real estate agents, those bloodsuckers, for? You rent places to tourists, put a couple in each bedroom, and here you are. Three hundred dollars every week.'

'See,' J continued the conversation that was unfolding in his head, 'if you stick with me, all this will be *ours*.' He pronounced the last word passionately, as if he were starved for its sound. J often swapped 'I' for 'we'. 'We painted the house,' he'd say. 'We think it's good to buy property in this area.' Despite J's bravado, loneliness always spurted out of him, overflowing the Melbourne streets as though we lived in a follow-up painting to *The Last Day of Pompeii*. He and I had become 'we' immediately after we met and then I found his need irresistible.

'And you don't need to work. Just look after me,' J completed his thought, waved the money at me again and headed for the shower.

I still didn't have a work permit and J's offer meant I could finish my novel without risking any trouble with the immigration department. While considering the proposition, I cleared the kitchen table and made tea for J the way he liked it, being the way of deprivation—a single teabag in a jug of boiling water. By the time I'd finish my cup of coffee, he'd have drunk the entire jug. J's gurus—usually white men dressed like Third-World sages, with the oratory manners of auctioneers and fees of lawyers— had taught him this way of tea drinking. It was part of their campaign against the mind, which they called 'mad monkey' and always wanted to defeat. Rigorous tea consumption was supposed to cleanse the body and the mind, and cleansing was something J understood deeply. He'd scold me for not washing my coffee cup immediately after I'd finished with it or for not washing it thoroughly enough, or for not drying it, because liquid could rust the sink, or, worse, attract ants into the house. J often cleaned after I finished cleaning, just the way he'd told me his mother, before she left him with his father, used to clean after he cleaned. J also followed her example in washing his hands many times a day, rubbing and rubbing them, soap foaming in the sink like spa bubbles.

I wondered what he was cleansing himself of. Sometimes it seemed that his mind was, rather than a monkey, his corridor, which was deep, poorly lit, with some doors open while others remained shut. I recalled folklore: Bluebeard gave keys to his bride with explicit instructions not to open one particular door but in the hope she would. The more I considered the matter, the less J's supposedly simple request I look after him fooled me. He, too, must have wanted me to bring him trouble, particularly considering that in our domesticity, potential disasters always lurked.

J, now clean, aromatic and naked, sat down at the kitchen table, pulling me onto his knee: 'I'm sorry about how I spoke to you, honey. Sometimes I can be an idiot. But quit the library.

Five dollars an hour is a joke! I'll pay you more than that if you help me. You can write my business letters, design houses. Or just be my travel companion, huh? I wouldn't mind a break. *We* don't need your money.'

I looked at his smiling face, feeling cosy and conflicted.

'Is that a yes?' J pressed me tighter to his chest. I nodded hesitantly.

'Hey, Lubochka,' he imitated my mother. 'I love you, Lubochka! C'mon, get dressed. Let's celebrate!'

I zipped up a flowery skirt passed on to me by my friend Natasha. J poked his head into the bedroom, still grinning. 'I gather you're going to give notice? I was thinking: if you get to see that pretty girl, who works with you, again … what's her name, Marina? Maybe ask her to come over? We could play with her, honey.'

I looked at J and saw a stranger. I told him to fuck off. To FUCK OFF. I slammed the door in his face. I then tried to do what I usually did during our quarrels—bury myself in a book. But Sartre's worldview was cold, his freedom was loveless; Nin's men repeatedly abused her kindness and her purse. J, I thought, had really overstepped the line this time. I picked up the suitcase I'd never bothered to unpack and trailed it onto the street past J, who, in his own state of rage, pretended to ignore me.

We lived far from public transport. I had no mobile phone, as I had no credit card, as I had no money, as I had no proper job, as I had no permit to work. My plan was to drag the suitcase to the closest main road and hail a taxi to Natasha's place. By the time I'd made it halfway, J caught up with me. His face was red, his eyes were liquid, like in our first week, when he'd told me the hiking story. 'You can't leave me.' He reached for my shoulders, hair, face. 'Where will you go, honey? You won't manage alone. You can't even speak English. You need me. I need you. Esther has already left me.' J finally reached for my Achilles heel. 'You've helped me to get over her, but I won't get over *you*.' He gave me the strongest evidence to make my final case for my worth. And he was right. I had nowhere to go. J carried my suitcase back to his house with one hand, while the other held tightly onto mine.

By spring I had quit the library and J had sold the Bundoora house and we'd moved into another, also large and empty, house in Ferntree Gully. We unpacked our few possessions, then took to the road. The distances stretched, silent, like elastic bands under our wheels—no one even hooted their horns here. I had noticed Australians talked of 'road rage' as a distinct phenomenon, not as a way of life. The silence, and the roominess of the green and blue horizons, ironed my crumpled nerves. In Australia, when I spread my arms I didn't bump into anyone. There seemed to be enough space for everybody here.

For the first time, I, the city girl, fell for nature: for the giant stars that embroidered the linen of night with gold; and the flowers, kangaroos, mountains and lakes that were all in bloom, aglitter. Even the black swans, vicious in Melbourne, appeared angelic here. I fed them, while J watched me. He never fed them himself, but made sure we always had a supply of bread. He acted similarly anywhere we went, be it museums or parks: never personally involved, but patiently observing the fuss his excitable woman made over the country he considered unworthy of his attention. He'd told me not to idealise a place where the youth suicide rate was one of the highest in the world. 'They blow their brains out here out of boredom,' J said, still watching me, as though I were, as Paris was for Hemingway, a moveable feast. I liked this role; my voice grew louder, I began pointing at things more often than I needed to. Still, being happy for two was draining at times.

Gradually, away from the kitchen sink, men's saunas and real estate agents, J relaxed. A dilettante comedian who had performed in some Melburnian venues, he practised his stand-up routines on me while I educated him about art matters. But in Mildura's gallery, which exhibited a pastel by Degas, J was less interested in the differences between him and the other Impressionists than he was in the scant security around the painting. While he considered the possibilities, I considered how to get us out of town quickly. Eventually, I prevailed and we took a hotel room at a nearby lakeside village.

So far on our trip, we'd forgone the news. Now, with the sunset through the window turning lush on us, J switched on the television. The screen released ammunition of snippets from Israel. Everything there seemed to be on fire: tyres, houses, bodies, souls. The familiar contours of hills and valleys were flooded with blood and visceral hatred. Apparently, as our trip unfolded, so had a national disaster. Horrified, we listened to the tribal chanting of death in Arabic and Hebrew, to the dry beat of bullets, the shrieking of stones cruising the air. The newswoman called it 'the Second Intifada'.

'I could never feel the future there,' J said, to my surprise. Usually, nostalgia held him in its grip and he'd endow his life in Israel with whatever his present supposedly lacked. Whereas I, then, wasn't interested in vacillation, but focused on being a newcomer for whom everything was possible. I disposed of chunks of my past, hoping to retrieve them later, once Australia became familiar. Despite my failure to reconnect to my Russianness, once again I deluded myself into thinking that getting my past back would be a piece of cake.

'Yeah, same for me,' I said. 'I'm not surprised. I could see this coming. But I can't imagine the end.'

Once I had, briefly, dreamed of a happy ending. But that wasn't a result of reflection; rather, upon my release from the army, some temporary mania overtook me and, for some months, all I thought of was sunshine, beaches, beer and my body. Otherwise, though, even in the magical bubble of Tel

Aviv, reality occasionally intruded into the chic of our cafés and the drumbeat of our music, particularly when buses and people would burst into flames. Then we would remember we lived on borrowed time and would party even more rabidly, dancing away the terror, as if the world were about to end. We were good at bravado, wielding it as a weapon against our history and geography. Now, a part of me wanted to switch the television off; another part was drawn in, hypnotised. If previously I'd entertained the possibility of escaping from J by returning to Israel, now I lost even that consolation. After tasting life in the world's greatest hideout, and in the face of this new political crisis, I knew I'd endure whatever it took to stick my roots into Australian bushland. But I also felt like a rat, that mythical deserter of sinking ships.

J, who under my tutelage had acquired a taste for wine, opened a bottle of shiraz as soon as I told him how guiltyguiltyguilty I felt about loving Australia—guilty despite all my complaints about Israel. Underneath my litany lurked the knowledge that I'd always need the country I'd called mine for fifteen years. Being a Jew meant you never felt secure anywhere, not even in the Antipodean haven. Whether I wanted it or not, Israel would always be my city of refuge. Here, by a gorgeous lake, abundant with swans, I felt even more ashamed of my banal desire for a comfortable life and of the conviction I'd developed that, whether in the short or long term, Israel was doomed. To walk away from a place like that, at a time when every able person was a much-needed soldier, felt cruel.

'Israel is like a Jewish mother,' I said. 'You love or hate her, but whichever it is, she's always making you feel guilty. We all have a national debt, don't you think?' J nodded and, I think, that was the moment when we finally tuned into each other. J put his arms around me and I *liked* him then, terribly: not for his life dramas, but for his beautiful deep voice, for our shared language and for the fact we'd both once donned khaki uniforms, and for the faraway, burning world we'd known and were still connected to—if not by an umbilical cord, then by a Jewish one. We switched off the television and lay on the bed entwined, and I don't think Esther was there that time. Outside, Australia lay so still, I could hear its heartbeat.

7

A Tale of Tragedy

'The spiritual disposition of a poet inclines to catastrophe.'
Osip Mandelstam

From Prichard's house, I called my parents in the Crown Heights neighbourhood in Brooklyn, to which they'd moved shortly after the Second Intifada began. It was in that place, where the air rippled with rap and klezmer deep into the night, and the black-clad Hassidim passed the time by mixing frivolously with their black neighbours until their dead leader, Rabbi Lubavitch, made his comeback as the Messiah, that my parents felt most at home.

'Where are you, *dochenka, moyo solnishko*, my little daughter, my sunshine?' My mother's lively voice was as clear as if she were in Perth.

I was acutely aware of how illusory that closeness was. For years now, the woman who during my early childhood had fed me pork fat had been filtering the world through a biblical lens. My father, a physicist, could straddle the worlds both of modern science and outdated divinities. But for my mother, the circumstances of Abraham, who nearly slaughtered his son for God, were more comprehensible than those of a female writer in the twenty-first century. At thirty-four, I had three books under my unchaste belt but no child yet. My mother framed this situation as her Abraham-style trial. To her credit, though, even if I remained childless, she wouldn't slaughter me. Not even if God ordered her to. From Russian–Jewish stock, she was a fierce, old-fashioned mother, the kind you no longer saw around much: a mother who was never polite or friendly to her children. Her love for us was bloody, animalistic. She still picked our ears and told us how to live our lives, as if parenting courses had never been invented. Although I hated to admit it, it was actually comforting having such a mother.

'I ...' I mumbled. 'I'm in Perth. It's very hot here ...'

'Is Noah with you?' my mother interrupted. My Jewish husband was the only story about me that made sense in her neighbourhood.

'No. I'm in a w-r-i-t-i-n-g r-e-s-i-d-e-n-c-y.'

'Aha ... So, bring Noah there. He can write too.'

Obviously, she wasn't as familiar with my Jewish husband as she liked to think.

'See, *mamochka*,' I said as I tried to open a window into my life for her, 'you don't just bring people into writing residencies. A residency is something a writer is awarded for her own use. The way it works is,' I said as I started enjoying myself, as minor writers rarely have opportunities to brag, 'many writers apply ...'

'It's not good to leave your husband alone,' my mother said. 'Men don't like to be alone. It's not good for marriage.'

'... then there is a selection process ...'

'When are you going back home?'

'In a few days.' And then what? Beneath the gear for work—my demure tracksuit and earnest spectacles—I wore around the writers' centre, lurked the secret of my lover, charging my every step with largeness. I was becoming addicted to life being felt so acutely.

'*Oy vey!* And where do you live there?' My mother had presented me with another problem, of having to explain what a writers' centre was.

I resorted to an easier option: 'I live in the house of an Australian writer.'

'Oh ... Lubochka, listen to your mama. Don't make your husband jealous! Also not good for marriage. Is he nice?'

'I don't know. *She* is dead. Her husband is dead too. He shot himself in this same house.' I couldn't resist upsetting her but forgot my mother liked such stories. Tragedies, beginning with the Bible, were bread and butter for Jews. Our collective identity was often defined and redefined by the many disasters that had befallen us throughout history. But we were also defined by our ability to laugh at our misfortunes. If Greeks were the progenitors of tragedy and comedy, then Jews must have invented the tragicomedy. Rather than classifying things, we complicated them. No wonder everyone hated us. No wonder I now finally got my mother's full attention.

'What's her name?'

What did it matter? I'd first heard of Prichard only when I was applying for the residency. As for my mother, nowadays she mostly read Tehilim, the Book of Psalms, and Mills & Boons novels, which were actually compatible, both being unselfconsciously tragicomic.

'Ah, Prichard!' My mother pronounced the name with the same ease she would say King David. 'I read her novels. We all read them in Russia. She was the only translated Australian writer, because she was a communist. Did you know she helped to found the Australian Communist Party, *dochenka*?'

I wished we'd never had that conversation. I felt dismayed that, once again, my mother was ahead of me. And I didn't like the idea of staying in the house of the founder of the Australian Communist Party. Ironically, the talk I was to give the next morning I had called 'Oppressive Regimes and Poetry'. The title was more strategic than didactic: I hoped to steer the discussion away from poetry, which I loved intuitively, and towards what I felt more capable of discussing intelligibly—my aversion to communism. Unlike many liberally minded Westerners, who viewed communism sympathetically—as a well-intentioned, if poorly executed, idea—I didn't think it was a good idea to begin with. In my view, full equality has always been more of a human fantasy than a human inclination, and a good fantasy it is, as long as it remains a loose guideline. To support my argument while retaining a literary focus, I decided to discuss the works and fates of four poets from the Soviet Union, where writers were not only censored but also instructed what to write. This was the same country that Prichard, I had now read in a biography of her, had kept supporting even after the details of Stalin's Terror leaked to the West. Many Australian communists left the party in the

1950s, but Prichard remained a loyal member until her death in 1969, a year after the Soviet tanks invaded Prague, crushing spring flowers and students under their wheels.

The poets I chose—Osip Mandelstam, Marina Tsvetayeva, Vladimir Mayakovsky and Joseph Brodsky—all shared literary greatness, the experience of state persecution and being the subject of my adoration. To make my talk more dramatic, I structured it according to the chronology of their premature deaths.

Poets' lack of longevity wasn't, of course, a strictly Soviet phenomenon; even when living under more lenient regimes, poets seem to have a fragile makeup. I once heard of a European writing residency that had a sign at its gate: 'Do not park your vehicle here. Poets must never be prevented from viewing the lake.' What is noticeable here, apart from the assumption about the necessity of lakes for inspiration, is the lack of concern for the prose writers. This made sense in light of a study finding that of all creative species, poets lived the shortest lives. Even the fiction writers with the most turbulent lives, like Hemingway, who shot himself at the age of sixty-two, might be thought of as having longevity when compared with the longevity standards of poets, and so might have got by without the lake view. But even among the poets, no one could beat the Russians; at least, not in their sheer volume of early deaths.

In Russia, Mandelstam once mused, poetry was truly respected—you could even get killed for it. Unfortunately, his musing proved to be prophetic for him. After writing poetry likening Stalin to a cockroach, Mandelstam was shot by secret police at the age of forty-seven. When the state didn't kill its poets, it made their lives miserable enough that they did the job themselves. Also living under Stalin, Mayakovsky shot himself at thirty-seven, Tsvetayeva hanged herself at forty-nine. Only Brodsky died of natural causes. But it was his death that particularly upset me. Brodsky, born in 1940, was too young to make Stalin cross before the great leader turned his belly up.

He had an even better chance at a long life after the Soviets expelled him in 1972 for his non-conformist poetry. In his new, American, home, Brodsky was a literary success, receiving the Nobel prize in 1987. Still, even he couldn't help himself. Being genetically unwired to Anglo-Saxon health worship, this ardent smoker, who once said, 'If you can't have a cigarette with your morning coffee, there is no point in getting up,' died at fifty-six from a heart attack. As I mentally finalised my talk, I noticed the 'no smoking' sign above the centre's fridge and hoped that tomorrow I wouldn't harm the reputation of Russian poetry in Perth. Then I changed my clothes, to head off to a jazz show with my lover.

In the morning, after an unslept night, I stumbled out of bed to the realisation that I was to do the talk in half an hour. Only now did I remember how much I hated public speaking and how bad at it I was. My eyes were puffy, my skin was still raw from my lover's touch. In order to fortify myself with caffeine, I went to the kitchen, where the members of morning writing groups—something I had considered an oxymoron before coming here—always lurked. Today, luckily, only one man was there to greet me and my blue dressing gown. The man, I noticed even in my dishevelled state, was an exception to the male writers who came to this centre. Usually, they were either the age poets were when they were still alive or the age that even prose writers rarely reached. This one, though, was mysteriously located between his forties and sixties. His thinning, greyish hair was brushed across his forehead in the futile attempt that some balding men make to preserve a look of luxurious abundance on their heads. He did have abundant hair elsewhere, though: under his nostrils, a narrow but potently thick moustache blossomed.

The man, who, I noticed, was clutching to his chest with both hands a brown case, seemed familiar, but I couldn't remember from where. To my relief, he introduced himself as a stranger would, enquiring shyly as to whether I was the visiting *Israeli–Australian* writer. When I confirmed that I was, his face lit up, transforming the thick moustache into a Christmas tree. For some odd reason, he relished my other nationality. Grateful for this, I asked him what he was writing. The man said it was about his life. But was there a particular focus for his story, I enquired politely. He seemed unsettled by my question. 'I don't really talk about my work,' he said. I apologised and went to my room, coffee-less and feeling awkward.

The minute I put on my dress, the door opened without anyone having knocked. 'You might like to have the phone number of my *Jewish* friend.' The owner of the case and moustache handed me a note with the details of a jeweller called Goldman, or maybe Cohen. Shaken by his puzzling offer and his sudden appearance, I waited in silence until he left my room.

Several seconds later, the door opened again. This time, the case was held more loosely, more frivolously, while the moustache seemed more erect. 'I need a ghostwriter,' the man said.

'A ghostwriter?'

'Yes. You'd be perfect.'

'Me?'

'Yes ... See, it's a very controversial story. But, as a professional, and *Jewish*, writer ... you'll understand.' At that, the case was blasted open to reveal a chaos of pages crammed with pencilled words and swastikas. The man grew more excited: 'The thing is ... but you must keep this a secret ... Hitler had a lost son. *We have to tell this story!*'

Finally I realised why the man seemed so familiar: the rounded shoulders, the toothbrush moustache, the long grey hair swept across the forehead ... My talk was about to begin and I ran out, accidentally brushing the man's case.

Out of the nine people who turned up for 'Oppressive Regimes and Poetry', only two, including Hitler's son, were possibly not of retirement age. A gentleman with a hearing aid who had a row of medals from one of the world wars pinned to his jacket also seemed vaguely familiar. I attributed his familiarity to my fragile emotional state; still, I surveyed the room to see if any other children of famous personages were in attendance.

Shortly after the introductions, it became clear that none of those present was familiar with Russian poetry. Apparently, my talk had been advertised as a generic writer-in-residence one, and now my audience and I stared at each other with apprehension. The only person unperturbed by the situation was Hitler's son. He kept sending gentle glances my way, as if to say, *You have my full support.* To my relief, I eventually learned that the audience's visible discontent related less to my topic and more to the lack of the morning tea that was expected at the centre's authorial presentations. The day before, Nina had taken me shopping, so I was in a position to sacrifice food for the sake of literature.

Once everyone was finally settled, I realised that the morbid angle I took on Russian poetry was an act of genius. The audience, fortified by my biscuits, proved to be even less keen than I was on the intricacies of poetic metre, but eager for the 'oppressive regimes' part. All I had to do was to mention the penchant of Cheka (the KGB's predecessor, formed by Lenin) for using ancient torture methods, such as skinning alive and crucifying their unfortunate victims, and I received the audience's undivided attention. The gentleman wearing medals even took notes. Only Hitler's son seemed uncomfortable. As I continued my oratory with a skill I never knew I possessed, he kept clutching his case, occasionally enquiring whether the chekist or poet in question was Jewish.

Fired by the audience's gasps, which were almost as frequent as their coughs, I launched into the most eloquent speech I'd ever made. 'The fate of Mayakovsky was ironic.' I paused for emphasis. 'He belonged to the Russian Futurists. But he was also an ardent supporter of the Revolution. In fact, he first became famous for the elegy he wrote for Lenin and for which other Futurists criticised him. But when Stalin declared the Futurists the enemies of communism, Mayakovsky got rejected both by the regime and its opponents. Attacked in the press, denied a visa to travel abroad and disappointed with the State he initially fiercely believed in, on 14 April 1930 Mayakovsky shot himself.'

The atmosphere grew tense, and even Hitler's son nodded sorrowfully. 'The aftermath of Mayakovsky's death was ironic too,' I went on. 'Now that he could no longer criticise the regime, Stalin named him the greatest communist poet. After glasnost and perestroika, though, Mayakovsky was denounced once again—this time, for his posthumous association with Stalin. But I think if you let his poetry speak for itself, then its virtuosic language and breathtaking rhythm will take over, making you actually *forget* politics.'

A lady with a white chignon dabbed the corners of her eyes with a handkerchief while helping herself to the last biscuit. To capitalise on my success, I read from the poet's famous suicide note: 'Mother, sisters, friends, forgive me. This is not the way (I do not recommend it to others), but there is no other way out for me. Lilya—love me!'

The medal man stopped scribbling and fiddled with his hearing aid: 'Who is Lilya?!'

'Was she Jewish?' Hitler's son asked.

I realised I'd made a strategic error. So far, in order to preserve the newfound popularity of Russian poetry in Perth, I'd deliberately avoided the romantic angle. Russian poets never, to put it mildly, excelled at romantic angles and now their honour was tied to mine. Luckily, out of my four chosen poets, Mayakovsky was only the first to die.

'Let's move on to Mandelstam now. He was born into a Jewish–Polish family ...' I glanced in the direction of Hitler's son and contemplated contacting the Baha'i handyman about installing a lock on my bedroom door.

Lilya was Jewish. And she was pretty, with her thick red bob, long lean limbs and large eyes. Lilya. Her existence spoiled my version of a heroic Mayakovsky who had sacrificed himself on the altar of his shattered ideals. But who would kill themselves solely for lofty reasons? Usually some pathology, or other personal unhappiness, mixes with political despair to create a lethal cocktail. Once Mayakovsky had shot himself in the heart in his Moscow apartment, competition over the title of 'poet's personal unhappiness' began. There was the beautiful Parisian émigré Tatiana Yakovleva, who had recently ditched him. Then, the young actress Veronica Polonskaya, the poet's most recent infatuation, claimed Mayakovsky had killed himself over *her* refusal to marry him. The most enduring hypothesis, though, was that those involvements were just more identical pearls in the string of affairs that decorated Mayakovsky's fifteen-year love for Lilya, who, in turn, had her own pearls. In the poet's suicide note, as in his life, Lilya held centre stage. To this day, the Russians blame her for his death. If only she had been faithful to their poet ...

Lilya confounded every Russian idea of what an artist's wife should be. For a start, she was a wife to *two* artists, living openly in the same apartment with Mayakovsky and Osip Brik, the essayist and literary critic. Then, rather than unconditionally adoring her man (or men) and self-effacingly forgiving the selfishness and promiscuity expected of male artists, she behaved like their peer. Unlike her compatriot and contemporary Gala, who limited herself to the role of muse (although one who had a business slant), Lilya was both a muse and an artist. She sculpted, wrote screenplays and acted. She was also a flirt and inspired obsession in men. She was witty, generous in spirit and, unusually for her time, confident. Ravenous for life, Lilya stayed up all night to dance and read poetry, traversed Uzbekistan (including its brothels), played tennis naked, wore large hats with feathers. No wonder people couldn't stomach her. No wonder she was irresistible. Throughout Lilya's life, men left much younger, sometimes prettier, women, to throw themselves at her feet. Unlike Gala's, her appeal didn't expire with age.

On that summer day in 1915 when Lilya met the great Russian poet-to-be she was only twenty-three. Mayakovsky, a year younger, later described the same day, when he walked into the Briks' apartment and saw Lilya, as the most joyful of his life. For him, it was love at first sight. But Lilya wasn't that impressed by the intensity of the tall, fierce-eyed, awkward (and, in my eyes, gorgeous) youth. Neither did she like the claims to genius with which he disguised his self-doubts. The poet's persistent adoration irritated Lilya as much as his bad teeth and general neglect of his appearance did. 'Volodya [a diminutive of Vladimir],' she later wrote in her memoir, 'didn't just fall in love with me, but laced into me.'

Lilya's initial ambivalence wasn't because she was married. Even before she wedded Osip, she was in the habit of having several suitors at once. Osip, inspired by the radical philosopher Nikolay Chernyshevsky, was also a freethinker. Besides, he himself fell in love (albeit platonically) with Mayakovsky after reading his poem 'A Cloud in Trousers', which indicates the emotional force of Mayakovsky's work as well as his personality.

> Tell the firemen
> to climb with love when a heart is burning.

Leave it to me.
I'll pump barrels of tears from my eyes.
I'll hold myself against my ribs.
I'll leap out! Out! Out!

With Russian extravagance of character, Osip committed himself to editing and promoting Mayakovsky's work. For some time, he even took to imitating the poet's bass voice. Meanwhile, in his own display of commitment to Lilya, Mayakovsky visited a dentist, and purchased a bowtie and a walking stick. Equipped with new teeth and fashion accessories, he resumed the courtship.

It is a famous story that, upon hearing from Lilya that she and Mayakovsky had become lovers, Osip was only disappointed that it took so long. 'How could you refuse that man anything?!' he exclaimed. Shortly after, Mayakovsky moved in with the Briks, and, from then until his death, lived with them for extended periods. Or, at least, this is how it is often told—as a piquant tale of a threesome. In reality, Lilya and Osip had probably stopped being lovers before she met Mayakovsky. Although she never changed her surname from Brik, she and Osip divorced, but remained bound to each other by deep, non-sexual love. They continued sharing a household and running a subversive artistic salon for years. Mayakovsky wasn't the third party in the Briks' relationship, but Lilya's lawful, if secret, husband.

This unconventional marriage was central to Mayakovsky's life and, probably, his death. He was addicted to Lilya: to her body, her laughter, her tenderness, guidance. Mayakovsky felt that she grasped his complexity: seeing straight through his formidable public image to his puppy-like essence. He signed his letters to Lilya '*Schenok*', meaning 'pup', and acted like a lovestruck puppy with her. In my favourite letter of his to Lilya, he fusses over her illness with his typical passion and originality:

> Dear and exceptional Lilionok! ... If Oska [a diminutive for Osip] won't look after you and drive your lungs to ... wherever is needed, then I'll bring a coniferous forest into your apartment, and the sea into Oska's study ... Love you, my sweet and warm sun.

Lilya loved Mayakovsky too, but the poet's possessiveness and extensive demands on her time went against her grain. She was more free-spirited than he could handle; it was she who insisted their marriage would be non-monogamous, even though his affairs caused her pain. But Mayakovsky suffered more: he was deeply jealous not only of Lilya's present suitors but also his predecessors, even Osip. The fact that as time passed, Lilya needed longer breaks from Mayakovsky and became more tolerant of his women, tormented him. Feeling unloved, he increasingly fled from Lilya into extended travels. A dominant theme in Mayakovsky's poetry is his pining for an uncommitted woman and he seems to be writing from bitter experience when warning young girls against love:

> I leaned just above her actually
> and actually,
> as I
> leaned,
> I told her
> like a good father:
> 'Passion is steep as a precipice—
> please, I beg you,
> stand further.
> Further still,
> I beg you, please.'

But Mayakovsky never managed to stand further back from Lilya. While it was probably his inability to possess her utterly that, at least partly, made Lilya so irresistible to him, it was also what eventually drove him to his death. While Lilya, I believe, wasn't intentionally responsible for Mayakovsky's suicide, as some Russians suggest, their relationship contributed to his demise. Once, years before 14 April 1930, the poet had aimed a gun at himself because of Lilya, but it didn't fire. He did better the next time.

On my one lover-free evening, the night was drawing its curtains over the fading sky. I often grew blue at such an hour, when the world wasn't yet dark but seemed diluted. I was most at home with intensity—of feelings, weather, art. The centre was atypically empty, if you discounted the ghosts haunting me— Lilya, Mayakovsky and, possibly, Prichard's husband. Since having encountered Esther, I should have known better than to provoke the dead. I felt uneasy and, to distract myself, decided to return to my writing project. I wanted to reflect on what fiction writers had had to say about non-monogamists' prospects; I needed hope.

However, in the few novels about non-monogamy that I was familiar with, the protagonists fared no better than Mayakovsky, which perhaps mirrors reality. And, unlike life, fiction can also have a moralistic air. Two notable works, *The Blood Oranges* by John Hawkes and Ian McEwan's *The Comfort of Strangers*, share not only a worldview but the archetypal narrative of good-girl-meets-bad-boy (or vice versa). In each book, a faithful couple falls prey to a sinister promiscuous one while on a holiday somewhere exotic, with the 'good' husband paying with his life for the encounter. But, while the storylines and their implied lesson never to play with strange couples are strikingly similar, there are also differences, which, to my mind, express the changes that ideas of morality have undergone.

In Hawkes's book, published in 1970, Cyril, an exalted propagator of free love reminiscent of the ideologues in *Monkey Grip*, is his narrator. By allowing us access to Cyril's mind, Hawkes shows some tolerance towards his beliefs, as Cyril is sympathetic even if you don't agree with him. His poetic voice ('Need I insist that the only enemy of the mature marriage is monogamy? That anything less than sexual multiplicity … is naive?') redeems him. And Cyril is capable of remorse in the face of the tragedy that follows his and his wife's seduction of another couple, Hugh and Catherine. When Hugh, unable to deal with the ensuing infidelity, hangs himself, Cyril, in an act of self-punishment, turns into a lonely, impotent man.

The Comfort of Strangers was published eleven years later, during the conservative decade of the 1980s that followed the sexual revolution. In the novel, McEwan shows the non-monogamists, Robert and Caroline, little lenience. No interest in their psychology is demonstrated, with the couple's pathological behaviour being narrated from the point of view of their victims. The bad couple here is truly bad, driven by a shared fantasy of seduction and murder. Their relationship is ridden with violence and unhealthy co-dependency, and the good husband, Colin, dies at their predatory hands.

Rick Moody set *The Ice Storm*, another novel about non-monogamy, in the 1970s, but explores this epoch through the prism of his own time—the 1990s' ever-increasing emphasis on fidelity. The two American families under Moody's microscope are trapped by the supposedly lacklustre pleasures of the sexual experimentation, the narrative revolving around one central event, a 'key party', a then-popular suburban variation on the sexual revolution. In such soirees, the men would jumble their keys and the women would randomly pick a set and spend the night with its owner. In *The Ice Storm*, while the parents and their keys are getting around, one of their children, who has been left unsupervised, dies of accidental electrocution. Being a fan of Moody's writing, I felt cheated by this easy equation of extramarital sex with parental neglect. Such a judgement seemed even shallower than McEwan's in *The Comfort of Strangers* in resorting to the easy rhetoric of 'What about the children?' so often exploited by conservative politicians, as if parenthood is synonymous with sainthood. It seems doubtful Moody has the statistics to prove that faithful parents are better at protecting their children.

In the Russian tradition, in which literature is prophetic and reading a moral duty, I often read novels as if they were manuals for how to live. Now I was getting increasingly pessimistic about my love life and sought solace in cinema, my other passion. But, once again, few films had non-monogamy as their subject and those that did disturbed me. In the 1962 classic *Jules and Jim*, directed by François Truffaut (and actually based on yet another novel), non-monogamy is portrayed as a psychiatric condition. Its heroine, the charming, spontaneous Catherine, who is married to Jules but also involved with other men, gradually turns into a vengeful psychotic, eventually plunging a car off a bridge and killing herself and her lover. And if in Woody Allen's more recent *Vicky Cristina Barcelona* no one dies, it's not due to a lack of pathological psychology but to the clumsiness of the striking, and strikingly volatile, artist Maria Elena, who is as passionate about knives and pistols as she is about her husband Juan Antonio, with whom she shares a lover.

What film and literature seem to be wanting to show us is that whenever couples open their gates, even only slightly, danger enters, and that committed non-monogamists are dangerous psychopaths. The only film I saw that depicts a non-monogamist as psychologically healthy, even admirable, is Max Färberböck's *Aimée & Jaguar*. It is based on the true story of Felice, a young Jewish journalist who has assumed a false identity and is struggling to survive in Nazi Berlin. She turns her life of daily danger into a party, drinking, smoking, dancing, writing erotic poetry and sleeping with women she desires because—as she tells her jealous lover Lilly—limiting herself to one person is against her nature. But to love fiercely, devotedly, *is* in her nature. It is Felice, not the faithful Lilly, a Nazi officer's wife, who risks her life for the sake of their affair by giving up her chance to escape Germany in order to stay with Lilly. Eventually, Nazis catch Felice and she dies in a concentration camp. But her story, despite the unapologetic centrality of non-monogamy it has, lives on. Perhaps Felice is allowed her dignity, and even glory, because she is a doomed Jewess and, what's more, in love with a Nazi housewife. Felice's faithlessness can be read as the Jewish revenge on Germany, which *deserved* to have non-monogamy inflicted upon it. The story's tragic twist also sweetens the bitter pill of the sexuality it celebrates. If Felice had survived, perhaps there would have been no film about her.

The night was closing in on me. I wondered whether, to paraphrase Mandelstam, the spiritual disposition of non-monogamists inclined them towards catastrophe; Esther had died too. I contemplated my own prospects. I didn't think I was a psychopath, and I didn't think I had any Nazi lovers looming on my romantic horizon (though the morning's incident had left me uncertain about this last point). Still, if previously I'd been considering such earnest titles for my book as *Non-monogamy: Territorial Negotiations of Coupledom*, *Non-monogamy: the Endless Misery* now seemed more appropriate. But maybe I just felt despondent generally.

I've always thought nostalgia is overrated. If I were Odysseus, I'd have forgone Ithaca and stayed with Calypso, the nymph. After all, I was most at home where I was a newcomer. To my horror, I no longer wanted to return to Melbourne. The closer the end of the residency came, the larger my lover loomed, while my memory of Noah receded. To lull myself to sleep, I re-read my lover's email about the next day's arrangements: 'Kindly note that I fully intend to kiss you (several times, probably) before we get to my abode.'

We decided to spend my last night in Perth in my lover's apartment, which, because of its distance from Prichard's house, I hadn't visited before. Nina drove me to the train station, so that I could meet my lover discreetly. I lingered, wet-eyed, in her perfumed, bosomy embrace. Then, once again, a man picked up the large suitcase containing my essentials—books, dresses and an unfinished manuscript—while, with his other hand, he pressed me tightly to himself.

Homes often betray, or at least complicate perceptions of, their owners. My lover's place rendered him even more opaque, being an odd melange of a nursing home and a nursery. I searched for his soul in CD racks dominated by the likes of Frank Sinatra, in his videotape collection featuring Fred Astaire and Humphrey Bogart, in the books that often predated the music and films he liked, but couldn't pinpoint it. I also couldn't grasp it in his bedroom, whose walls he had covered with expensively framed images of Batman.

One of my lover's charms was that he was a gifted listener, though he rarely said much in return. Stories, just like love-making, I used as a panacea for most discomforts. To draw us back into familiarity with each other, I told him about my favourite essay by Joseph Brodsky, in which he describes how, as a child in the Soviet Union, he was overwhelmed by the ubiquity of Lenin's image in public spaces: 'There was Lenin, looking like a cherub in his blonde curls. Then Lenin in his twenties and thirties, bald and uptight …' Since then, Brodsky wrote, he'd detested any repetition. To him, a few trees were acceptable, but a forest was banal. I said I shared his view. My lover looked at me surprised, perhaps assuming I was hinting we had no future. Once again, spoken words failed me. What I'd really wanted to tell him was that our affair was singular in my life.

I always found sleeping with someone new harder than making love. I disliked emerging from the oblivion of sleep into a sudden close-up of strange skin illuminated by the sharpness of daylight, into unfamiliar morning breath and sweat. My lover had always left in the dark, before Prichard's house would come alive with people. Now I was afraid of the morning, and kept shifting, restless, in his spotlessly neat bed with the blanket tucked in hotel-style. Trees, loaded pistols, even Hitler, ambushed my head that night.

At the airport, my lover handed me a parting gift—*The Cat in the Hat*, his favourite childhood book. Surprised that I had never heard of Dr Seuss, he laughed almost soundlessly, as the Israeli writer used to. I wished he hadn't. Hadn't laughed, hadn't bought the book. It complicated everything, bringing innocence somewhere it didn't belong.

'I'll come to Melbourne next month. If you don't object,' he said, and I wondered if I could handle all this—Noah, the book, this man, my flesh. I wanted to freeze time, to live in the airport, where guilt, pressures, plans, regrets always melted away. We still hung onto each other when the final boarding call for my flight came. I etched my lover into me.

Would he really come, the senior financial advisor?

8

A Tale of Domesticity, or— Who Really Killed Mayakovsky?

'*Normal people do not know that everything is possible.*'
Friedrich Nietzsche

My parents never understood the poetry of freshly baked bread and crisp sheets, or even that of swept floors. For years, they've been in the business of survival, battling the windmills of communism and then those of free market forces, all for their children's sakes. In some ways, they derived pride from their difficult fate. But their perpetual lack of peace and money meant they developed an intimidated wonderment at conveniences others accept as their natural prerogatives, be these cars or modular couches. I, on the other hand, grew up interested in equal measure in adventure and domesticity. In the children's books I read, the battles with dark forces and the cosy fireplaces where hobbits congregated were equally fascinating. In my teens, I took to hitchhiking and knitting. Vases and teapots make me happy. Wherever I live, I dust regularly, hang art on the walls, arrange plants and candles, keep the pantry stocked with lentils and preserved lemons. But the apartment I shared with Noah was the *chef d'oeuvre* of the kind of domesticity I desired.

Noah had purchased this place in the year we mostly spent apart, following J's threat to report me to Immigration for breaching some law or other if I kept seeing Noah. By then, he'd already damaged Noah's car. I'd worried that next time, he'd harm Noah and about my vulnerability in having only a temporary visa. Later, though, when I was still under J's surveillance but living separately from him and working at a proper job, I'd bought my first car in Australia, a tattered station wagon, and driven to Noah's newly purchased apartment.

That night, as I drove along Beach Road and past Luna Park and the nunnery-turned-fancy apartment building and the houses with telescopes supposedly positioned for watching the ocean, I felt frightened and not just because I was finally driving on the left side of the road. I was worried J might be on my tail. Even more, I feared that, after all this time, I'd discover Noah wasn't the man I remembered, wasn't the man I could love. I also worried I was spent, done with love, and I probably was then. But Noah's apartment—more extravagant than practical, with its deep carpets, fake marble and brass in the kitchen, views of the city's towers, the sound of the nearby ocean's ancient chords—soothed me. Noah had said he'd chosen this place with me in mind, and, several weeks later, I finally unpacked my suitcase, and hid in the womb of the apartment for the next six months, until J left the country. Then Noah and I bought a purple couch large enough to seat a dozen, planted rosemary and mint on the balcony, and filled the place with friends to celebrate our, now-free, life together.

There was something deeply nourishing about Noah and the home we had made. I nestled within the two, soaking up their goodness, fruiting rapidly. My skin shone. My hair thickened. When I lived with J, I oozed passion and darkness. I was unhappy in a fierce way that made me feel alive but also ate at me. With Noah, my occasional unhappiness was never crushing, never terrifying. In the company of my husband, the couch, the plants, I'd often felt complete. Like I belonged. Like I was where I needed to be. But perhaps any growth is finite?

When I was back in Melbourne from Perth, Noah felt almost as strange to me as my lover. I spoke to him like he was my husband, held him like he was, but I was now constantly swarmed by the dazzling butterflies of yearning for something else. This yearning clouded the space between us. Befuddled, I kept losing hair clips and took to tying my hair with itself. Being naturally unruly, my locks came undone at any opportunity, tickling my nose, getting stuck between my teeth, covering my eyes. I saw nothing anyhow. I was all skin and nerves waiting to be touched. There were weeks to come before the teaching semester would begin, before my usually dense routine would, hopefully, flatten my edges.

In the meantime, I tried to recover my married self. I marinated chicken in garlic and coriander, vacuumed the carpets, baked a blackberry pie. I sent Noah an email titled 'Things I enjoy'. The list included: 'when we kiss', 'when you stroke me' and 'some things I'm too shy to write about'. That was the ridiculous limit to how far I dared to proceed in my approaches. But, even to this, Noah never responded and the butterflies kept following me around. In his defence, the longer we lived together, the more I got into the habit of reducing myself to two incompatible personas who made intermittent appearances on our marital stage: his formidable mother and his spoiled child. One told Noah what to do and squeezed his nose; another liked baby talk. That would be a tough mix for any man to handle, even someone as patient as Noah, and not one that would ignite passion. But then, even that description of us was generalisation, a linguistic escape from the sticky mess that our marriage had become. We had so much happiness among the muddle. How does one sum up a marriage?

Since domestic affairs failed to distract me sufficiently, I retreated into books. Lying on the couch under Chagall's naked bride, I tried to imitate her languid pose and re-read *On the Road*. I wanted to be in the company of people who believed lusty living wasn't the prerogative of adolescents; people who were reluctant to walk the so-called 'mature' path that required yearning be de-clawed:

> At lilac evening I walked with every muscle aching among the lights of 27th and Welton in the Denver colored section, wishing I were a Negro, feeling that the best the white world had offered was not enough ecstasy for me, not enough life, joy, kicks, darkness, music, not enough night.

I viscerally got the protagonist's addiction to ecstasy: 'I was having a wonderful time and the whole world opened up before me because I had no dreams.' I envied him too. I had too many dreams now, and they got in the way of what used to be my life. Even the arrival of doctorate scholarship offers couldn't distract me from my flesh. I kept wasting the precious days on which I could write full-time. Eventually, I locked myself in my study amid the hundreds of books I'd collected over the years and that were in the kind of bookshelves I'd always wanted to have—white with glass doors. Still I couldn't focus. I panicked. This ceaseless desire wasn't the price I'd thought I'd be paying for my affair. Instead of writing my book, I wrote my diary: 'WA changed me. Maybe for good. In both senses of the expression.' But I wasn't sure I meant it; more confusingly, I wasn't even sure whether my yearning was directed at my lover. But a stranger wouldn't do either. I desired not only sex but also that slippery dance of courtship that was possible with a lover you knew—but not too closely.

Feeling too wild to be still, I set myself in motion. That week, a rain of Russian potency was whipping Melbourne into cream. My wipers stopped working, the road became a blur. I drove anyway, amid the ambulance sirens and the screeching of cars breaking down, as though the risk were worth it, as though the movement could put me back together, as though putting myself together were desirable at all. I returned home to Noah dripping wet and he, who in practical matters always knew what I needed—coffee, hugs, petrol in my car—helped to dry me. Yet, what I really wanted was to talk—about my confusion, even about the pleasure I'd just known.

My initial hope, when I'd envisaged a non-monogamous marriage, was that by setting each other free, we'd actually be drawn closer together. Instead, there was now all this secretiveness between us. I tried to say one true sentence, as Hemingway once put it, but the fear of causing Noah hurt seized me by the throat.

So I suggested we go to Harvey Norman to realise one of my old dreams. We bought a dining set for our balcony to replace the old one that was made of rough wood. The new set was cushioned thickly. When the delivery men unloaded it, I sighed with relief. Meanwhile, my lover emailed me to say he'd booked his second trip to Melbourne, even though the first one hadn't happened yet.

Desperate to talk about my confusion, I phoned my friend Ronit. She and I were close in age, and also in the timing of our arrivals in Australia from Israel. But Ronit was a real *sabra* (native Israeli). I met her at an Israeli gathering in my second year in Australia, when I was still trying to bond with people only because they had a connection with either of my former countries. Most of those relationships proved unsubstantial and dissipated quickly, but Ronit remained a close friend. With her outlook being a complex mix of prejudice and freethinking, like that of many Israelis, in Australia she struggled to transcend her origins. She handled aptly administering a complex organisation, but its politically correct etiquette was a mystery to her. There were some unbridgeable gaps in our worldviews too, particularly Ronit's being a fatalist. For me, though, such gaps only made our friendship more delicious. I often found her observations about anything—the film *Titanic*, chicken soup, female writers—disagreeable, and wonderful in their sheer unexpectedness. I delighted even more in *how* she expressed her opinions. Ronit was a linguistic acrobat devoted to black humour. While to strangers she could seem shy, among friends her tongue ran rampant.

Not daring to reveal my affair at once, I began the conversation by telling Ronit about my book. '*Eizo zohama!*' she said with gusto. 'What filth you're writing about!'

I was surprised by her response. She wasn't a prude; once, Noah and I had kissed her simultaneously. And she knew all about powerful, complex longing. When Ronit fell for someone, she did so in a way that was full of tears and booze, with passing out in bathrooms and the tearing up of photographs. Since I'd known her, Ronit had usually been unhappily in love. It didn't help that her romantic choices in Australia were limited. She viewed non-Israeli men as a form of alien life, and the few Israeli men who were around were either taken or were young travellers, and generally weren't bookish enough by her standards. She craved stable love, but since her divorce, she and her young daughter lived mostly as a sovereign country. In her habitual air of melancholy, and with her dark bob, pale skin and fine nose, she reminded me of Juliette Binoche.

I now recalled that Ronit once told me that her divorce, which had happened not long before she came to Australia, had had to do with some involvement she and her husband had had with another couple, something that she similarly described as filth. I didn't probe her then; she still seemed pained by the story. But now I couldn't help myself.

'You wouldn't let me off the hook, would you?' Ronit sighed. 'I suppose it's good to get things off your chest, as they say in Australia.'

Noah was at a cricket match, so Ronit and I could smoke inside. Shrouded in a cloud of tobacco, Ronit told me how the marital crisis ensued shortly after her daughter was born. The stress of becoming parents shook the already wobbly edifice of Ronit's six-year-long marriage to an IT wizard devoted to high culture. The bespectacled man with a somewhat portly physique I had seen in the photos at once appealed and didn't appeal to Ronit. She had felt sexually bored long before becoming pregnant, which, she hoped—as people do—would improve the situation as, of course, it never does. Things became even worse when Ronit's mother came from Australia to stay in their lovely, spacious apartment in the heart of Tel Aviv, to help with the baby. Her mother—who was never content with anything, including her only daughter—and her husband yelled at each other for a month. In the renewed silence after her mother's departure, Ronit noticed she'd lost interest in anything, including her child.

'I think I had postnatal depression.' Ronit's voice flickered faintly, like the city lights through the windows. In 1999, postnatal depression was still largely unknown in Israel; mental maladies were often seen as signs of individual weakness. Despite his intellect, her husband didn't understand Ronit, but got increasingly angry about her sadness, whereas Ronit's yearning for a more thrilling life intensified to an extent fit for Chekhovian heroines. To introduce some excitement, she booked a vacation in a European resort for her husband, hinting he could have some adventures there. 'Really, I did this for myself,' Ronit said. 'I wanted credit for later.'

On his return, her husband told Ronit he'd had an affair, and that he and this woman had feelings for each other but he'd put an end to it. He sounded proud of himself, not knowing the damage his confession caused. Like me, Ronit could handle sexual infidelity but the word 'feelings' cut her deeply. Instead of energising their marriage, the European vacation led to more arguments. The husband, who made his living solving problems, suggested that partner swapping might fix theirs. 'I think,' Ronit said, 'he offered this more for me, so that I also had fun. And I was enthusiastic.'

The internet was still a novelty then. In the largely vacant cyberspace, particularly its tiny Israeli share, websites for partner swapping were, contrary to assumptions, used mostly by inoffensive IT people like Ronit's husband, and this threw up its own unique surprises. The man from the first couple they met, over bottles of rosé in a posh restaurant, turned out to be one of Ronit's husband's managers who worked in a different office and whom he'd never met before. After suffering that embarrassment, they decided to be more careful before making any more arrangements. While that may sound reasonable, even amicable, at the same time their fights, mostly about domestic trivia, kept escalating. But at twenty-eight, most people are hopeful, particularly in matters of the heart. Ronit and her husband clung to the idea of partner swapping as a magic wand.

'Then we met *them*,' Ronit said, 'and everything turned much worse.'

Youth meets age. Innocence meets corruption. Ronit's was a tale worthy of Hawkes or McEwan. Even if no one had died, this was about my friend, and so I puffed nervously on my cigarette while the tape recorder strained to catch her voice.

A man walked into Ronit's and her husband's apartment. In tragedies, there are always apartments—those cursed places where people fall into doomed love, and hang or shoot themselves. Trailing behind him was a wife who, Ronit said, looked older than her early forties; used up. But it was the husband on whom Ronit focused her attention.

The thing about husbands who work in IT is, even if they read all the right books, their professional concerns lead to harassed glances, early nights. The man who walked in wearing—unnervingly like my lover—a ponytail, and a trimmed beard, exuded an aura of having more bohemian priorities. Later, Ronit would indeed find he was a minor actor and a film studies lecturer.

'It was a great night.' She restlessly tapped her foot in its green snakeskin sandal. 'It wasn't like the conversations you'd have with Australians. It was a competition of minds. They said they'd been doing partner swapping for ten years now. But mostly we talked books and music … See, Lee, I was falling in love.'

'What was the wife like?'

'Oh … she was one of those Russian migrants …' Ronit often forgot my origins, indulging in the habitual Israeli disdain for Russians. 'She had that mentality. You know the one, when they give you their last shirt and then slap you. She was also a bit like me, depressive. But I had some balance at least. She was totally off the rails. She didn't work, neglected their children. She needed constant excitement, young men, you know, internet sex chats. She was miserable, really …'

Ronit's husband felt more kindly towards the wife, later telling Ronit he wouldn't have minded having sex with her. Oddly, at hearing this I felt a pang of envy. After five years, I hardly knew anything about *my* husband's desires …

A tryst was arranged. Ronit's husband went to the other couple's place, while Ronit waited at home for the lecturer, peeping nervously through the blinds: 'The best moment in all that filth was when he walked in with a bottle of wine. We just stood in the corridor for a long, long time, embracing. It felt like a real date. He seemed so in control. I felt I could relax with him, that he'd be responsible for everything. This made me really want him.'

Under Chagall's red demonic bride, on the couch meant for reclining, Ronit sat very straight. 'He knew how to be a man. But he was a predator, really …'

'What happened next?'

'What do *you* think happened?' Ronit laughed bitterly, as though a part of her wanted to keep talking while the other wanted to slap me. 'Obviously, I had sex with him, in the same bed where I slept with my husband. I don't even remember if I enjoyed it. I thought I wanted sexual excitement. But the real excitement for me was that he seemed infatuated with me. I actually wanted something romantic.'

'And was it?'

'It was ugly, disgraceful! We woke up really early and sat in the kitchen, drinking coffee. Then my husband came in and saw this man wearing his slippers. He got so angry, his face got all distorted. And that was it!'

'What do you mean?'

'You're tormenting me … That was it. The point of no return. See, my husband couldn't get over those slippers. Later, every time he justified his decision to leave me, he came back to those damn things.'

Ronit thought that her husband seeing another man's feet in his slippers must have trampled his most fundamental aspiration: to have a solid family life. Possibly even more offensive to him was the fact that she colluded with the man, offering him his slippers. But that morning, her husband said nothing. After all, he too had just slipped into someone else's wife.

From then on, the older couple, like the fictional sinister spouses I've talked about, courted them relentlessly. The foursome went to the theatre and movies, and spent time with the lecturer's friends, who liked pot, Dostoyevsky and pornography in equal measures.

'They didn't give us any space. It was like they wanted to have one big open family. They didn't get marital intimacy. He always said, "I love my wife." But I didn't see any love, only his egotism transferred onto her. Look, they had two children. And they shared all that filth no one else could understand. They were addicted to a lifestyle they could only do together. But she hated him, I think. And he hated that she didn't earn money. He had a terrible temper. He'd yell at her, slam doors, all that in front of their friends. It was like they lived publicly. I think there was an emptiness between them. I even felt sorry for the wife. Sometimes I felt closer to her than to my girlfriends because, after all, she was in the filth with me.' One night, the wife suggested Ronit join her and Ronit's husband in bed. Ronit felt sick at the sight of her vagina—shaved and prickly like a hedgehog. In fact, by then everything made her sick but she didn't know how to stop doing it.

Ronit said that coquettishness overtook her: she turned feline, hormonal, and would stare at mirrors for hours, admiring her reflection. As the frequency of the phone calls and unannounced visits escalated, Ronit's husband was getting more sarcastic about what he called 'the situation'. Once, they had had soulful conversations, but now they barely discussed what was happening. Ronit, still the romantic, began fantasising that she and the lecturer would elope and live together, happily ever after. But he had other fantasies. One day, they took a bath together and he pointed out a rubber glove.

'That night, I realised he was a pervert and lost my respect for him,' Ronit said.

'I don't get it. What did he want you to do with that glove?'

'Lee, do you have to ask? Just imagine!'

But many possibilities entered my mind and I couldn't choose between them, let alone stop the tape recorder, even if I was no longer sure Ronit wanted to keep talking. I could be selfish like that sometimes, when a voyeuristic opportunity came along.

About a month after the slippers incident and soon after the glove's appearance, Ronit and her husband finally found the strength to ignore the couple's calls. It took some weeks, but eventually the lecturer and his wife left them alone. Six months later, Ronit's husband left too. In between, Ronit and her husband had sought help from a psychologist who told them that after *such things*, people usually don't stay together. At this point, I could see, Ronit was on the verge of tears, possibly over her former husband, or the lecturer, or her current loneliness.

'I think,' she said, 'for my husband, our involvement with those people supported a conclusion he'd reached much earlier, maybe when I booked his vacation, that I was bad, corrupt. He probably fell out of love with me then. Because by the time we got rid of them, he didn't give a damn about me, or our baby. He hasn't seen her since we moved to Australia. But it's all my fault, Lee. *I* brought this on us. I was light-hearted. I knew *I* could put the past behind me, but I should have known my husband was different.'

The delayed flood of tears eventually erupted and it wasn't the kind that brings relief. I asked for Ronit's forgiveness and she asked for another cigarette. Then, after a year of persuasion on my part, we created a profile for her in English on an Australian dating website.

A TALE OF DOMESTICITY, OR—WHO REALLY KILLED MAYAKOVSKY?

Ronit said she now believed non-monogamy could only lead to disaster. If you really need 'that man', as she referred to my lover, keep it a secret, she advised. After she left, I mulled over her advice and the question of *my* credit in our case. Was I the bad wife, who took advantage of her agreeable husband, or was our situation more mutual than it seemed? I still didn't know how Noah had spent his time in my, and his, absences. Or maybe, through guesswork, I had some idea. Certain Jewish men living in Melbourne were notoriously inventive in how they dealt with marital tedium. But Noah told me nothing and wanted to know nothing. What kind of marriage was it if we didn't talk about what really mattered?

Hanukah, which celebrates a rare Jewish victory, when the Maccabees drove the Greeks from Jerusalem, arrived with its miracles, potato latkes, and tales of the rededication of the Temple. Possibly, Noah thought the time was right to rededicate us too. As, before going to an Israeli Hanukah party, we rested in our bed that was bubbling with summer shadows, he made a joke about my hypothetical rendezvous in Perth and I confessed.

Noah didn't un-embrace me. He even retained his ironic little smile. How did we meet? Did I enjoy myself? Was the man attached? I told the story in spare brushstrokes, only what I thought was necessary. 'He is a senior financial advisor'; I emphasised this fact as though it made everything tame, reversible—as, initially, I hoped it would be. My trick seemed to work: Noah appeared only mildly upset, and even somewhat amused. If this conversation had been with J, I'd have been howling with loneliness at his lack of jealousy. But now my stomach unclenched.

In the classics I'd grown up with, the most independent and powerful female characters were the femmes fatales. Theirs was my sort of feminism—dark, practical, full-skirted, scheming, shimmering with bare skin and jewels. It was an art, not a vocation. I never forgave the Three Musketeers for helping condemn Milady to being beheaded. Even now, when I write *beheaded*, I feel uneasy, as though this really happened, and happened to offend me personally, like something dirty between Dumas and myself. After all, I, too, had a streak of the femme fatale.

Now that I thought Noah saw me as made more attractive by the affair, I felt stronger, prettier, freer to go wild. Coquettishness overtook me too. I went to the Hanukah party wearing a hot pink lace dress, feeling like Ronit did—feline, hormonal. I danced, hot pink, on the concrete floor to the electronic beat of hard house that used to be played relentlessly in the Tel Aviv of my youth. I drank too much, smoked too much. The men from my former country could be mad but also painfully handsome. I chose one to dance with, then Noah tapped me on the shoulder. I turned to him and, even through the haze of glittering darkness, I could see in his face the ancient ruins of our marriage.

In the car, he finally asked, 'Are you going to see him again?'

'I don't know …'

He kept quiet, kept driving. Meanwhile, the wine I'd drunk evaporated, leaving the two of us alone. Then I realised. I realised what I'd done. Noah was aching. So was I now.

'I won't see him,' I crossed my arms over the suicidally deep cleavage of my dress.

I can't remember whether we shared a bed that night.

In the following day, while Noah was at work, I thought more about Ronit's story. On reflection, I had spotted a contradiction. Non-monogamy can only lead to disaster, Ronit had said, in the tradition of the tragic narratives I recounted earlier, explaining her divorce as the tragic outcome of non-monogamy. But she'd also said, 'If we'd had a good relationship before we met that couple, we may not have separated.' I recalled Ronit's complaints about her former husband that I'd heard over the years. What if they'd have divorced anyway? And what if tragedy weren't necessarily the reality of non-monogamy but the standard framework to tell its stories? If our spouses are often our cities of refuge yet the temptation to break free is always there too, then we might be afraid to imagine non-monogamy occurring within the range of manageable difficulty. This may mean we too could try ... Besides, tragic narratives also provide us with a complex pleasure, possibly akin to the philosopher Gaston Bachelard's suggestion that seeing there is stormy weather outside enhances the comfort of being at home. Tragic tales can render the hearths of monogamy infinitely cosy. So, who killed Mayakovsky?

To solve this riddle, I visited Dr Gribovsky. Once my glorious career at the Russian video library had ended, and to weave myself into the Australian fabric, I broadened my friendship circle beyond migrantland. But Dr Gribovsky, a poet and dentist from Moscow with a sizeable library, remained dear to me, satisfying some primal longing I had for the vanished country of my childhood. He was the kind of Russian I considered a 'real Russian' in line with my nostalgic dreams of Russia, which, for me, will always remain the land of soul, sadness and intellect. Dr Gribovsky was the kind of Russian I expected to meet, and was daily disappointed *not* to meet, in the video library. He read books in seven languages (two of them classical), recited Brodsky, had no social manners and had lived an adventurous life about which he didn't have the patience to talk. Instead, he'd show me where in Toorak to pick edible mushrooms and took me to lectures on mythology conducted by an unemployed Russian professor. For my part, I amused him with my hideous Russian pronunciation, and admired his poetry. I also stole from him phrases I used whenever I tried to appear smart, like 'We haven't come up with anything new since the Greeks.' Now, over that favourite Russian drink, tea, I asked Dr Gribovsky whether he thought Mayakovsky died of love. Always averse to verbal communication, my friend gladly shoved into my hands some books in Russian, barking: 'You read these and tell *me*!'

In my search for clues, I began by re-reading Mayakovsky's poems. 'Lilichka' particularly depressed me. In it, the poet concludes that while for him Lilya is essential ('outside of your love/I have/no sun'), for her his love is 'a great weight/hanging on you'. But when I reached the end of 'Lilichka', I had an 'It's elementary, my dear Watson' moment:

> I won't plunge down
> or drink poison
> nor will I raise a gun to my head.
> No blade
> holds me transfixed
> but your gaze.

This detailed description of exactly how Mayakovsky wouldn't kill himself, written fourteen years before his suicide, aroused my suspicions. I picked through Lilya's memoir, which Dr Gribovsky had given me. Mayakovsky, she wrote,

> had an insatiable thief in his soul. He needed to be read by people who didn't read him, to be visited by those who wouldn't visit, to be loved by that woman [I suspect she refers to herself here] who—he presumed—didn't love him.

Other contemporaries also described him as excessively needy. Despite being held in the highest regard by so many, the poet often felt misunderstood. On that, and many other accounts, he was prone to fits of anger.

The public, and I, to some extent, thought Lilya culpable for the poet's death. But, I realised as I kept researching, he'd never been stable to begin with. It was probably no accident that one of his first works was titled *Vladimir Mayakovsky: a Tragedy*. Deeply troubled by the prospect of ageing, in 'A Cloud in Trousers', he wrote:

> Of grandfatherly kindness I'm devoid,
> there are no grey hairs in my soul!

Apparently, I was learning, Mayakovsky had never intended to live beyond thirty-five, as if he guessed that as he grew older, his poetry would grow worse. Yet, even when that happened and his suicidal thoughts intensified, Mayakovsky still outlived his planned death by two years, and it was often Lilya who kept suicide watch on him.

Examined in its entirety, his relationship with the Briks seems to have offered the poet more support than grief. Some scholars think that without Osip's critical guidance, Mayakovsky wouldn't have achieved his poetic depth. Both Briks spent many nights discussing his work with him. They collected his reviews and royalties, and their finances became interdependent. Most importantly, the Briks loved Mayakovsky. Their close relationship comes through clearly in their affectionate correspondence. 'Dear, dear, dear Lilyuk. Sweet, sweet, sweet Osyuha …' Mayakovsky addressed them repeatedly. 'Boring, boring, boring, boring without you. Without Oska it's also not great,' he complained to Lilya from Paris.

The poet's premature death was probably the unfortunate result of his temperament, combined with his disillusionment with communism, the state's marginalisation of his work (which increasingly contradicted the official line), and his creative block, rather than his relationship with Lilya. In fact, it may be more than a coincidence that he shot himself while the Briks were in Europe. Of course, it is also not implausible that Mayakovsky could have lived longer if Lilya had loved him exclusively. But, considering that the Stalinist atrocities were about to begin and Mayakovsky had no talent for self-preservation, and that even the mighty Lilya couldn't halt his ageing, he was probably doomed anyhow. The poet was crystal-fragile, and Lilya held onto him for as long as she could. But even she had her limits.

'Don't blame anyone for the fact I'm dying,' Mayakovsky's suicide note begins. Forty-eight years later, when the eighty-six-year old Lilya, happily married for a fourth time but crippled by terminal illness, took her life too, her own note began, 'My death I ask not to blame on anyone.' It seems that right until her last moment, Lilya was still in a dialogue with the great poet.

The sadness of Mayakovsky's story, combined with my own, weighed on me. But at least now that I thought it wasn't Lilya's infidelities that killed him, my ideas about marriage appeared less sinister. I tried to return to my book but, instead of writing, kept looking out for the daily email from my lover. My skin crawled at the thought that his interest in me might have dampened. In this way, I was like Mayakovsky, who wanted to be the first priority of *all* his women, even if his own priority was Lilya. My mouth, like my hair, came undone. I muttered, 'He doesn't care about me.'

'Are you talking about *him*?' Noah said sharply. He'd developed the habit, long before he needed to, of quietly sneaking up behind me when I worked in the study, as though he'd predicted my treacherous nature.

I felt my face burn with humiliation, which was less about being found out and more about revealing my lifelong anxiety of not being deserted by a man. I recalled how, years ago, I'd come home to my boyfriend, the writer, with dark marks on my arms—signs of passion from another man. I'd told him it was an allergic reaction to an insect spray and he'd pretended to believe me. But I hadn't wanted him to believe me. I'd wanted to live with him more dangerously. Shortly after, I left him and the man who made the marks took his place. That man was the social worker from whom I fled to Australia.

I didn't want Noah to believe me, but felt nauseated at the thought of causing him more pain, and of my weakness being revealed. The things we do not to hurt each other … 'I was talking about you,' a lie that tore the gap between us wider. I, who wanted to fly with non-monogamous wings, was now trotting head down in the miserable footsteps of Anna Karenina, Emma Bovary and the subjects of women's magazines. The word *filth* fluttered clumsily in my head, like the Israeli cockroaches that were always trying to fly.

Later that night, my lover's email arrived, alongside another email from Western Australia—Nina's second confession. There, to my great surprise, she wrote that after dropping me at the train station, she stopped across the road and watched me waiting for my lover on the bench, with my suitcase in front of me and the evening sun streaming onto my face. Nina felt strange, wondering if she was going mad, hoping I wouldn't see her. Then my lover emerged from behind the parked cars. Nina went on describing how I approached him and folded into him; he wrapped his arms around me. She wrote that at that moment we looked as lovers do, as if we were the last people on earth and that there was a quiet intensity to our greeting, a palpable relief at being together again. It felt surreal, reading Nina's descriptions of us as if we were characters in some romance.

Nina went on to confess her own sadness at the sight of us, which—she wrote—wasn't just at our imminent separation, but was also a more generalised (and simultaneously deeply personal) grief at the thought that most people experience this kind of intensity and aliveness so rarely. Mostly, Nina wrote, we all live in a semi-coma, staying inside the rules and feeling safe yet dull. She kept apologising for 'spying' on us, but also explained that she had to see the two of us meet because she yearned to witness people standing on a pathway of their own making, and to remember how that felt. He lifted your suitcase, Nina wrote, and walked you to his car with his arm around you as if he couldn't bear to have any distance from you. And then you two disappeared from my sight.

9

A Tale of Expanded Couples

'Ah, I'm always so ashamed when I buy a new dress! Much more ashamed than when I have a new love.'
Marina Tsvetayeva

In four weeks, my lover would arrive. In a week, another year would slip away. It was that time in Melbourne when shopping centres drew in more people than beaches did, to crowd their painfully lit passages barricaded, as in greengrocers, with crates but of jeans and facial creams. It was when you bought mocha ice-cream in food courts, between expeditions into Beyoncé-filled Aladdin's caves to fulfil your wishes; when the heavier your arms felt as you held plastic bags, the happier you were. Noah, eager to take me shopping, as if this would normalise our marriage, drove me to a DFO, where all I wanted to do was purchase lingerie.

I loved clothes, but for some years now, I'd lost interest in underwear. Under my carefully chosen frocks, I'd unself-consciously wear an array of discoloured bras and comfortably oversized cotton knickers. Now I was immersed in my new project, even if I was unclear what its aim was—was it to impress my lover or save my marriage? While Noah perused *The Age* outside boutiques, I dipped into silk, satin, lace. The slippery slinkiness of the fabrics I tried on in fitting rooms soothed me. I couldn't stop shopping that afternoon, as though tomorrow there would be no more lingerie shops, and bought sixteen bras and thirty-four pairs of panties. My husband showed no curiosity about my unusual shopping or how my new acquisitions looked on me.

I wrote in my journal: 'It is difficult to focus on anything but the waiting. Even the photos of the apartment he rented in Melbourne turn me on …' I put off preparations for teaching and my writing, and began visiting salons where my feet and hands were manicured and pedicured, lotioned and massaged, my eyebrows were plucked, my face was steamed like broccoli and smeared with cream. The grooming hours left me dazed and in lust, but also satisfied. I felt smothered, perfumed. Now that I was finally getting out of my own head and finding relief in that, I more understood J, who thought his enemy resided within him.

These days, my lover was written all over me—in my languid body language, my smooth legs, the midriff tops I'd stopped wearing after I turned thirty but had now retrieved. I was regressing to my Tel Aviv self, when my skirts were merely extensions of my panties, and stilettos turned me into a Tower of Babel with my head in the clouds; when my smiles shone with pink gloss and shaky bravado. Oddly, I actually felt more whole now than I had in years, but also the loneliest that I had felt for a long time. I reached for Noah's hand more often than I normally would and, unusually for him, he shook me off.

I wanted to party, party, party, beat my mind into submission. Our neighbour, an Italian drug dealer, invited us to his New Year's Eve soiree. I stretched a tiny shock of blue lycra above my navel and, arm-in-arm with Noah, walked into a flat that was brilliant with stainless steel.

'For passion, guys!' The drug dealer poured Dom Pérignon into our plastic cups. 'For hammer! Know what hammer is? It's the best orgasm you can have.' He smacked Noah on the shoulder, winking at him. My husband, usually merry in company, drew back. I suspected he was thinking about us, about our shortage of hammers. About the hammers I wanted to have with others.

'Hey, hey, meet my girlfriend, guys!'

The girlfriend, who was paler, shorter and much older than the neighbour's usual companions (stunning, gigantic African girls with little English), told us she had a celebrity relation. Her sister was a bestselling author who wrote about the kind of spirituality J liked. 'Last night,' she said as she sipped from a blindingly fluorescent drink, 'my sister and I went to a dinner party at her friend's, a gay priest. We sat there with his Dalmatian dogs and his boyfriend's mother, who wore a diadem, under a chandelier for a six-course meal. Now, *that* is a party, darling.'

She turned scornfully to the hammer man, yawning with her mouth open. Noah and I used this gap in the conversation to escape to Brunswick Street, as though there, where we'd spent many pleasurable hours together among students, barflies and poets, we could begin the year the way we ought—as though a marriage were a videotape you could rewind.

We pulled the car's roof down, and drove with our heads stewing in the cauldron of the night, jammed with fireworks and boiling air. My hair, tangled in the wind, floated up into the inky sky. Once we neared Fitzroy Gardens, Noah, who nowadays seemed to be more at ease with me when we were in a car than when we were at home, asked if I planned to leave him. His question left me feeling hollow. I always thought that 'leaving' was the kind of way of living I had left behind once I met Noah. Now that he mentioned an end, I instead thought about our beginning.

Every new love carries the thrill of exploring the wilderness that constitutes another person, with its distinct images, sounds, smells, places. I thought about the single rose that Noah gave me on our first date. About the mint-and-Marlboro scent of his breath. And the piano bar in the city where a black singer dressed in blue sang Billie Holiday songs to us. J and I never braved such establishments—their coolness exaggerated our foreignness. But Noah introduced me properly to his country. I could not separate any longer our beginning from my beginning in Australia, that beautiful and terrible time with J and Esther, when I held onto this continent with my fingernails, scraping my way in. Since I had met Noah, because though, I'd thought all that was behind me: that a husband equalled salvation. Now, arrogantly but also with crippling despair, I also thought I could never remove myself from Noah, because I could not do this to him. The emptiness inside me felt unbearable. I wanted to say, 'Of course I won't leave,' but the nightclub-ambiguous smile from my youth took over my face.

Whenever I wanted to wean myself off blue cheese, or something else that was potentially bad for me, I'd indulge in it freely until the thing lost its appeal. I hoped this rule applied to men too. I wanted to be honest, to tell Noah about my lover's imminent arrival, so that I could ask him to wait this out and promise him I'd get myself back together afterwards. But I lacked the guts. I kept smiling as though someone had stretched my lips and then nailed them down. Noah, who was almost as reckless and virtuosic a driver as J was, turned the corner with one hand on the wheel and stopped sharply. It was way past midnight when we had our New Year's kiss.

Shared domestic spaces, I've noticed, have dividing lines that go beyond doors and walls. To map those is to map relationships, which can be sobering. Or unsettling. Over the years, Noah and I had silently, subtly divided our home. We were supposed to share the study, but, as time went by, my books, notes and the assignments of my students advanced, while Noah's paperwork retreated to the writing desk's corner. The kitchen was always my domain. The living room, with the monster-sized television, was Noah's territory, unless we watched DVDs there or entertained guests. I'd stopped watching television years before, but sometimes I yearned for Noah to invite me to join him in his channel-surfing, to hang out together. He never did, though; perhaps he was afraid I'd reject him there too, and I was too stupidly proud to make the first approach. So I left him alone there and he left me in the study. The main problem, though, was our bedroom, the place that best expresses a marriage by what happens, or doesn't, there. The bedroom was rarely ours outside of sleeping time. During weekends, and some afternoons, we'd lay there, chatting, though never for long, and in the mornings, the bedroom was all mine. I read there, with the bedsheets crisp against my skin, while Noah browsed newspapers in the living room.

Now, unaccustomed to asking each other for help when we were sad, we spent the early days of the new year licking our wounds in our separate spaces. Perhaps unjustly, I never felt Noah could carry the weight of my sadness. In fact, I'd always felt like that with men. None of them seemed strong enough for my sorrows. Perhaps that was arrogance on my behalf, but it was also a longstanding habit. As a child, anxious not to burden my already burdened parents, I used to console myself secretively, often through reading and writing. In adulthood, being so deft at self-soothing, so self-sufficient, made me feel powerful. But this skill also became the barrier between me and my lovers, making me feel estranged from them, even resentful, as though it were their job to break the barricades I erected. With Noah, I sometimes tried to drop my guard and he responded. However, during his dark moods, he'd fortify himself within the couch–television circle, unapproachable. For five years now, we had made each other happy, but when we were in the space of unhappiness, we were useless to each other.

Finally, Noah's reply to my 'Things I enjoy' email arrived. Against each of my items, he'd added in capital letters 'I LIKE THIS TOO'. I responded instantly: 'This is what I call better late than never.' It was time to desert our troubles, we decided almost in unison, leave them behind while we searched for happiness somewhere far away and cool. On the *Spirit of Tasmania*, I wore a lilac G-string with pink rosettes and a matching cami bra.

During the ten-hour cruise, Noah watched cricket, while I battled nausea and read the letters of Marina Tsvetayeva, the dark-haired and dark-souled Russian poetess and non-monogamist (curiously, she was Gala's childhood friend). Those letters were dispatched in 1926 from Paris, to where Tsvetayeva had fled after the revolution. She was thirty-four then, the same age I was now, and married. By then she had already been heartbroken so many times that she redirected her cornucopian romantic energy into chaste correspondence with the German poet Rainer Maria Rilke, whom she never met but whose work she admired.

I was a fan of Tsvetayeva's poetry, but that wasn't the reason why I brought her letters and diaries, and a biography about her, along on this trip. I was interested to find out more about how she managed her unconventional marriage to the striking Sergey with his tragic, dark eyes, whom she'd married in her early twenties. Sergey Efron—Tsvetayeva and her biographers agreed—was one of the few who truly grasped her unique personality, even her need for other men. But that understanding didn't make either of them happy. Once, during her involvement with another, Sergey wrote to a friend: 'Marina is ... a huge stove, whose fires need wood, wood and more wood ... It goes without saying that it's a long time since I've been any use for the fire ...'

One of Tsvetayeva's biographers, Claudia Roth Pierpont, wrote that in her poetry, love was

> not meekly awaited or gratefully accepted but demanded as a right ... Next to the keening violins of women's traditional love poetry ... Tsvetayeva's instrumentation is for brass: bold, charged, indignant.

Tsvetayeva's poetic persona of a tragic adventuress braving the brutal wilderness of love was a fairly accurate reflection of her life. Her emotional intensity, demands and penchant for drama were grandiose even by Russian standards. Once she wrote to a lover: 'I cannot tolerate the slightest turning of the head away from me ... I HURT, do you understand? I am a person skinned alive, while all the rest of you have armour.'

Tsvetayeva believed that her exposure at the age of six to Pushkin's verse novel *Evgeniy Onegin*, about a woman rejected by a man to whom she declares her love, doomed her to become an unsuccessful pursuer of men. Possibly, though, it was Osip Mandelstam, one of her first extramarital lovers, who set the pattern, leaving her soon after their affair began. But I suspected that it was mostly Tsvetayeva who, maybe unconsciously, positioned herself for unhappiness. She seemed to need to self-destruct in order to write. The pain of losing Mandelstam expressed itself in a string of striking poems, whereas her adoring husband, who once wrote to her that 'a day I haven't spent with you is a wasted day' couldn't feed the dark fire of her poetry. Unlike Tsvetayeva, I almost always was the one to leave. But Tsvetayeva's penchant for having a disastrous love life struck a chord with me. I now reflected that I'd been doing a variation on this in some of my relationships—self-destructing to have something to write about. Particularly when it came to J. And possibly now too.

Tsvetayeva felt no guilt about her chronic unfaithfulness and nor did she want (for most of the time) to leave Sergey. She thought herself able to maintain several parallel loves. 'Was I ever indifferent to someone because I loved another? Honestly, no ... One star for me doesn't outshine the other—others—all!' she wrote in her journals. I wondered how well she had thought this metaphor through. Stars seduce and inspire in their brilliance but they cannot give warmth. Tsvetayeva's lovers dazzled her; Sergey was her hearth, she knew that much. Her diaristic descriptions of him are lovingly indulgent:

> A beaut ... his hands are like from an ancient engraving ... the face sits unique and unforgettable under the wave of dark-gold, thick, luxuriant hair. And I haven't mentioned yet his steep, high, blindingly-white forehead, within which the entire wisdom and generosity of the world have concentrated ...

Tsvetayeva saw Sergey as her moral compass and placed him on a pedestal. But in loving him in this way, she stripped him of the wilderness aspect required to evoke sexual desire. Perhaps Noah and I did just the same thing to each other.

Sexual tepidity notwithstanding, Tsvetayeva stuck by Sergey through their exile years after they fled communism. That time, spent mostly in Paris, was marked by abject poverty. Sergey, a former White officer, never adapted to life outside Russia, and was often unemployed. Tsvetayeva took on any odd job to provide for him and their two children. At times, she even resorted to petty theft. When the despairing Sergey once offered her a separation, she begged him to stay. Several years later, unable to handle life in France any longer, Sergey returned to the Soviet Union. Tsvetayeva followed him. Soon after their arrival, on Stalin's orders, Sergey was executed and their daughter sent to a labour camp. Aged forty-eight, Tsvetayeva hanged herself.

At this point, I decided not to draw any further parallels between me and the Great Russian Poetess. Instead, I redirected my attention to the language of her letters, which were pure poetry. 'The first dog you'll stroke after reading this will be me. Pay attention to its gaze,' Tsvetayeva wrote to Rilke, who, by then permanently confined to his sickbed with leukaemia, was unlikely to encounter any dogs. Soon afterwards, in keeping with his profession's tradition, Rilke passed away prematurely, aged fifty-one.

I was still feeling morbid and seasick when Noah asked if I was hungry. This wasn't what I wanted to talk about; I wanted to quote to him Tsvetayeva's wonderfully strange line about stroking a dog. It was a fleeting urge, though. In Noah's company, I often jettisoned chunks of my personality. Our marriage was based more on action than talk. Instead of arguing over housework, we did it. We didn't discuss the family budget, we spent it. Noah shopped for meals, I cooked. We walked on the beach. I chose Noah's clothes. He bought my jewellery without consulting me and usually got it right. We looked after each other during sickness. It really was a good marriage, and our cultural narratives reinforced my assessment. Particularly given my experience of J, who would get nervy when performing the smallest acts of kindness, and always made sure that if he brought me a cup of coffee or massaged my feet that his credit for it was paid in full, I had come to see love through the prism of mutual care. I can't say that it was on the boat that I started doubting my theory of love, but the long journey did bring forth what I'd so far been pushing to the back of my mind. Perhaps, I thought as we discussed the shortcomings of the ferry's café, mutual care wasn't enough. Perhaps we should take snapshots of our minds and display them, in all their complexity, to each other. After a lunch of stale schnitzels, Noah bought me socks printed with koalas to keep me warm, then retreated to discuss the cricket match with fellow watchers. I wished he'd stayed by my side.

Not far from Devonport, Noah and I climbed to the upper deck, to watch the sky dip its long, white feet in the ocean. We embraced tightly, as if entrusting our flesh with keeping us together. Noah's mobile rang. It was our friend, telling us that her recent affair had just ended. I knew how exhausted she had been by that package deal of single life: fucking that goes nowhere satisfying, and energy-depleting waiting for love. Now in our natural habitat, we put our friend on speaker, sending her kisses, reminding her what a loveable woman she was.

In our friendship circles we willingly, gladly, fulfilled the role of the rock-solid couple, akin to Hope and Michael Steadman from *thirtysomething*. More adventurous people circled like wild planets around our home. We were 'the consolers', whose couch occasionally served as a sickbed for ailing hearts. Even when Noah and I argued in public, our fights didn't worry our friends but cracked them up. Although we genuinely cared about the problems of others, we must have also thrived on them. Once our friend had hung up, I felt that familiar mix of sadness for her but also smugness at Noah's and my survival. He and I finally had a substantial conversation during our trip, analysing in detail that expired relationship while growing more and more joyful. We kissed deeply. Noah's mouth felt velvety, fresh; he was a great kisser, my husband. It was easy to pretend now that the cricket, nausea, Tsvetayeva's suicide and the man from Perth had never existed. I felt the urge to tell Noah I loved him, but the words came out of my mouth like something from a farce. 'I love you, sweetie,' I said as I might have to a child. As much as there were things about Noah I didn't understand, in some ways he felt too familiar. This was my doing. I took after my mother, who always tried to eliminate the distance between her and the people she loved by pulling them closer to her, by not listening to what they said, by telling them what they thought. There was warmth and comfort in such familiarity, but it also cheapened feelings. I kissed Noah's face tenderly.

The only other time I'd been to Tasmania was during a weekend I'd spent in Launceston with my writing group years before. We were so content with our books, wine, laptops and conversation that we never left the house. But Noah always helped me to get back into the world. We crisscrossed the island in his convertible, listening to dub music. For some time, I again felt free of my mind and full of that wild, dizzy happiness I'd often felt in the Australian countryside. It was there that I most acutely felt I couldn't do without this country, that even my time with J had been worth the end result. I loved everything I saw now: the mountains and rainforests; the roadside cafés with oil-cloth tables; the towns that beat all other Australian ones in the contest for the kitschiest and most ubiquitous souvenirs; the crystalline water of Wineglass Bay; the giant shrubs and ferns that made the island appear so prehistoric that at every turn of the road I expected dinosaurs to emerge.

For an injection of civilisation, we stopped at Hobart, where, for the first time ever, I was stung by a bee. Several hours later, I received a text message from my lover, informing me that, for my sake, he'd bought his first mobile phone. Swollen with the bee's bite and with pride at my importance, I reflected on life's whimsical nature, against which marriage seemed the best buffer. But what was the buffer for a marriage? Some degree of honesty, I eventually decided.

I always did this—calmed my men, made a home for them, nourished them with food and caresses, then disturbed them at my peril. Over dinner in a wooden pub full of ageing musos, I told Noah about the nature of the book I was writing. 'Would you agree to open our marriage?' I asked shakily. *To open* were the only fitting words I knew to use. They described an action, not a definite arrangement. Noah looked away and I hated myself.

'We can find some arrangement *for you*,' the businessman, or the husband, in him offered. He insisted upon two things, though: people we both knew were off-limits, and so was the man from Perth.

'But what do *you* want?' I asked, instead of using this opportunity to be truly honest about myself. Yet, even now, Noah wouldn't say. And he wouldn't tell me what had happened on that all-men weekend at his friend's holiday house while I was in Perth. I'd heard rumours, and was pretty certain by now, that he, too, was unfaithful to me—if not on that occasion than on some others. But I had no tangible proof and whenever I asked Noah directly about such matters, everything was always vehemently, very vehemently, denied. This disappointed me, since I had told Noah several times he could have some erotic adventures as long as he told me about them. Still, instead of confronting him I clutched at his hand and wouldn't let go of it until we finished our dinner.

Now that at least some things between Noah and me were in the open, my book felt urgent again. I hoped it would become a crutch that would help us hop forward in our marriage. Back in Melbourne, I asked a friend who, for years, had been experimenting with his sexuality if he knew anyone I could talk to. He told me about polyamory ('many loves'), a term signifying a lifestyle of having more than one intimate relationship at a time. I composed an ad asking for interview subjects and my friend posted it on the website of PolyVic, the Victorian organisation of polyamorists.

While I waited for a response, I educated myself about polyamory. I learned that the word was coined in the late 1980s by Morning Glory Zell-Ravenheart, a Californian resident who describes herself as a priestess and Goddess historian, whatever that means, and is a partner in a several-person relationship known as 'the Ravenheart family'. Despite her obvious busyness, Morning Glory partook in establishing what is defined today as the polyamorous community, which stretches across many continents and countries, including South Africa and Japan. Although still a small subculture, its membership is growing. In America alone, there are about half a million families now openly identifying as polyamorous, and probably many more undercover polyamorists. As for Australia, I discovered that since the early 1990s, it has been home to one of the first polyamorous organisations in the world, Beyond Monogamy Inc. It is difficult to estimate how many polyamorists live here, but, suffice to say, the PolyOz website has about 1000 members and every state capital city and some regional areas have their share of polyamorous gatherings.

My lover, meanwhile, did his own research. He emailed me something he called a 'photo essay': he'd retraced and photographed places where our story had been playing itself out. The pub where I'd first reached for his lips and whose entry sign 'Life begins at Woody' I now took seriously; the former asylum; Kings Park, jewelled with limestone; the Prichard house. I wrote back:

> Even though I've left Perth, Perth hasn't left me. I've been to two Christmas gatherings now (quite a lot for a Jewess …), and at one I met four people from Perth. Unaware of the undercurrents of our conversation, they delighted at my vivid interest in their city. Their conclusion was probably that there is something about Perth that appeals to Israelis. Then this morning I heard on the radio that Perth is on fire. Is this true? Is it as romantic as when Rome once was? Are you in danger? Can you smell the smoke? Please, don't tell me the truth and put out my inflamed imagination … I do find myself nowadays taking personally any news coming from your city. As to your essay, something was missing there: your photo. I looked at the photo of me you attached and my first reaction was to cringe: I look so dishevelled there, with dark circles under my eyes. But then I really loved it—not myself, but the signs of exhaustion, the melancholy. I love it—not sleeping with you.

As days passed, I was feeling increasingly romantic, both towards my lover and my husband. And, it seemed, polyamory was about just such stuff. This movement, unlike the sexual revolution, apparently had a feminine bent. Many polyamorous leaders, activists and authors were women—a fact that challenged the usual assumption that non-monogamy was a male agenda. The emphasis was on feelings: people identifying as polyamorous wanted to *love* more than one person. The more I read about polyamory, the more I fantasised about personal salvation.

An email from Anne, the co-establisher of PolyVic, arrived: 'I am in a (or multiple) polyamorous relationship(s) …' My first *proper* interview, I thought, exhilarated.

Anne lived in a western suburb of Melbourne, where art students, veiled women and yogis lived side by side. The morning I walked into her apartment, so small that I could almost touch the ceiling, I was as tense as I was when I met Bianca. For some reason, non-monogamous people frightened me as much as they attracted me. I searched nervously for neo-pagan signs in Anne's living room, but all I saw were shabby-chic brown furnishings, artworks of nudes and drag queens, and a piano. I didn't know yet that Anne, the priest's daughter, was as averse to divinities as I was.

'Coffee …' Anne began, in a deep, dramatic voice that didn't match her willowy beauty. With her dizzyingly high forehead, short, thick hair, and eyes as large as plates, she looked younger than her forty-four years. I thought of Bianca again. People who didn't love by the rules seemed to be marked by physical incongruity. I, too, always fluctuated between the librarian and libertine look. So maybe, I was, after all, fit for the life I wanted to live?

Anne's offer was cut short by the emergence from a hallway that probably led to a bedroom of a young woman with glasses and an appetizing, plump cleavage. She stretched her white arms, yawning. 'This is Shelly, my partner,' Anne said. 'You can interview her too, if you like.'

Shelly nodded. I liked the dark alertness of her gaze, but I'd have liked that coffee even more. While I tried to appear casual in the face of the interview becoming less intimate, a pale-faced man with longish locks appeared from the same hallway.

'Peter, my *life* partner,' Anne introduced him.

'What do you mean—life partner?' I worried I was being too intrusive too early, but no one seemed to mind. They must have been accustomed to explaining themselves. Anne said that she and Peter expected to be together for life. I wondered about Shelly's status then, as a *mere* partner.

'And we've been together fourteen years now. So we're doing better than many marriages.'

Peter laughed while another man stepped out from the, apparently endlessly fertile, hallway. This one had a red ponytail. Tall and a little potbellied under his t-shirt, he seemed too large for this apartment, and for his childlike face. But, despite his size, this man-boy's presence felt light, even hovering.

'Justin is Shelly's partner and …' Anne stumbled, possibly struggling to articulate his relationship to her, or perhaps remembering my coffee.

'Is anyone else going to come out?' I laughed too hard at my own joke, overwhelmed but also excited by the goings-on in this apartment, as unpredictable as a magician's hat.

'We didn't plan this,' Anne said. 'Shelly and Justin came last night, to return Peter's car, and ended up staying. And Peter just turned up now.'

The next thing I learned about polyamory as it's lived was that even the logistics of sitting down could be complex. Or, more likely, I was projecting my own concerns onto it. Careful not to interfere with anyone's still, to me, mysterious alliances, I took the furthest armchair, which stood amid strewn papers and jars filled with cereal. Anne and Shelly settled, embracing, on the two-seat couch. Peter moved the other armchair close to Anne. Justin perched on a chair near Peter and placed a hand on his knee. I watched them all huddled together. Nothing in my past had prepared me for interviewing such a cohesive-looking group about their love relations. But, somehow, their thick intimacy felt inclusive and, combined with the sunshine coming through the windows and the steaming coffee Peter deposited in my hands, it soothed me a little.

Once we began talking, I realised that, despite the somewhat ideologically adventurous origins of the movement, whose initial members, like Morning Glory, often came from New Age subcultures and political movements that propagated communal living, these people were … well … Anne was a massage therapist. Justin was a scientist. Peter was a musician and a writer, and Shelly was doing a PhD in engineering. Aside from being in the academy, she and I were of a similar age and shared burdensome Jewish origins. Later, I learned that the middle classes had discovered polyamory. The movement now contained more geeks than hippies, and also considerable numbers of academics, therapists and artists. I could see I could fit in … I collected myself and tried to map out the relationships between my interviewees more accurately.

'You can say it's two couples here, but there is sexual interaction between all the corners,' Peter said.

'And all the threes from any direction,' Anne added.

'The only lack of interaction is between Anne, me and Peter.' Justin's correction to the equation confused me even further.

'And that hasn't happened yet because we've been close only for a short time.' Peter reassured me.

'Peter and I have a mostly chaste relationship. We're cuddle buddies.' Shelly joined the conversation, unprompted, for the first time. Like me, she seemed to reside uneasily within the verbal realm.

'Cuddle buddies?'

'People you cuddle with but not necessarily have sex with,' Peter explained.

'I'd really like to have a sexual relationship with Peter,' Shelly said, 'but I have a problem with older men. But there was that time when Justin and I were having sex, and Peter joined in very mildly.'

No one but I flinched at this latter detail, as the voyeur in me lifted her dishevelled head.

'With no touch between me and Shelly, she felt safe. Justin was the focus of the action,' Peter added.

'Poor Justin,' Shelly laughed.

'With Shelly, Justin and I, it's hard to say where the line between close friendship and intimacy lays. Polyamory gives me this freedom not to define,' Peter summed up.

'Yeah,' Justin agreed. 'I like that in polyamory, intimacy and sexuality can be expressed on the continuum, rather than pigeonholed.'

In places where polyamory is more established, particularly across the USA, heterosexual polyamorous relationships are common. In Australia, polyamorous and bisexual communities often, but not always, overlap. Everyone here but Peter thought of themselves as bisexual. Peter called himself *hetero-flexible*, meaning he wasn't interested in anal sex with men, but as long as there was a woman, he'd engage with men in a 'low key' way.

Still searching for some clarity, I asked more questions about their relationship arrangements. Anne said she didn't want to define hers with Justin and Shelly, but they stood apart from her casual lovers. Justin, I learned, lived alone and had a second partner, Debi, in another state, with whom he'd been together for eight years. He and Shelly had met a year before, not long after she attended her first polyamorous gathering.

'I worried I'd find tree-hugging hippies there or creepy internet people,' Shelly said and I didn't admit that that had been my worry too, 'but I met all these intelligent people who thought about their relationships deeply and worked on their personal growth. At the second event I attended, I ended up having group sex, which was very nice,' she added casually. I liked the way in which an ease with psychological clichés (shared, to a varying extent, by everyone here) and wilderness coexisted in Shelly.

Justin and Shelly had other lovers too. For some time, they consulted each other about their numbers. 'Look,' Shelly eventually said, 'there are many people we're on snogging terms with, and perhaps more with some …'

She continued to talk, while I thought that the only thing I was certain of so far was that Anne lived here alone. But even this wasn't straightforward. She had bought the flat jointly with her other partners, a married couple who lived in another state. 'Your life partners?' I tried to demonstrate my growing familiarity with the polyamorous lexicon.

The husband, Anne said, was her *life* partner. But the wife, who used to be her *partner*, wasn't anymore.

I thought that, while they might seem chaotic to me, these arrangements were a way of life for Peter, Anne, Justin and Shelly. In preparation for this interview, I had read about how diverse polyamorous arrangements can be. While some, like Anne, had permanent and casual relationships, others practised *polyfidelity*—exclusive commitment to several people. *Triads* were arrangements where three lovers were involved with each other. In *vee* relationships, like the one Justin had with Shelly and Debi, one person had two partners who weren't lovers. *Quads* were relationships between four people, usually two couples. And these were the simpler examples. Elaborate hierarchies that distinguished between primary and secondary partners were common too, whereas some polyamorists refused to rank their lovers. In polyamory, I learned, a couple wasn't always the basic unit unless you had a distinct primary relationship. But the couple was the basic unit for me. I wanted to find out what it was like to be a polyamorous *couple*. I asked about this, and learned that, once upon a time, there was a couple, and, as is often the case, God, at the bottom of this story.

Nineteen years before, when Peter and Anne were in their twenties, they had fallen in love. But, even back then, their relationship was complicated by others—Peter's wife and the holy trinity. Peter and Anne belonged to a Christian community in which they had both been brought up. They tried to suppress their forbidden feelings, Anne even marrying someone else.

'I'm so embarrassed to say it but I'd been a good Christian girl. I hadn't had intercourse before I got married at the age of twenty-eight!'

'Me neither,' Peter said. 'I figured out at twenty-three that it was better to get married than burn in hell, so I walked to the altar.'

'I thought if I kept myself pure for my husband, my reward would be a great sex life. But sex in my marriage was appalling.'

Two years into Anne's marriage, her and Peter's passion for each other only grew stronger. Peter decided to leave his wife, and God, and Anne followed in his footsteps. They finally became lovers; yet, the 'happily ever after' ending was still to come. In their first years together, Anne struggled to reconcile her love for Peter with all the yearning that had accumulated within her during her chaste years. She told Peter that, although she felt he was her soulmate, she didn't want the usual stuff: monogamy, children, or even living together. Peter agreed to be with her on her terms, but it was difficult. *He* wanted to live with Anne, and monogamously. 'But now,' he said, 'I'm grateful she didn't give in. I'm much happier being polyamorous.'

It was a gradual process, though, his finding happiness. Peter liked having other lovers, but Anne's affairs, and her desire to talk about them, pained him. He said that now he knew Anne just wanted to share her joy with the person she loved the most, but back then he'd get angry. He wasn't yet experiencing what Anne did: what polyamorists call *compersion*, a pleasure in your beloved's enjoyment with another, which is the opposite emotion to jealousy.

'We used to argue until four in the morning,' Anne said. 'I was hard on Peter until I understood it really hurt him. Still, he had to take responsibility for his feelings.'

The points Peter and Anne were making actually had the opposite effect on me of the one intended. Listening to them, I regretted having told Noah about my lover, even though I had been spare with details. I thought that sometimes the urge to tell can be closely bound with selfishness. If I told Noah the full story of my affair, I'd probably relive the exhilaration of it, and maybe even redeem myself in my own eyes as being honest. But what about Noah's hurt? And what if this wish to protect me was why he was secretive about his own whereabouts?

Peter, though, was clearly now on Anne's side. He said: 'I knew I had double standards. That made me even more upset. I felt feelings I had were wrong. I really wanted to get over my jealousy.'

The wrongness of jealousy is a common view in polyamorous circles (although it is milder there than it was among the 'sexual revolutionaries'). Anne, too, saw jealousy largely as an emotion that was socially fostered, in order to sanction people controlling their partners' behaviour and thus preserving the monogamous order. Such an attitude offered an alternative to the sweeping, clear-cut way in which those in mainstream society often speak of sexual jealousy as the *right* reaction, which indicates love. However, thinking of jealousy as being right or wrong implied that it was answerable to notions of fairness and logic.

To me, such an implication seemed naive. Even the most ardent and sophisticated theorists of sexual freedom weren't immune to jealousy. When anarchist and priestess of free love Emma Goldman fell in love with the handsome Doctor Reitman, who was ten years her junior, his infidelities obsessed her. H. G. Wells got incredibly jealous about the doings of his mistress Rebecca West, even while he was married to his beloved Jane. I thought that a better conversation would be about nuances of jealousy. I, for one, could live with the thought that Noah had been sexually unfaithful to me. But I knew that if I ever found he was *infatuated* with a woman, even if he didn't have sex with her, I'd be devastated and would have no qualms about expressing it. After all, allowing yourself to express jealousy can be also about affirming your worth by demanding to be loved in the way you think you deserve.

While all these thoughts were revolving in my head, Peter said: 'I tried something that was like a phobia de-sensitisation technique. I visualised Anne with men in ways that made me mildly unhappy, before I visualised something that made me even unhappier, and so forth. I'm not sure if that did the trick, but now I have very little problem with jealousy.'

His words reminded me of such polyamory educators as Tristan Taormino, who offers techniques to help to 'get to the root of jealous feelings and transform them'. Polyamorists seemed to believe jealousy was amenable to interventions. And perhaps it was, but did one have to be immune to jealousy to be happily non-monogamous? Even if some of Taormino's, or Peter's, techniques worked for Noah and me, I didn't actually want to have a non-jealous husband—this could make me feel unloved. Rather, I *liked* jealousy. I thought that if I wanted to be with Noah for life, as Peter and Anne said they wanted to be together for life, we needed occasional jealousy injections first to find, then recharge, passion. The challenge here was, of course, to know how much each of us could tolerate without going mad. Perhaps Noah was right—for us, discreetness could be as good as disclosure was for Peter and Anne. The problem was that, at the moment, our so-called discreetness resembled the secretiveness of infidelity.

I escaped from my confusion back into Peter and Anne's story of expansion. Eight years before, Peter had met Nuo, and it was Anne's turn to feel unsettled. She said she had realised from the start that to live non-monogamously meant always putting yourself at risk. But now theory became reality. Peter had strong feelings towards Nuo, and Nuo wasn't prepared to settle for the role of a secondary lover. Then, during the same week, Anne's other lover, a married man, became Nuo's lover too and, more significantly, Peter and Nuo announced themselves to be life partners.

'This is the intensity you can get in polyamory,' Anne said. 'All that week, the five of us, including my lover and his wife, were having these conversations: "How are you feeling about that?", "What do you need?" When all your relationships are going well, it can be heaven. When they all go wrong, it's hell!' she continued, resorting to metaphors from her upbringing.

Peter and Nuo moved in together, in a coastal town near Melbourne. For a while, Anne worried *she* would become Peter's secondary relationship: 'Partly it was because I had a problem communicating with Nuo. We're very different. I like to be direct and she …'

'Subtle?' Peter suggested.

Anne chuckled: 'All right, say "subtle" … I felt she really wanted to be monogamous. And that she wasn't always honest with me. One of the things that helped was, we started to do energy work together. Now we have a very good relationship.'

The three of them eventually worked out an arrangement to suit them all. Nowadays, Peter stayed in Anne's apartment two to three days a week. Occasionally, Anne spent coastal weekends with him and Nuo. 'Caress the detail, the divine detail,' was Nabokov's advice to writers. I wanted to know more about the logistics of their life, to imagine for myself what shape such intimacy took—affection, attention, all those things couples take for granted, and therefore sometimes struggle to preserve. I also began fantasising about commuting between Melbourne and Perth.

Peter, a writer himself, understood what I was after and offered me if not his caresses, then, at least, the details: 'If the three of us are together in a lounge room, I might be sitting on the couch with Anne, and Nuo will sit on a chair, or maybe on the floor between my legs. She's more likely than Anne to come over and cuddle me. When we're in public, the three of us may walk arm in arm, or just two will hold hands. It's quite fluid, really. At first I used to go nuts, because I'd cuddle Nuo and think, "I need to cuddle Anne now," to keep it equal. Now I think it's just my problem.'

Anne happily confirmed it *was* his problem. When she stayed with Peter and Nuo, she added, she slept in the spare bedroom. Sometimes Peter joined her; other times, he remained with Nuo. 'These things can be so funny! Nuo and I might go "Okay, who gets him tonight?" or "I don't mind, you can have him."' Anne squeezed Peter's hand.

I noticed that everyone's hands were constantly at play, occasionally shifting targets. I loved this flow of affection. There came a moment when the four of them sat with their hands interconnected like a human wire, possibly passing messages I couldn't understand. Still, I didn't feel left out. The tiny room brimmed with possibilities, with a playful suggestiveness that monogamous couples rarely exude in company, as though everything here, including my position, was fluid. For a moment, I wanted to fuck them all.

'There has been some tension,' Peter qualified Anne's story. 'But the last years have been much easier, because Nuo now really believes I'm going to stay.' He and Anne exchanged glances of tacit understanding. I envied how freely they seemed to talk.

Peter and Anne's relationship kept expanding to include more partners. Two years before, Anne had met Robert and Elinor, the couple from another state, through a polyamorous website, and added interstate flights to her coastal commuting. Since both Anne's life partners lived with other women, it would be easy to assume that these relationships weren't truly committed. But since her recent diagnosis of chronic fatigue syndrome, Anne told me, Peter and Robert had been helping her financially. She was also involved with Robert and Elinor's three children—a teenager and two pre-teens who, Anne said, understood and accepted the complex dynamics of their family better than many adults would. I wasn't surprised to hear this last point. Despite the moral panic surrounding non-monogamy, a longitudinal study by American sociologist Elisabeth Sheff showed that children did well in polyamorous families, as long as their homes were stable and loving.

The findings of this study, and of the few other existing studies of polyamorous families, indicated that, moreover, these children were likely to *thrive*, since they had more caregivers.

I got progressively nosier until Peter used a pause in the conversation to ask me about my own circumstances. Why was I writing this book? Uncomfortable at the sudden shift in roles, I mumbled something vague about marital difficulties. He nodded sympathetically and Anne said that polyamorous relationships weren't for the fainthearted. 'Some monogamous people,' she said, now looking at me intently, 'see us from the outside and think "This is great!". But they have no idea about the emotional work, maturity, energy and time that it takes. If someone is not clearly committed to polyamory, I find them less attractive because I find them less trustworthy.'

'I see …'

Swept up by the intelligence, humour and easy conversation of my new acquaintances, I was, notwithstanding the jealousy question, seriously considering attending one of the polyamorous social gatherings. The problem was, Anne's language, and that of the polyamorous websites and books I had perused, ran counter to my desire. The PolyVic website typically defined polyamory as 'the practice of honest, open, ethical multiple relationships'. Intellectually, I liked this and other, similar, definitions that challenged the mainstream perception that morality belonged exclusively to monogamists. I also liked how polyamorists addressed the issue the non-observance of which, I thought, had caused the sexual revolution to fail: insisting on a secure base between lovers as an essential ingredient of non-monogamy. However, the polyamorous emphasis on communication and honesty was also strangely in tune with the mainstream view of intimacy that didn't appeal to me. Most therapists today believe that the more spouses know about each other, the better. David Schnarch's writing typifies such a belief: 'Intimacy requires letting someone know you as you know yourself to be.'

But now listen to this. 'You have no cruelty,' Anaïs tells Hugo in *Henry & June*, meaning it as an insult. Earlier, as the couple had entered their living room, where they were dining with the Millers, they'd caught their visitors caressing on the armchair. The voyeuristic shots of the faceless Henry smudged on June's body, his crude hand on her perfectly bare shoulder, instantly made Anaïs, and me, swoon with desire. So did the couple's sly, slow disentanglement—not a gesture of politeness, but a tease. Now imagine, instead, June saying: 'How would you feel, Anaïs, if I kissed Henry now?' And Anaïs responding: 'Yes, let's set the boundaries. Hugo, do you feel safe?'

Like Anaïs's, my desire was darker than polyamorous and mainstream discourses allowed for. I associated excessive trustworthiness with predictability and boredom, and preferred dwelling in the shadows (and not only where love was concerned). Perhaps this had something to do with the place of my birth, Siberia, where the sky has a permanent grey film stretched over it. I never completely took to Israeli ways that, actually, resemble Australian ones. Brought up under the relentless sunlight that bleaches or blackens everything, Israelis like describing themselves with the colloquial adjective *dugry*—a sharper, rougher, but also more naive, version of *honest*; the in-your-face honesty that is a way of being in a world where everything has to be named. I liked this mode of being but also found it tedious. For me, Salome with her seven veils was endlessly more seductive than a stripper. I hoped that Noah and I could restore some degree of mystery between us.

'There is a lot of information and interaction in the community,' Shelly said. 'It's not about who's sleeping with whom but more how they're handling their relationships. Everyone does know about everyone else. If you cheat, outside of your partner and children there is an enormous amount of other people you're affecting.'

'You have to be committed!' Anne joined in. 'Committed to really enjoying relating to people, to spending a lot of time relating to people. You have to be committed to your own personal growth because things you can get away with in monogamous relationships, you *cannot* in polyamorous relationships. You get very exposed. Your deepest, darkest things tend to come out. *I had a constant problem with being judgemental that I had to fight, fight, fight!*' I was growing horrified.

'What Anne means,' Peter calmly interjected, 'is that when your lover says something critical of you, you might not listen. But when you have two lovers saying the same thing, you think maybe it's true. I hate it when Nuo and Anne start comparing notes ....' We all laughed, but it was only I who did so hysterically.

'Another difficulty in polyamory,' Peter continued, 'is that sometimes I have to make difficult choices. For example, on Friday both Anne and Nuo were sick, and I really wanted to be with both of them. Several times, they were in crisis at the same time. Luckily, they're very independent, but if they weren't, our relationship wouldn't have worked.'

The stories kept coming. Apparently, being considerate could get in the way sometimes. Once, at ConFest, where the polyamorous community meets regularly, Anne decided to sleep in Robert's tent, because Peter would be jamming till late at night. To be fair to Peter, Robert woke Anne in the middle of the night, saying Peter had just returned. Would she like to see *him* now?

'The first time Shelly and Debi met,' Justin broke into the laughter, 'I realised everything was going to work when they decided to squeeze out the blackheads on my back. The shared grooming ritual worked!'

Now that we were having fun again, I swiftly reconverted to polyamory, and decided to ask the question the answer to which was what I had really come here for: was polyamory compatible with romance? I'd read *The Ethical Slut*, a book co-authored by therapists, and former lovers, Janet Hardy and Dossie Easton, to which polyamorous people, only somewhat jokingly, refer to as the 'poly-bible'. Its tone, once again, had reminded me of mainstream self-help books: 'With practice, we can develop an intimacy based on warmth and mutual respect, much freer than desperation, neediness, or the blind insanity of falling in love.' But I liked that blind insanity.

'What do you mean by *romance*?' Shelly stared at me sternly—the first rift so far in our Jewish idyll. I noticed she and Justin sat away from each other, and, generally, didn't demonstrate the easy intimacy I saw between Peter and Anne. Once again, I found myself questioning who was truly in love here. Oh, yeah, what *did* I mean when I spoke of romance? Some of my long-married friends had also asked me that, and with the same accusatory note. But what was I guilty of? Immaturity? Hopeless dreaming? Or maybe I was dreaming now, feeling highly strung and accusatory myself? Perhaps, like Anne, I needed to fight my judgementalism.

'I guess …' I mumbled, 'it's about protection, lighting candles …' Protection? Candles? Forget traditional feminists, even I cringed at the words that had slipped out but that I didn't mean.

Anne joined in. 'I'm still not sure what you mean.'

'Are you talking about the *constructed facade of intimacy*?' Justin pronounced the last words with distaste.

Oh … Unfortunately, and in the most reactionary way, I did love the constructed facade: yes, candles, and flowers, tears, sleek cocktails, fragile evening frocks, oozing fruit, whispers, red curtains. I wanted from non-monogamy what I wanted (and sometimes got) from life generally—beauty, urgency, poetry, unapologetic decadence, meaning. In short, romance; I wanted romance. But I wasn't an idealist, expecting continuous ecstasy. I considered myself a pragmatic romantic. All I hoped for was bursts of excitement threaded through my life.

Before I said more wrong things, Peter, who had so far gallantly acted as the go-between for the others and me, clarifying our questions and answers, said: 'I think Lee is saying that romance, like a candlelit dinner, in our society is reserved for couples. Is that right?'

Not really. But instead of explaining myself, I, the meek interviewer and wife, giggled with embarrassment.

'I don't like candles, for that matter.' Anne said. Somehow, it was my stupid candles that captured everyone's attention. 'The joy of polyamory for me is that I can share the specialness of Shelly and the specialness of Justin and the specialness of Peter. And they are all different kinds of specialness!' she said, expansively, theatrically. 'In polyamory, we talk about "new relationship energy", when you fall in love and have these romantic days. And then it fades, as you'd expect, and translates into something deeper.'

'I'll be the devil's advocate now.' I hid behind the convenient idiom to avoid discrediting myself, once again, as a seeker of unworthy pursuits. 'I've heard from you about rules, and some therapy kind of language …'

'Yeah, we do sound a bit like we do counselling …' Peter interrupted, smiling.

'We do, don't we?' Shelly chuckled.

I laughed too, in love with them all again. Yet, this time I persevered: 'Do you think the openness of polyamory can be detrimental to Eros?'

'Ah, the naughtiness!' Shelly exclaimed joyfully.

Peter looked thoughtful: 'Some kinds of erotica that occur naturally in monogamous relationships, like flirting, don't translate as well into the polyamorous setting, because it's more responsible, more ethical. Potentially, something is lost there. I think it's because polyamory is new, it's still developing its eroticism … but once a polyamorous relationship has been established, the erotic play becomes really interesting, because there is usually more than two people. There is the eroticism of knowing your partner is having sex with someone else. There is also a lot of kinkiness within our community, like BDSM.'

I actually felt Peter's words on my skin; this conversation was arousing me all along. 'The usual way we find new lovers,' Peter had said earlier, 'is when, let's say, someone wants to do an interview for a book …' I had laughed that off, but for a while now, I'd had the feeling I could easily move my armchair closer, slide in … This might just have been my vain fantasy. Still, if as an interviewer, I usually felt I was merely a vessel for people to make sense of their lives, or pass on their messages, the interaction here constantly tottered on the brink of mutual therapy and seduction. Perhaps, like Peter said, polyamory offered a different desire, and I should try it.

I now watched my interlocutors shift positions and make the vast potential of polyamory palpable. Shelly came to perch on the arm of Peter's chair, her hand around his neck. Justin moved to the couch with Anne and, as I turned to ask them a question, I found them deep in a kiss. They noticed me and politely stopped. 'No, no, go for it,' I said excitedly.

Four hours into the conversation and the heat of the afternoon, we all appeared somewhat crumpled, dishevelled, red-faced. When I finally got up to leave, Peter said: 'You know, Lee, I'm ridiculously lucky. After all these years, I still feel in love with Anne and Nuo. I know they're both the best. It's completely illogical, but it makes sense to me that they are both the best.' And I believed him.

'Come to our socials,' Anne said, hugging me at the front door. 'Bring your husband.'

The conversation's energy pumped through my veins as I drove home to Noah. I was thinking about what Anne had said, once her combative mood receded: something I, too, sensed but struggled to articulate when I was thinking about everything I wanted from non-monogamy. Anne thought being polyamorous could become a catalyst for experimentation in other areas of your life as well. I wanted to talk to Noah about this—and to suggest we go to a polyamorous gathering.

I asked Noah if he wanted to listen to the interview. For the first time in a while, we shared the study, sitting side by side. I felt thrilled he was partaking in something I cared about. I leaned my head on his shoulder, marvelling at how little it can take to feel romantic.

Me: 'What about saying "I love you"?'
Peter: 'It's easy. I can say this to Shelly.'
Shelly: 'I say this to all the people I love, whether it's sexually or otherwise.'

Noah paused the recording: 'But wouldn't polyamory make you feel lonely?'

Just like that, in an instant, my husband clarified what I'd so far struggled to articulate. To be a polyamorist, you needed to be more like Ryam Nearing, a polyamorous author who described herself as a 'creature who is most comfortable in a tribal band'. But I was a solitary cat. In groups, even among writers, I often felt claustrophobic and lonely. I wasn't interested in spending time 'relating to people' and preferred one-to-one friendships. Like Noah, I had the need to retreat from the world to the one person I loved.

Later, I learned even more about to what extent polyamory wasn't just a 'lovestyle', but an identity bound with communal, and even public, life. Like many other identity-based minorities, polyamorists often engaged in the politics of rights and responsibilities, talking about coming out, fighting against discrimination; all worthy pursuits but ones in which I didn't want to partake. For now, though, I just sensed loss, as I had previously when I came across groups I liked the sound of but realised I didn't have the right personality to join them. I needed a subtler version of non-monogamy. Or should I say we needed? At that moment, I felt close to Noah in *our* study. I inhaled him. Then I remembered. Tomorrow.

Now I knew that even non-monogamous people could live in the light: pay membership fees, and hold AGMs and family-friendly picnics, as polyamorists did. But I needed darkness. I was descending to Hades, but told Noah I was going out dancing. I wore my new black panties under a backless dress, slipped my feet into red stiletto sandals. Before I left to go into the smoke and fire of the night, I wrote in my journal:

> I'm going to see him and I feel no desire. If only I could understand how my erotic self works. Why didn't I feel attracted to him at first, and then, on that afternoon when we drank beer together, I was suddenly burning? I can't put that down to alcohol, since I'd drank before in his company. And on that night, when I seduced him, I wasn't drunk (only later, for courage). My stomach is fist-tight. My body has been telling me something lately. It's not just him, of course. It's my marriage …

10

A Tale of Pleasure Seekers

'I had love at home. I sought only pleasure outside.'
Catherine Millet

I played Frankie Goes to Hollywood's 'Relax' as I drove to the man who'd just flown nearly 3000 kilometres to see me. I opened the car windows to the scorching night, thrust one arm out, while the other lay loose on the wheel as though I were J, or Noah, and blasted the song until the car rock-and-rolled with it. The music enhanced me: I felt bolder, younger, stronger, more dangerous. I even felt I could face my lover again.

The first time I heard 'Relax' was in the late eighties, when I was a teenager and watched Brian De Palma's notorious film *Body Double*, the characters in which were mostly voyeurs, exhibitionists and murderers. Among this creepiness was a scene that for me was pivotal and that had 'Relax' as its soundtrack. In it, Jake Scully, the nerdy protagonist, arrives at a glamorous nightclub, where masked men in leather, and women in leotards and garter belts, slink up and down winding staircases or devour each other against leopard-spotted wallpaper and the jade glitter of curtains; all to the song's conflicting instructions not to do it *and* to live their dreams. To this day, the sexual push-and-pull of that scene and the song linger somewhere deep inside my erotic soul, alongside *Henry & June*. As an adult I, usually unsuccessfully, had sought to access that place. Now I hoped to find it where my lover was staying: in a building appetisingly called Plum Serviced Apartments. As I drove on, I thought of plum-red satin sheets, plum-plump pillows, the sweet allure of plum wine, the rain of yellow plums spilling down in slow motion in the film *Perfume*. About my lover, I tried not to think.

In the real Plum Apartment, the air-conditioning wasn't working properly, the bedding was made of polyester and the mattress was hard. My lover's touch was as tender as my husband's. We held each other for a long time, but I felt no fever; nothing that evoked 'Relax'. Darkness was, once again, eluding me. I thought that perhaps this was happening because I was domesticating my disorder through the choice of an amicable lover. After J, I was less enthusiastic about risk-taking. Still, even in this shrivelled-plum apartment and no longer framed by the sinister West Australian landscape, my lover was a foreign country to me, and I could re-experience with him something of what I felt in my first months in Australia, when my sandals drummed the sidewalks as though they were dance floors.

Later that night, which was already early in the morning, luxuriating in our nakedness, I began dreaming in 'What if?' style: What if I didn't go home? What if I had no husband to report to? What if my life were as light as the floating island, all egg whites and custard?

Then I had to leave.

Freud said having a good life was all about work and love. I'd always agreed with him, but could never prove him right on the latter. Work *did* help to keep me sane. Now that the lover was here, once again I couldn't write, but at least I could do interviews. This time, I wanted to talk about pleasure. Not that there wasn't pleasure to be had in polyamory, but it wasn't at the centre of its discourse; and it wasn't the slippery, murky pleasure of 'Relax' I was after, the kind that carried a waft of rot. Karen, a friend of a friend, agreed to talk to me about just such things, even at the end of her demanding day at her managerial job in the government, followed by a gym workout.

It was late evening when I arrived at Karen's split-level terrace house in an inner-city pocket of Melbourne that was rich with boutiques, veterinarian and counselling clinics, wine bars and other therapeutic enterprises, and conveniently close to Plum Serviced Apartments. Ben, Karen's partner of six years, was out, working a night shift in a restaurant. But the story I'd come for wasn't his anyway, even though Ben and Karen, to borrow a polyamorous term, were in a vee relationship with an older

Italian businessman. There, Ben was at the centre but, before meeting him, Karen had been a pleasure seeker.

In preparation for hearing about that time in her life, I cleared some room for myself on the sofa amid shopping bags with Playboy and David Jones logos. The bags fitted in with the overall expensive chaos of her living room, which housed a treadmill, fish tanks, an enormous—more decorative than practical—chess set, and bookshelves. Karen settled further away, on the carpet. Even there, everything about her seemed outsized: Karen had a bulky, athletic figure, and a wide face framed by short black hair. But, really, this was due to her most striking feature: gigantic—perhaps more practical than decorative—hazel eyes that rolled restlessly under the swollen balls of her eyelids. They scared me. Karen scared me. Only three years older than me, she exuded that intensely adult aura that people in powerful positions often exude. Karen was a woman who knew how to make money and her way in the world, and was at ease in a way I never could be with words like 'strategies' and 'planning'.

'Ask me whatever it is you want to know and I'll see if I can answer,' Karen said in a businesslike manner. I felt I was intruding into the little spare time she had, and was unsure why she'd agreed to meet me, as she seemed to be not just short of time but of interest in the conversation. Still, I was at home asking questions and soon found out that Karen couldn't be easily summarised as just a 'power woman'. She was another of those people I'd been meeting recently, who had undergone many metamorphoses, living their lives not so much progressively as in parallels. In her youth, Karen was wounded so badly by an affair with a married man that she'd retreated into separatist lesbian circles for some years. When, in her mid-twenties, she became more optimistic about the world, and its men, and to compensate herself for her prolonged isolation, Karen plunged into what she kept referring to as 'naughtiness'. It was as though she thought the cuteness of this word could exorcise the darkness that people usually associate with the world of swinging.

I felt uneasy at the turn our conversation had taken, because of my ambivalence about swinging. I was a voyeur and liked creeping around the edges of sleaze, but the two swingers parties I'd attended with J weren't pleasurable experiences. I'd gone reluctantly, mostly at J's urging. I might have enjoyed myself more if J hadn't been so eager. I was also reluctant to blend in by undressing, more because of my scars than out of modesty; besides, I never liked doing what everyone else did. I kept my bra, miniskirt and stockings on, and felt somehow relieved by the mediocrity of the nudity I saw: overflowing bellies, cellulite, grey hair. I mostly spent my time at those events alone, hiding in dark corners with a drink, hoping for J to come to my rescue. But J had his own agenda. At the second party we'd attended, he at first stayed with me, rather than taking off as he'd done at the previous one. I was glad, holding onto him amid the chaos of arriving guests.

'Look, she's got herself a black man.' J pointed at a middle-aged woman borrowing a clean towel from the bar, and at a lanky black man beside her, who stared blankly at the woman's veined thighs. This scene depressed me; I'd come to those parties to find something smoky, delicious. Instead—there was a towel.

J kept whispering into my ear. 'You know, honey, you could do it in the back room, where no one is watching …' For an instant, I thought he was offering himself, and softly brushed my fingers through his hair. But J's breath was short, in that familiar way: 'Don't worry. I'll be so quiet he won't notice me watching … We'll trick him …'

'Who the hell are you talking about?! Who is *he*?'

J's eyes turned shiny, his voice childlike: 'You said you like black men …'

At that moment, I felt so alone beside him that I had to leave. 'I'll be back,' I said, staging a smile, then slipped away into the smoking room. I wanted to cry. I wanted to stay.

The light in the room was abruptly bright, eliminating any remaining illusions. A woman wearing only pink suspenders and stockings was talking to a short man: 'I tell ya, Collingwood will never make it to the finals.' I'd seen her before, in a flesh pile on the mattresses in the first room. The short man had sat nearby, occasionally patting different body parts, muttering quietly, 'Fuck you, fuck you.'

'It's my first time here,' a man with large, melancholy sheep-like eyes told me. He offered me a cigarette and I wondered whether he liked me. And if he did, what would we do? Line up at the bar? A towel, please, thank you? I slipped away again, this time looking for J. I wanted to go home.

In the narrow hall, peeping through half-opened doors at men and women entertaining themselves with strangers' flesh, I finally recognised J's muscled back; he was sucking off a blonde, marble-chested guy on a bed piled with sheets. I watched them, more curious than anything else. J noticed me first and, his mouth still busy, waved to me to come in. The blonde gave me a nice smile. His teeth were snow, his hair was sun. His was a clichéd beauty, like Apollo's. I drew closer, watching J's head going up and down, briefly considering joining in. J released the long, slender penis from his mouth, smiling at me with shiny lips, as if he'd just bitten into a slab of butter. Strangely, I couldn't feel any relationship to him anymore. All I wanted was to go home, alone. But J had the car keys and the money. Meanwhile, the ring of his lips closed again on the divine penis. All this happened a long time ago, but that giant yearning for aloneness I felt then is still fresh in my mind.

Sadness, awkwardness, imperfect bodies … It occurs to me that my memory favouring the repulsive details reflected the unhappiness I felt with J more than the people I observed. Besides, I should have given the party guests more credit, as they had the courage to strip down to their imperfections while I never showed my scars in public. In my recollection of those parties, I must have echoed the prejudice that surrounds the culture of swinging. Contemporary media usually evokes swingers in relation to tragedy (the death of Herman Rockefeller comes to mind), or comedy, like stories about nude fistfights in a Queensland-based swingers resort, or panic about sexually transmitted diseases. But an open-minded investigator, American academic Brooke Wagner, attended a swingers conference and thought the couples there seemed in love and 'were normal'.

More systematic studies of swinging reached similar conclusions. Canadian journalist Terry Gould interviewed swinging couples and concluded that most people he met had strong, loving relationships. Even more counterintuitively, academic research reveals that swingers *epitomise* the mainstream: they weren't abused as children at a higher rate than that of the general population, and are likely to be white, educated, middle class, politically moderate, in long-term relationships and even to hold religious beliefs. Lawyers, doctors and other health professionals are prevalent among swingers. Still, something does differentiate them, and the difference is in their favour. Swingers tend to be less racist, sexist and homophobic than those in the general population. And, according to two large American studies, swingers rate their marital satisfaction *higher* than does the general population, claiming swinging has *improved* their relationships. The general wellbeing of respondents was also rated as higher than average compared with that of society at large.

If there is something about coming together in a casserole of flesh that makes people happy, then swinging must go deeper than being just another sexual fantasy. Some say swinging helps them recapture their youth and confirms their sexual appeal, but you can potentially say this about any sexual adventure. In order to try to understand swingers, I thought back to the ancient Greeks, who made orgies a part of their religious worship, so as to induce an ecstatic state in the worshippers, bringing them closer to the gods. Yet, as often happens with religious rituals, the underlying goals were more pragmatic. The Greeks believed an occasional disordering of the senses helped people release stress, and made them happier, more orderly citizens, just as today's swingers indeed appear to be.

Most swingers, according to research, follow the Greeks' moderation, swinging only several times a year. In this, and other aspects, swinging differs greatly from chaotic 'free love'. Rather, as in any group games, rules and rituals are as intrinsic to swinging as the emotional bouquet of pleasure, competitiveness, fervour and passion—all that the famously reckless Russians sum up in one word, *azart*, and that Karen calls 'naughtiness'— the players experience. The more advertisements for swinging I browsed, the more I became aware of how important it is to know the rules. At some parties, you must participate in sex; at others, you can just watch, if you wish. Sometimes, full nudity is compulsory; elsewhere, you can keep your underwear on or even remain fully clothed. And at a dance party that was part of the swingers conference that Wagner observed, she noticed that during the faster songs, guests mingled, but that during the slow ones, they danced with their spouses.

Love seems to be as important for swingers as it is for polyamorists. But if polyamory is an organised group romance, then swinging is organised pleasure seeking, where love and sex are separated. Like a football game, it is 'event-focused': limited by time and space. You play, then go back to your domestic haven. But I wouldn't summarise swinging as impersonal sex with strangers either. In reviews of swingers clubs I read, there was more talk about the friendliness of attendees than about their attractiveness. Indeed, according to some studies, for many, swinging is also a chance to befriend like-minded people. Some swingers clubs are even based around shared hobbies, such as boating. Particularly since the arrival of the internet, which offers easy access to these usually secretive activities, swinging often occurs in the context of communities that are reminiscent of the polyamorous level of organisation and interconnectedness.

Polyamorists, though, may not like my comparison: their websites and blogs go to great lengths to differentiate between 'good polyamorists' and 'bad swingers'. English sociologist Christian Klesse even thinks polyamorists are at heart puritanical when it comes to sex. But perhaps they just try to avoid the bad publicity attached to swinging. In any case, after doing my research, I could put a finger more precisely on my ambivalence about swinging, which is that the stuff of 'Relax' is unlikely to reside in swinging's communal, ritualised pleasure. But possibly it is because of this orderliness that swinging not only didn't fade away in the aftermath of the sexual revolution, but expanded. In Melbourne alone, where Karen used to swing, in any given week about twenty-five swingers parties take place.

Swinging is often called, derogatorily, wife swapping. But single people swing too and it's not uncommon for romance to ignite at the modern-day orgy. Karen met Hayden at a swingers party she attended with a casual lover. Hayden, a plumber, looked like a gorgeous beach boy—lean, muscly, with yellow hair and white teeth. He was also a natural charmer. When he talked to Karen, he made her feel that she consumed him, no matter that he'd come to the party with a girlfriend. The four of them retreated to a private room and the encounter was so delicious that soon the foursome spent a whole weekend together in a holiday house. Not long after that, Hayden left his girlfriend, and he and Karen moved in together.

'People would ask us, "How did you two meet?" and I'd say "Socially!"' Karen roared with laughter, her eyes in bloom.

'Oh,' I said excitedly, 'I have so many questions to ask you.'

'Go, go, go, go!'

With Karen having suddenly dropped her adult demeanour, I relaxed a little and she continued with her story. When you meet your partner at a swingers party, it's not surprising if you then continue swinging together. However, after getting together, Karen and Hayden turned to a different variety of pleasure seeking.

'We hunted,' Karen said.

While polyamorists want love and swingers want sex, hunters' pleasure is bound up more with the *azart* of the quest and the sleaze of seduction than with consummation. Hunting is a murkier affair than the more organised forms of non-monogamy. Karen and Hayden kept swinging occasionally, but they much preferred to hunt wherever they could—on beaches, in bars, on websites. They set some rules, though, mostly at Hayden's insistence.

Non-monogamous couples often need to decide whether to venture outside their union together. People who cannot bear to see their spouse with someone else will conduct their affairs alone. Those who temperamentally are loners and seek independence and personal space in non-monogamy are also more likely to take lovers on their own. But some couples seek the opposite in non-monogamy—to strengthen their bond through the pleasure of a joint adventure. As a swinging couple in *Mating in Captivity* says: 'Instead of having secrets from each other, we have secrets from the world.' Shared escapades may not just spice up a couple's sex life and bind them through excitement, but also help contain a certain type of jealousy. Separate rendezvous are not confronting to the eye, but can fuel anxiety akin to that arising from other declarations of independence from a lover (such as them having a night out alone). Bringing third parties into a couple's space may turn affairs into shared projects. Hayden insisted he and Karen could only hunt together, and—a trickier condition—Karen could make love only to women, as otherwise he'd feel jealous.

I'd already glimpsed Karen's curious book collection: Jackie Collins paperbacks, books of the *Men Are from Mars, Women Are from Venus* kind, along with those by feminists such as

Naomi Wolf. At least as a reader, Karen was upfront about her conflicting yearnings for passion and fairness. I asked how she felt about Hayden's stand.

Her 'Go, go, go, go!' cheerfulness visibly receded. 'He was very naughty. He had double standards, and loved having a relationship with two women where he was the centre of attention ... At the time, I said it was okay, because I'd done enough. I wasn't desperate to be jumping on other guys. It was more the principle that was never resolved.'

Another problem with their hunting was finding single girls, particularly as they hunted at the same time when Ronit and her husband were looking for lovers, in the relatively early days of the internet. At swingers parties, single girls were nicknamed unicorns because of their rarity. But hunting thrives on solving obstacles. Karen placed a newspaper ad, posing as a single girl seeking another girl to go out with to pick up guys. To whoever responded, she said she knew an interested man (who was Hayden, of course). They also wooed prey in bars. There, too, Karen had to do the work of striking up conversations, since women tend to be more at ease with other women. Hayden's role was to test whether the woman had a prey's willingness about her. He'd say something lewd, like 'Wouldn't it be a fun thing for you girls to play and I'd watch?' He'd then assess the reaction. Did she laugh nervously, look shocked or just smile? If the prey was ready, they'd take her home, and sit her between them, so she didn't feel like an intruder. Women in this situation, Karen said, don't want to relate to you as part of a couple. During their hunting expeditions, she and Hayden behaved more as accomplices than as lovers. Since hunting lacks the boundaries that swinging has and the seduction process can last a long while, it might be difficult for hunting couples to draw clear lines between their time with others and being alone together. The risk of them becoming merely hunting buddies, defined by third parties—or even rivals competing over the lover—is always there.

'How often would you … hunt?' I asked and Karen looked away. Apparently, it had been Hayden's primary hobby. They'd set out to do it almost every weekend.

'I wasn't always in the mood, but if I didn't approach the girls, he'd get upset and ask me to make an effort. We both got a bit focused on that. I think if we hadn't done this, we probably wouldn't have stayed together. We'd have got bored with each other. But, anyway, eventually I got bored. We started saying, "Tonight we aren't going out looking for a girl, we're going to have fun and if something happens, it's a bonus".'

But once they were out, Hayden would become restless, his ears pricking with the hunter's instinct, tuned to prey.

'I was fairly patient then. Now I wouldn't be,' Karen said flatly. But, just as her story was turning into the clichéd one of a woman victimised by her man, she qualified it: 'But, look, it was my thing too. We were partners in crime. It was exciting! Like being high on something.'

Her voice now sped up the way J's would when he was turned on. 'It was like "What are we going to do now? Are we going to talk to her?" All that manoeuvring, scheming. Everything was orchestrated down to "Is this the right moment to ask her?" We had code words and gestures. If I said, "Your mother called," it meant something. All was practised. We worked at it, we worked at it.' Karen sounded proud. 'We bought a black book in a sex shop and wrote in it about every girl we met. It was very graphic!' She went into such a laughing fit that I worried her eyes would jump out of their orbits.

'What happened to that book?'

'I lost it when I moved. You'd love it, wouldn't you?' For the first time Karen addressed me directly, and I averted my gaze.

Karen probably had the makeup of a huntress; the problem was that Hayden wasn't a good team player, to use her professional jargon. Initially, the discord between them was minor, even funny, like on a night when Karen brought a girl home, but Hayden thought her too chubby (Karen herself was much slimmer then, she told me). The three of them had a drink and undressed. Then, in the midst of their foreplay, Hayden got up and left, complaining about a headache. 'And I'm like, "Mate, I was doing all this work, getting her here for you!"' Karen roared with laughter again.

The incident that upset Karen the most happened at an important point in their hunting history, when they acquired a girlfriend. She was an honours psychology student, Karen said with pride, a slim beauty with long dark hair. The three of them spent five romantic months together, the way dating couples would, meeting several times a week, cooking dinners, going to movies and picnics. The girlfriend would stay the night and there was no talk of hunting then. However, she was still categorised as prey, since Hayden and Karen only had sex with her together. So, what went wrong?

'He was a pig!' Eight years later, Karen still sounded angry. One day, without telling her, Hayden phoned the girl to say it was all over. I asked whether he did this because he'd missed hunting. Karen shrugged her shoulders. Maybe, but she thought Hayden's main problem was that while it was supposed to be *his* show—one man with two doting women—Karen and the girl fancied each other too.

'He really hurt her. She was attached to us.' Karen seemed flat again; I noticed her moods swung swiftly. After that incident, she lost interest in their games and the relationship deteriorated swiftly. She wouldn't tell me exactly how it unravelled, which was what I, in my current state, most wanted to know, but she ended her story with one striking detail: 'We were fighting a lot. Hayden said he needed a break and went to stay with his sister. Five days later, it turned out that instead he'd gone off to marry a woman he'd met on the internet …'

With Ben, whom she'd met not long after Hayden left, Karen never hunted. Not because of her bad experience with it, she said: she did offer Ben the option to try it, but he didn't have a hunter's bent. The first person they met and liked became his boyfriend. Since then, the three of them had been in a vee relationship, the kind that Shelly, Justin and Justin's interstate girlfriend had.

I saw what Karen meant about his not having a hunter's bent as soon as Ben walked through the door. Small, skinny and with light-coloured, almost white, hair, he looked painfully young and girlish. He gave us a bashful smile and at once hid behind a computer screen. Karen shifted restlessly. I gathered she'd had enough of me, and of the kind of memories and introspection I was trying to elicit. Still, I couldn't help myself. As Karen walked me to the door, I asked why she'd remained with Hayden until he ran off. Was it love? A tram rattled past us, illuminating Karen with its headlights. I noticed that when her eyes didn't sparkle, they looked bottomless, like wells.

'I don't know,' she sighed. 'I've never left anyone. They've always left me.'

'Why is that?'

'I just can't … My biggest fear is to be left. Maybe I can't do it to someone else.'

I walked out into the night that was heavy with dark birds and the perfume of jasmine, thinking about what Karen had said. I, too, was terrified of being left. So I always left …

For six days, he came. For six viscous mornings and afternoons, in a bed jammed under a large window with its wooden shutters down, in a failed attempt to shield us from the sun and the city. Outside the window, Melbourne stretched like a feline, meowing with ambulance sirens, accents, motorcycles. The Plum Apartment disoriented me, pretending to be Marguerite Duras's love den in Saigon. My lover wasn't as wealthy as hers, but just as passive. We pretended not to hear the city, or be hot, and all the questions my lover never asked and things I didn't tell him about my marriage pushed between our damp skins, pulling us apart. Still, I was happy. Or rather, exalted. The exaltation took me in wild, sharp bursts. The whole world opened in front of me in that room, but not in Kerouac's orgasmic void. Rather, it seemed as mysterious and appetising as a foreign land, and I piled myself into it, limb by limb, bone by bone. But my lover, who, at heart, I was realising, was an eternal tourist, needed to get out. Always the good hostess, I offered to show him Mount Dandenong.

During the six months when I'd lived in hiding with Noah, leaving the apartment mainly to go to work, we'd escaped several times to the countryside. Noah would drive and I'd bend over, covered with a blanket, to avoid J until we'd exited the city. Now I was the driver, but I felt as if my head were once again covered. I navigated Melbourne's streets furtively, in loops, to avoid suburbs close to home. My lover knew why I was taking the detours but said nothing. Instead, he attempted to relieve my anxiety by massaging my neck and with anecdotes from his travels. I knew he traversed the world often—that was the only real passion he smelled of. He talked excitedly about the shades of wintry sunsets in the Romanian countryside and the nature of ghosts in Irish graveyards. I noticed now that the more kilometres we consumed, the more colour appeared in his long, usually pale face. He watched me intently, as though I, too, were an exotic location. His many emails came to mind. There he recalled in detail the words I wrote or said, jokes we shared, books we discussed. What if I were mistaking his explorer's drive for emotion? And what if he were less impenetrable than I wanted him to be? I kept driving towards the majestic mountain, which finally appeared on our horizon, green and fresh like an apple, thinking, Here I am in the company of another alluring and restless man with whom I have the shape, but perhaps not the flavour, of an affair.

I put on St. Germain's *Tourist*. The music made me think of Noah, who also loved this album; made me think of the tale of my marriage as bookended by furtive countryside drives and triangles. Bookended … Was that a Freudian slip? In one of my favourite fairytales, 'The Little Prince', which is also an essay on love, a fox tells the prince: 'You become responsible forever for what you have tamed.' I had never thought I was noble enough to follow such high moral standards, but now whenever I thought of leaving, the phrase appeared to me, punching me in my underbelly. Bent and breathless, I made my way into the mist and spiders of the familiar mountain that, in my lover's company, appeared strange.

Several hours before my lover flew back to Perth, we drove to Werribee Zoo. That day, Werribee was overflowing with rain, and rap music was pouring out of dented cars sporting obscenely large spoilers. We'd come there for the lions.

We were the only visitors to their enclosure, even though by now the rain had become lighter, shooting in sharp, thin drizzles. I pulled my lover's shirt out of his jeans, scratched his sharp ribs with my pink fingernails, and pushed him against the glass that separated us from the sand-coloured, thick-buttocked animals who observed us from an impertinently close distance with what appeared to be ironic looks on their faces. Anxious but excited, my lover wriggled against the glass wall. I pinned him back, rubbing against his loins until he gave up all resistance. I felt nothing. Not knowing what else to do, we remained locked together next to the animals and surrounded by gnarly tree trunks until children's voices sounded nearby. It was time to head to the airport anyhow. I wanted him to go. But his departure meant I'd now have the space to think about what I should do. 'You'd never manage without me in Australia,'

J told me every time I'd tried to leave him, and although I did leave and did manage, I must have carried his words with me, transferring them onto Noah …

My lover's plane took off. On the way home from the airport, I drove past a glitzy bar. In its large window overlooking the street, a middle-aged man with coarse, dark features sat between two women who, with their piles of fluffy, pale hair like fairy floss, appeared to be replicas of each other. *When you have two men, look for a third one.* My mother's advice, which she used to give me whenever I dated more than one man at once, echoed in my hollowed head.

I kept moving like a hurricane, in feedback loops, but at the same time still searching for a pathway to follow. I wasn't a swinger, or a huntress. I fancied myself as a pleasure seeker, though. I wanted something composed of translucent fabrics thrown upon naked bulbs and bodies, Louis Armstrong's hoarse music, 1920s cigarette holders, and sweet sherry painting glasses and lips crimson. I wanted to find the realm of 'Relax' in which to exhaust myself, then settle back down with Noah.

My friend Ophelia called to suggest I interview her older brother. Brad was in a monogamous relationship now, she said, but the story of his former marriage might interest me. I felt uneasy about doing this interview because of its terrible timing—their mother was nearing death. That was why Ophelia's many siblings had gathered in Melbourne from all over Australia. Brad had flown in from a little coastal town in Queensland, where he lived with his partner Eileen, her two children, and his sixteen-year-old daughter. I wasn't sure Brad would want to talk to me now, but Ophelia thought his visit was a rare opportunity for me. 'Besides, talking to you can brighten him up,' she said kindly.

I had a secondary, vain anxiety to deal with too. I'd seen Brad's photo. He appeared handsome in a boyish way that didn't reflect his fifty-one years, with curls, round cheeks, and bright lips and eyes. Then there was Ophelia's remark that Brad was prone to recklessness. This unsettled me further. I wanted a brush with someone else's recklessness, now that my own was leading me nowhere. Eager to impress this reckless, handsome man I'd never met, I chose my sexy librarian look—always a winner with men. I left my glasses on, wore a short dress with a doll appliqué on it and fishnet stockings and walked, nervous, into Ophelia's spacious house filled with echoes, books, guitars, complicated cooking appliances and the sweetness of her children.

Brad was a copy of his photo: a slim, compact adult-child. Although his face had hardly been touched by life, I knew from Ophelia he lived intensely in many ways. I was relieved that he, too, seemed tense, smiling at me incessantly. I reciprocated. Once we'd smiled ourselves to death in front of the perplexed Ophelia, Brad grabbed a bottle of white wine and we went into the backyard studio, to settle on a curvy orange couch underneath eerie abstracts streaming with silver.

'Sue and I are both sexual,' Brad immediately told me. Sue was the wife who had walked out on him two years before. 'But before we met, I was also inclined …'

Brad owned now a burger shop, but once he'd been a butcher. He told me that for butchers, flirting is second nature—he glanced at me apologetically—with all those women coming in, spilling their cleavages onto the counter as they watched him dissect poultry breasts and backsides, his white-gloved hands smeared with intestines. He could see beauty in every woman, Brad said, and I adjusted my too-short dress. But he was also awed by the beauty of forests, mountains, the sea.

For a while, he spoke about island sunsets, treetops in the morning light, the moods of the ocean. He had dyslexia, and found language a strain. He couldn't read or write fluently, and the internet was a foreign country to him. Perhaps to compensate for that, but also through sheer talent, Brad had turned into a man who lived with all his senses entangled in the world—something I'd never managed to do. Now I thought that perhaps a shortage of language could be a blessing of sorts. Although was Brad really short of it? I liked the passion with which he spoke, sucking in air whenever he got especially excited, repeating in a shamanic fashion his praise of beauty. In his way, he was actually a poet. The more I listened to Brad, the less I remembered the real subject of our interview. But Brad did.

Apparently, he and I were similar in our approach to love: greedy but also needing an anchor—the beloved—to stabilise us within the chaos of desire. One night, Sue walked into the apartment of a friend of Brad's where he was staying that night. He saw the shapely blonde woman with lush breasts, all flirtatious smiles and dancelike movements, and thought this was his female match. In hindsight, he wasn't really wrong. Or right.

In the small hours of the morning, after much wine, the friend—a shy, older man—told Sue she could stay at his place, rather than drive drunk. She happily dived into the bed, naked, between the two men, pressing herself to Brad, all warm and curvy. Brad and Sue made love while the friend watched from his end.

'It started like that, but it wasn't always like that. We had years when we wouldn't pursue anything,' Brad hastened to tell me. Sex with others wasn't something that his marriage revolved around. They had two daughters to raise, a busy shop to manage, and each other, of course.

Brad was also keen to make the point that, contrary to the rumours that trailed him and Sue in the small rural communities they lived in, they weren't sex addicts, or swingers. Brad wasn't a hunter either. Rather, he was a *gatherer*. He gathered around him people to share pleasures with—hiking, drugs, dancing, diving for crayfish, and, sometimes, sex. Such sex, at once a raunchy and intimate affair, wasn't usually planned, but arose spontaneously, like when he and Sue spent a weekend away with another couple and, at the last moment, decided to swap spouses for the night. Another time, a handsome Italian fireman, a friend of Brad's, came over and Sue felt like seducing him.

'We were smoking joints. Sue sat close to him and kissed him. I just let it happen, because …' Brad hesitated, as if unsure how open-minded I'd be about his sexuality. 'It's nice to watch people kissing.'

'Oh, yeah, yeah …' I said, to indicate I didn't think this was odd.

Unable to sit still, Brad fidgeted on the couch, his lovely face brilliant with the tender afternoon sunshine. He said, animated again: 'I love watching live sex. It's better than pornography. We ended up going to bed together. He made love to Sue. Then I made love to her. Having sex with a woman after another man has come inside her is just … ' he seemed suddenly shy.

I twiddled with my hair: 'Exciting?'

'Exciting, yes! Everything is wet and slippery,' Brad laughed nervously, sliding glances in my direction, possibly to check whether he'd overstepped the line. I smiled to indicate I actually liked how, in a rather Israeli way, he called things as they were. Besides … I felt turned on by his story.

'Were you jealous?'

'No, no, no! It was just nice to watch them kissing, caressing. He might be fucking Sue and she might be sucking my cock, so it was all nice …'

For gatherers, unlike hunters, longevity of relationships enhances the pleasure. Their affair with the fireman lasted a while. During the two decades of Brad's marriage, other friends became their lovers. Things could turn comical, like one night when Brad and Sue were staying, along with several other guests, at a friend's place on mattresses in the living room. They all went dancing, but the women came home earlier. When Brad returned, tipsy, they were asleep in the dark. He wanted to make love to Sue: 'I started licking her. I touched her breasts, but they weren't the same size! But the woman didn't mind and it was too late to stop, because I was already inside her! She was so wet and my cock slipped in easily ...' Brad laughed with childlike joy. Apparently, no one minded what happened.

But Sue wasn't always that easygoing. Like Hayden, she was less keen on giving her partner the freedom she claimed for herself. Brad said he didn't really mind: 'I was never into having sex behind Sue's back. I'd fuck with a woman if Sue was there and agreed to it. But, really, it was best for me to go to bed with Sue. I loved her and knew her intimately.'

Brad, I was gathering, although he was a flirt, was a candaulist at heart, and an affectionate husband. His strongest sexual fantasies were about Sue. He said what he loved most was making love with her or watching her being fucked by someone else: 'It looks great, you know, and from different angles ... It's a joy to watch your partner being pleasured by another man and then have sex with her.'

Sex was probably the language Brad spoke best. Yet, now he sounded regretful about the form his self-expression had taken. He gulped the rest of his wine in one go: 'The outcome wasn't good, Lee ... It broke my family.'

Three years before, their friend and her housemate, an accountant, invited Brad and Sue to a dinner party. Softened by ecstasy and Latin music, they ate filet mignons and drank champagne. There was a palpable feeling of sex in the air. Sue was keen on acting it out, but not how Brad wanted it: 'My idea was we'd all get together. But Sue just went to bed with that man. I felt hurt, excluded. And the next day, she said to me, "You opened a can of worms ..." This man was successful and focused ... different from me. Sue thought he was the Holy Grail.'

Sue, I was finding out, wasn't as good a match for Brad as he'd initially assumed. She gathered with him, but also liked hunting, alone. She'd occasionally go to bars to pick up strangers, then regret it and tell Brad. 'I loved her and forgave her,' Brad said. 'If you're totally a saint yourself, it's one thing. But I decided to move on. I don't consider one-night flings major. If you both love each other, you move on.'

But the accountant wasn't a fling. During their eldest daughter's birthday dinner, Sue broke the news that she was leaving. 'I was heartbroken and devastated ...' he said, with such emotion that I spilled coffee on my dress.

This wasn't the first time Sue had fallen in love, or thought she had, and opted out. Some years before, she'd made a similar confession, about a secret affair she'd had with the town's squash captain, who was married too. They were going to live together.

Brad poured the remains of the bottle into his glass: 'My eldest daughter asked Sue then not to go off with that married guy and, at the fifty-ninth minute, she agreed. I forgave her, because she wasn't happy. We worked together in the business seven days a week. She wanted to escape to something that would make her happy. Happiness wasn't something that came to her easily ...'

At that, our conversation veered to matters of happiness and its opposite—depression. It took Brad a while to realise that although Sue carried herself in an agile, smiling, pretty body, her soul was shot through with heaviness. During their marriage, she went on and off antidepressants. Her illness got progressively worse as life stresses escalated. Their first daughter, he said, was very ... free-spirited, might be the word? She and Sue always battled. The second one was born with a faulty heart.

'In our last years together, we had a beautiful house on the beach, with no neighbours, and absolutely beautiful views of an island, rocks and trees. But Sue couldn't see the beauty ... She wasn't happy with what she had.' Brad himself now sounded intensely sad.

I knew what he was talking about. In my family and work, I saw the mightiness of depression, how it could lop people down as though they were trees. Perhaps in her sexual ventures, Sue hadn't sought pleasure as much as escape the sadness. But no matter how fast she'd run, how hard she'd partied, it had trailed her. Antidepressants helped, but they dulled her, which was why, time after time, Sue would stop taking her medication. It was tough on Brad and the girls: during those times, they'd have to walk on eggshells.

Still, Brad thought in their years together, he and Sue had much fun, whether with their girls or when it was just the two of them. They'd drive to Brisbane to go clubbing until morning; or throw grand parties in their house, with DJs, revolving mirror balls, lasers, smoke machines. Since the divorce, though, the house had gone. The parties had gone. The accountant, perhaps frightened of Sue's moods, still saw her but wouldn't live with her. Brad felt sad for Sue, for their daughters, and for himself.

I asked him whether he really believed it was their pleasure seeking that had come between them, or was the marriage bound to disintegrate anyway? If Sue hadn't met the accountant, wouldn't there have been another catalyst, akin to the squash captain? And with the latter—hadn't it been rather 'ordinary' infidelity? Did it matter who the man had been? I was probably talking about myself too.

'Yes, yes. The downfall, from my perspective, was that Sue didn't want to take antidepressants anymore. I think for a non-monogamous relationship to work, you have to be totally in love with each other, but also …' Brad struggled for words, 'you need to be happy with yourself.'

He looked at me closely now and wriggled his body, as if to free himself from the verbal labyrinth my questions had sent him into. 'Can I turn the tables? Ophelia said you're in an open relationship. Did your man want it?'

Ahhh … 'It was my idea.'

The simplifications.

'So, you wanted this, because this brought something out of you that you enjoyed?' Brad's tone was urgent. I wondered how much his current relationship suited him.

'Yeah ... I feel like different men bring out different parts of me.' That was the most honest thing I'd said since I began the interviews for the book. 'But I prefer to do this alone.'

At least in this regard, I matched Noah, who—I kept hearing, and by now was quite certain—also occasionally sought pleasure (while insisting he wasn't) on his own. But was I really after pleasure? My scars always inhibited me, and being comfortable with your nudity seemed essential in pleasure seeking. And what inhibited me even more was my princessy nature. With men, I needed to feel unique, chosen—a feeling that was impossible to achieve with sex that was purely for pleasure. So what did I want?

Brad had to head off to a dinner, but I had one more thing to ask. As always, I was on the lookout for a happy ending. Was he happy with Eileen? Brad examined the wine bottle, as if to make sure it was empty, and said he *probably, more or less*, preferred monogamy now: 'It's nice living with someone who is more stable ... Eileen, she didn't even let me kiss her at first. She was very cautious. And now she's head over heels in love with me. And I'm with her. But it's getting ... like, she doesn't have many interests. A few weeks ago, I said, "I need some space." She was clingy. "I also need to do things that I love and you don't, like fishing."' Brad said he hadn't told Eileen about this interview. But she is head over heels in love with him and he is with her, he repeated, to make sure we both understood.

Brad walked me out to my car. In the open space, we tried to deflate the intensity of our conversation through chitchat. But once I got into the car, he dropped the niceties. 'If only we'd met earlier, before I became monogamous—I'd love to fuck you!' he shouted and that was the warmest, nicest 'I'd love to fuck you' I'd ever heard. I smiled, exquisitely embarrassed, and drove off.

On a brilliant-yellow Saturday morning, our friends Nicole and Joseph came over and we sat on the balcony on Noah's and my new cushioned chairs, eating almond croissants and drinking Coronas. The men talked cricket, American politics, and other things involving teams and rules. Nicole and I discussed less structured pursuits. She was writing a PhD on poetry and we considered the wisdom of mixing writing with the academy (I doubted it, she was in favour). We drank more beer and watched the city buildings swelling with heat, billowing at a distance. Underneath us, cars accelerated and wheezed; several young men crossed the road to a pokies barn, chanting merrily, 'Fuck, fuck, fuck!' as if it were a Christmas carol. In short, Melbourne was shaking off its holiday zombieness. I, too, wanted to return to normality. I noticed the sunshine spilling in buckets onto the tanned face of my husband, and that Nicole was smiling at Joseph from across the table. They were about to do their weekly walk along Beach Road and were finalising their plans for the night. Noah was tapping away at something on his mobile. It suddenly hit me that since our guests had arrived, we hadn't exchanged as much as a glance.

I usually make my most difficult decisions in an instant. I'd deliberate over a problem for months, then a moment of clarity would come, like on the night my boyfriend had tried to kidnap me and I finally knew it was time to leave Israel. Now, something akin to it happened. I could no longer ignore what I'd sensed all along: that what had unravelled inside me since I'd first reached for my lover was irreversible, irreparable, and that it wasn't just the desire that had trailed me around from that moment. It was time to admit that too much bitterness and estrangement had seeped into the space of my marriage in the course of five years. That we'd lost our vision of togetherness. By the time Noah said he'd walk our friends to their car, I knew there was no hope for us anymore.

Why are you with me? Noah had asked me several times in recent years, usually when our fights escalated. I said it was because of his hands and lips that relieved my loneliness, his heart that was kind, the twinkle in his lively eyes, the spring in his step, the way we danced and ate ice-cream together and slept entwined. Because we made a great home. Because he made me happy more often than he made me miserable, and because, when I tried, I made him happy too. But was that enough?

Was Tolstoy right when he wrote that happy families are all alike? My happy experiences, familial or not, contain as many nuances as the sad ones. With Noah, I'd had times of feverish, desperate happiness when I was still with J and would escape to Noah when I could, burying into him like a hamster. There had been the giggly, light happiness of us when we'd roam the streets hand in hand, and the melancholy variety when we were apart and I'd take pleasure in my solitude, filled with the knowledge that soon I'd see Noah again. And just before I'd left for Perth, I'd been happy too, in a kind of sedate, resigned way.

There had been times when Noah had wondered whether I loved him at all. I'd always said yes. But I'd never admitted that my love for him was an injured love, the love of someone worn out from previous intimacy battles, chiefly the ones with J. And what kind of love did he have for me if he didn't want to fuck me ferociously, lustfully?

'Hey, babe, why are you crying?' Noah sat down beside me on the couch, where I'd been slouching since he left. He put his arms around me. The tenderness in his voice and touch seized me by the throat. I wanted to rip off my tongue, where those final words perched. Instead, I dragged myself away from my husband: 'Please don't. You won't want to hold me when I tell you why I'm crying …'

I was right. As soon as the words squeezed their slithery, snaky trunks through my throat, Noah flew off the sofa. His arms flew up in the air. His legs paced. There were words of fury: *You didn't try hard enough. You didn't give us a chance. You can't just go ...* The sunshine kept pushing through the windows, illuminating the bitter nothingness that settled between us. I heard a door slam. Finally, Noah claimed the study for himself. Finally, I was sitting in the living room as if it were my territory. As if this were my life. As if I'd found someone to grow old with. As if I could ever stop passing through my life as an eternal newcomer.

11

An Asymmetrical Tale

'I feel, even at the lowest moment, such endless vitality inside me.'
Iris Murdoch

I now came to see those swingers parties J and I attended as a signal that we were sinking into the type of non-monogamy most likely to turn tragic: an asymmetrical one, driven by one partner while the other trudges along unwillingly. But first, there was more to play out in our relationship. J sold the house in Ferntree Gully and bought a flat in a quiet street in East St Kilda, near the Chabad synagogue. I felt happy about that. While we were living in Melbourne's suburbia, I'd begun doubting my existence. Israelis, and even more so Russian–Israelis, were as rare in Australia as single girls were at swingers parties. But now I was back in a place where I had some point of reference, some validation of myself. I could buy herring if I wanted and every day I saw lively Israeli boys with curly ponytails stroll around.

At our new home, I set up a study for myself in the spare bedroom, stocked the pantry and cooked Israeli meals: capsicums stuffed with rice and beef, spicy soups, *shakshooka*. J developed a little potbelly and, in this newly found domestic happiness, even went as far as to purchase a brand-new coffee table, with a kitschy marble sculpture as its base. J was also happy with the opportunities for salvation our new neighbourhood offered. Normally, his soul received a periodical cleansing in men's saunas, ashrams, real estate lectures, brothels, chanting sessions and, since we'd met, in my arms as well. But most of that stuff was pricey, whereas the Shabbat dinners the Chabad offered, to save the souls of Israeli tourists and local Jewish misfits, were free. Soon after we moved, J became so content that he even lost interest in looking for new lovers.

To keep J satisfied and out of trouble, I now trailed him on Friday nights into an enormous, aggressively lit Chabad hall that reminded me of the depressing communal dining rooms in Kibbutzim. There, we ate dry chicken drumsticks and were told by a youngish, cocky rabbi why we happened to be the chosen people. In between the chicken and the sermon, J offered cash-in-hand work to handsome Israeli tourists. He also befriended

Shimon, an Israeli of uncertain age and mental health, who had lived in Melbourne for a decade in a tiny flat that resembled a monk's cell. Shimon was a short man whose face was spotted with curly sprouts unsuccessfully attempting to form a beard. According to the Centrelink records, he was unemployed, but according to Shimon and the World's Creator—as he referred to his employer—he worked overtime. A self-proclaimed Cabbalist, Shimon's job was deciphering divine messages hidden in the shadows cast by the three-dimensional shapes of Hebrew letters. Shimon never revealed what he found there, but J took an interest in him anyway.

He offered Shimon some carpentry work on his investment properties, which were now mostly in the city, where newly built apartment buildings soared into the sky like Towers of Babel. I often joined J in inspecting those projects. The luxurious granite kitchen islands and the glittering views of Eureka Tower sedated me. I decided that if only we could move into one of these apartments, J and I would become a *forever and ever* couple. J, too, read coded messages of happiness in those places, and promised me after each inspection a future of love, luxury and travel. I'll work and you'll write, he'd promise. A part of me still remembered J was wrong for me, but wrong things often made me happy. So I began thinking of *us* and my future as a writer in one breath. At night, I'd watch J asleep in the filigree of starlight, how he shifted and shifted, edging closer to me.

Yet, even at the peak of our entanglement, when I reeked of J, I could envisage a future without him. Could that be still love? The novel I was working on then was about love. This was what I've always done through writing: tried to figure out my confusions. I was obsessed with romantic love, but I didn't understand it. Since my teenage years, when I first began having boyfriends, I'd never been sure whether what I felt towards any of them was the desire for a particular man or the generic desire for love. I needed to be loved grandly and I was careful with my romantic choices, fancying those who already loved me. Love seemed instrumental to affirming my worth. When I had a man, it showed in the confident way I moved, talked, smiled. Besides, I arrogantly assumed that I deserved to be loved with the same mad intensity that my mother loved me. So I was usually partnered and usually restless, though not always unhappy. Often I was even content. For that contentment, I was prepared to pay the price of never being certain about my own feelings. This may not be an inspiring romantic history, but at least I got through the battlefield of my youth with a healthy dose of self-respect.

But now, at twenty-seven, I wanted more from *love*. I was hoping the novel would answer the question *Do I love J?*. In our first months together, he often walked alongside me with his hands stuck in his pockets. I became preoccupied with his hands, insisting he pull them out. After a while, I succeeded and the pockets were left to their own devices; J's hands moved firmly into mine. It was only then that I responded to his love declarations. The problem was, my 'I love you's had a mechanical, impersonal sound to them that even I recognised.

While I was contemplating all this, J arrived home, wearing a zipped-up leather jacket. His face was as bright as if he'd just been to a beauty salon, though in fact he'd come from a meditation retreat and I knew that for the next few days even an unwashed plate wouldn't pose a threat to our love. 'Hey, *neshama sheli* [my soul]'; these days, J's vocabulary was rather divine. He kissed my neck, long and good. I drew in the freshness of his aftershave and the leather smell—the odours of a fuckable man—and thought myself a fool for doubting my feelings.

A few months later, and white dust began swirling throughout our apartment day and night, clinging to our clothes and hair.

We lived clouded in it, breathing in acidic paints. What I had thought was, finally, our love den, J saw as an investment. Or perhaps he just always had to pay his dues for something. Whenever he made a good profit, he gambled it on the next deal. Whenever he had love, he put it at risk by inviting in others. Whenever he had a home, he demolished it. The wall between the kitchen and the living room was gone now. Then the kitchen was gone. We now ate our meals at La Porchetta.

To save money, J did most of the renovation work himself, with the help of Shimon. Similarly to my mother, whenever J wanted to appropriate someone, he'd rename them. I was *neshama* or 'the damn princess', depending on his mood. Shimon was *tzadik*, 'the saint', whereas the saint, in common Israeli fashion, took to calling J *ahi*, 'my brother'. While I was in the throes of finishing my novel, the brothers ripped out carpets and knocked out more walls, all while listening to the latest Israeli craze—recorded lectures of Rabbi Amnon Yitzhak. This rabbi of Yemeni descent, equipped with ceremonial Yemenite robes resembling my mother's dressing gowns and with dizzyingly long *peyos*, toured Israel converting people to his vision of Judaism, which excluded public singing and the existence of the state of Israel in the one breath.

Day after day, working in my study, I heard the rabbi's high-pitched voice: 'When someone wants to make *teshuva*, to repent, his friends laugh at him. You wanna be a nutcase? Be a man, they tell him. Pierce your ear, pierce your tongue!'

The rabbi's rise to stardom coincided with Arafat pulling out of the Camp David talks and, shortly after, the launch of the Second Intifada, when despair hung heavily in the air and a vengeful Jewish God became a consolation to many. Yitzhak made his reputation through excelling in performance. He was skilled at hyperbole, slapstick and the absurd, and was easily God's most entertaining representative in Israel. His comedy was never self-directed, and had a shamanic quality that relied less on content and more on sound. The rabbi's penchant for chanting and his distinct voice, steeped in the throaty 'khhhs' and 'aaas', transfixed his audiences:

> Pierce your foot, your bellybutton, your finger! Do loads of holes! Insert some thorns too! Paaaaint your haaair hhhhaaaalf gold, hhhhhaaalf green. C'mon, be a maaaan! Tear your paaaants!

Tzadik's and J's laughter followed the live audience's. The rabbi accelerated the shouting: 'Get torn jeans aaand paaay a lot! Not cheap! Waaalkkk aaaround like a nut, be a maaaaaaan!' By now, the audience was clapping so hard, it was clear they were ready for the inevitable message: 'So is this a man, I ask? Be a Jew, be a righteous man, have a soul—that's a man!!!' The clapping became thunderous. But even this wasn't enough for Yitzhak, who wanted to ensure the benefits of such a choice were clear. For that, he was even prepared to draw on the environmental science he usually despised:

> The day will come when it will be 1500 degrees on planet earth. Then the secular Jews will burn like mosquitoes in electrical traps, giving off the same sounds—*tzz, tzz, tzzzzzz*. And their saintly Haredi neighbours won't understand what these sounds are or why their secular neighbours have vanished. *Tzzzzzzzzzzzzzzzz* …

The night pitched its dark tent and lit celestial campfires. Shabbat expired. It was spring, but planet earth was already sizzling. J thought installing an air conditioner was a waste of money, so we retreated to the cooler bedroom, watching mosquitoes fly in and out of the open windows while our saintly neighbours carried their overheated bodies, over-packaged in dark caftans and fur hats, to the Chabad house. We lay for some hours, sweaty, hardly touching. This lack of touch threw me into a panic. When I couldn't feel J physically, I couldn't feel him emotionally either. To get closer, I suggested we go for dinner to the air-conditioned buffet restaurant at the casino. Like many Israelis abroad, we were keen on all-you-can-eat places for their abundance, unheard of in our country. It wasn't so much the quantity of food as the variety and limitlessness that we craved.

On the way to the casino, J put on another Yitzhak tape. Lately, he was also keeping a flimsy white yarmulke in the glove box of his car. I resented this and not just because of my upbringing. The archetypal fantasy of metamorphosis that had made its way from myths and folktales into television makeover shows was central in my life, and I extended this ambition to my men. With my passion for remoulding my lovers, I was naturally a haven for salvation seekers. J must have sensed this when we met, and I must have sensed his need to be transformed. I wanted to be in charge of J's salvation, but I faced too much competition. At least the rabbi always put J in a good mood.

The more I listened to the tapes, the more Yitzhak revealed himself to be a multi-tasker. A prophet, a greenie, a fertility specialist (during his lectures, at least, he was always trying to help women get pregnant), and now he also exhibited a historian's ambition: 'There were two great criminals in the history of the Jewish people: Hitler and Herzl. Hitler wanted to destroy the body of the Jewish nation. Herzl wanted to kill the soul.' At this point, J parked the car and said, 'We'll wait until many people come in all at once, then get in.' As always, he was eager to sneak in for free, if only to prove, once again, his hypothesis that Australians were gullible. He said all we needed to do was to walk in confidently, looking straight ahead. 'They only catch you if you're scared.' And, at least on that matter, he was right.

In the restaurant, once the air-conditioning had cooled me down, I wondered, and not for the first time, why, if Australians irritated J so, did he want to live here. J said Esther and he had had enough of struggling for a living. I said I didn't buy this: they owned an apartment and could afford overseas travel. J said he'd be back soon and returned to the table with a plate piled with shellfish. I peeled prawns for us both. J always struggled with this task, perhaps because shellfish wasn't kosher.

'What was the real reason?' I asked.

Oh, there was also a criminal record. Or, not really a record, just an attempt to charge him. Assault charges. False, of course. Well, at least, he'd never been found guilty. But if he returned to Israel, the case could potentially be reopened. We ordered wine. He hadn't done anything bad, really. He'd been driving taxis for a living then. The women were his passengers. He'd felt playful that night and, just as a joke, he'd asked them for something other than money as payment ... Nothing serious; their feet, maybe ... He'd just asked: they didn't have to go crazy. See, *they* attacked him. Someone got a broken nose. Not his fault. It was all an accident, self-defence. It shouldn't have been a big deal, but the problem was, there was another complaint against him ... Another passenger, she, too ...

The electric glare underlined the gluttony all around us, performed to perfection. The orderly queues for food were heavy with flesh and silence. The stillness was shattered only once the patrons were back at their tables with their loot of chilli mussels, burned potatoes and pale roast pork. Their virtuoso fingers then travelled purposefully between their plates and mouths. The knives lumped butter onto wilted bread rolls, while poison-green jelly painted children's faces. I watched everything closely. The more unravelled I became by J's story, the more comfort I drew from this spectacle of plenty. Until Esther came to mind. Esther ... She was alive then, and J's willing accomplice whenever he wished to play. Still, there were the feet, the broken nose, the trouble. Could J ever get enough? Apparently not with her. And with me?

I said I wanted to go home. That night, once J fell asleep, I made sure we didn't touch. Several days later, as we drove along Fitzroy Street, we noticed Tzadik coming out of a sex shop. I giggled, but J didn't.

J's friendships tended to be highly charged and, as with most intense things, had a short lifespan. He'd clutch onto people, promising them mountains while sapping as much life from them as he could. Then, once they, or he, didn't live up to expectations, he'd become bitterly disappointed. Now that J held Shimon in contempt, the word *tzadik* acquired a devilish ring in his mouth. They still worked together, but these days, Shimon—who needed the money—sheepishly circled around his brother, often doing unpaid errands. I felt sorry for Shimon, but at least we didn't have to go to Chabad any longer.

On the rebound from Shimon, J embarked on a new friendship, with an obscenely rich, obese and diabetic Frenchman. He lived in a penthouse in South Yarra. His luxurious abode was strewn throughout with bottles of expensive cognac, half-smoked cigarettes, empty pizza boxes and a zoo's-worth assortment of stuffed animals he'd either imported or would export. The man had some tax problems back home and was counting on staying in Australia. His need became J's new project. In return for J's efforts to find a local bride for the Frenchman, we received a giant blue bear, with fiercely black, maniacally bulging eyes, who took over our sofa.

Between the dust, the demonic bear, the parade of prospective brides comprising those overweight, wild-haired women from J's past, and Amnon Yitzhak's prophecies that kept growing more apocalyptic, we began bickering again. The longer we lived together, the less J noticed the boundary between us. When he looked at me now, he must have seen his own soul. This could either delight or make him cringe. Increasingly, J was finding faults in himself and, consequently, in me. He wasn't spiritual enough; he was too focused, or not focused enough, on making money; he was misplaced in this country of fools who wouldn't listen to his wisdom. I, too, wouldn't give him what he deserved. I didn't wash the dishes enough, or not properly. I ate dinner without waiting for him. I was a dreamer. 'Life isn't all about books, princess,' J took to saying every time he found me reading or writing.

I suspected that, in part, J's agitation stemmed from the fact that he was no longer enjoying the sexual liberties I'd allowed him, particularly now that I'd begun encouraging his occasional visits to Grey Street girls or men's saunas. My motivation was no longer voyeuristic: rather, I wanted to be alone, to finish my novel. However, the more lenient I became, the less J wanted to go out or, rather, he didn't want to go out alone. He took to singing in my ears the virtues of a handsome Israeli tourist who now did the work Tzadik had done. During sex, he'd whisper in my ears his plans for the tourist's seduction by us.

Yet, although I still wore Esther's dresses—now because I had no money left to buy clothes and was too proud to ask J for any—I had no inclination to be her. I wasn't a man's pal. I wanted to be a princess who was fought over. When a boyish-looking girl asked me for a dance in a nightclub, and J pushed himself between us eagerly to act as a broker, I lost my nerve and punched him in the chest. I hoped he'd beg me for forgiveness. Sometimes he did.

Life continued to eat at J. In the mornings, I watched him do his push-ups, his nakedness glistening like oil, his undirected anger pumping through his veins, inflating his already large muscles. I decided I'd leave as soon as I got my work permit. Anyway I still hadn't unpacked my suitcase, in which I could never find what I needed but everything I didn't want was always accessible.

As the spring drew to its close, J's appetite flowered. Now that he was clear I wasn't going to turn into Esther, he began indulging in a different voyeurism, which hurt me to the bone. In public spaces, he'd evaluate any attractive summery women, with their bright eyes, naked skin, heat-cracked lips; he'd raise his eyebrows and stretch his words like toffee—'Look at thaaaat, *neshama*'—and something in me would violently crash.

We farewelled the end of the year in Natasha's place in the Russian way, with herring, toasts of vodka and poetry recitations—all those things J didn't understand. Still, he seemed content that night, as he kept relating the history of his economic success in Australia to Natasha's sister, who wore her long hair up in a thick bundle and her lips starkly red. For the entire party, J hardly glanced in my direction, and as we said our goodbyes, I saw him kiss the sister's hand.

J had the looks, I had the scars. He had the money and I didn't. Still, I'd never been that easy to purchase, I thought furiously on our way home. Once we got to our apartment, I fastened my suitcase. I had no idea where to go, but it didn't matter. I told J that was it.

'Please don't go! I'm sorry. I don't deserve you! Let me make it up to you, let me …' J's voice escalated nervously, yet excitedly. In retrospect, as much as he thrived on my missteps, he seemed to thrive even more on his own. Despite all his complaints about me, I probably gave him exactly what he wanted, since J's favourite way of apologising was between the sheets. There, I had full rein to design any punishment.

So, once again, I put my suitcase down for a man. I lacked a plan, and means, for leaving. Besides, I was then arrogant and naive enough still to believe I could tame J. My thing was never trailing bad boys, but conquering them. I now know that when I told J I loved him, what I really loved was how undone he could become at my will. I still like that audacity of my younger self. But the price I paid turned out to be higher than I expected. I was coming undone too; from that night on, I ate less and kept coughing more. Writing remained my anchor. I was revising the novel's end, where my protagonist realises that the story's bad boy is her soulmate and they get together, happy ever after.

The more unsettled we felt, the more we travelled to the countryside, driving for days through the ghost-grey bush, occasionally set on fire by flames of galahs, to the melancholy soundtrack of ballads about love not working, which J had now substituted for Yitzhak's sermons. We'd stop to make love in the privacy of dirt roads, among the dense, humid foliage and its blue shadows tangled with spider webs. The country flies, fat and suicidal, kept smashing across our windscreen. The rows of gum trees disoriented me with their Escher-like repetitions. I had a tacit hope the bush would smooth us out. It's hard to believe now, but at the time I was so gripped by a yearning for a stable life that, in between my fantasies of escape, I still sometimes imagined a happy ending for us.

When the ballads, trees and flies all got too much, I'd ask J for more stories about Esther. What kind of love was it? Did they touch each other when they picked up strangers? What did the two of them do when they were alone? I was really trying to find out what the future held for me. One day, after we stopped near a pier with a restaurant at its edge, J told me that, before they left Israel, Esther had done a stint with an escort agency for some months.

The ocean around us lay so still that it resembled a carpet; Matisse-pink brushstrokes smudged the evening sky. The sun turned swollen, turbid, low enough to crash into the water, but I kept my sunglasses on, as a shield.

'Really?' I feigned neutrality, but here it was—the first time I really, intensely, didn't want J to continue a story. It wasn't that I couldn't understand such a choice. It was that I could clearly picture J's thrill at it. It was that I didn't want to kiss a pimp.

'She worked in luxury hotels. I always waited for her in the car, to make sure she was okay …' J sounded sheepish, possibly noticing my distress. I imagined him, waiting, with that glint in his sapphire eyes I knew all too well. The image made me sick.

'It was good money,' J said.

I asked whether he thought it'd been difficult for Esther to do that job.

'Maybe … Sometimes. But I think she mostly enjoyed it.'

'Or *you* did!' I said, more fiercely than I'd wanted to.

That night, we stayed in a lovely eighteenth-century-themed cottage, with antique furniture and a hearth. The autumn was advancing outside our windows, where large, wet leaves hung; inside, firewood crackled. I lay down on the four-poster bed with my clothes on, feeling relentlessly fatigued. I wanted to go back to Melbourne: I needed the comfort of home, or something I could try to call home. But I no longer believed J could stop moving. My desire to become his oasis, his saviour, to contain him, was no longer there either.

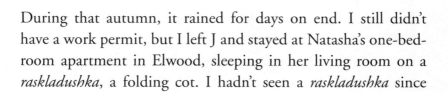

During that autumn, it rained for days on end. I still didn't have a work permit, but I left J and stayed at Natasha's one-bedroom apartment in Elwood, sleeping in her living room on a *raskladushka*, a folding cot. I hadn't seen a *raskladushka* since

I'd left Russia, where it was an essential piece of furniture. Most apartments in major Soviet cities were partitioned to allocate one room per family, often composed of three generations. Although my family escaped the 'shared apartment' fate, our flat was small too and we used a folding cot. I came to associate the *raskladushka* with forced proximity to others' intimate sounds and scents, with an accompanying loss of dignity. I had thought *raskladushkas* expired with communism, but here one was, and it stood for my new freedom or, rather, it sank under me.

Natasha was a dancer. Her mind, too, moved constantly, as if attempting to catch up with the rest of her body. Like J, she was at war with her thoughts and, to stop them, Natasha spoke to the universe on a regular basis. To deprive her mind of stimulation, she painted her flat white, furnished it sparsely and avoided spicy food. Around ten pm, Natasha would bind her curls into a tight plait, as if to ambush her brain, and all the lights would go off. I had to be quiet and keep my nightly toilet trips to a minimum. Still, even then, Natasha's mind would race on.

But I was a night owl. Sunk on the *raskladushka*, I'd read, with a torch under the blanket, fat nineteenth-century novels while the rain hammered the windows, trying to fall asleep. The rain's potent flow, accompanied by lightning and thunder, reminded me of the Odessa of my childhood, where the rain had a similar force. In Odessa, I was often confined to my sickbed, waiting for the rain's arrival. For some odd reason, I believed in its magical power. When it did come, I'd close my eyes and focus on the rhythm, to ease my pain.

Melbourne's rain was more a beautician than a nurse. It rendered the city marvellous, smoothing its fidgety electronic advertisements, filling the streets with myriad reflecting surfaces. I walked the wet streets in search of cash-in-hand work. Yet, as J had noted, I was too much of a princess for my own good. Every time a prospective employer placed a metaphorical pea under my mattress, I got found out. I was no good at stitching sheepskin slippers, or as a deli kitchen hand, or as a waitress in a busy Italian restaurant. The deli owner never paid me my wage, but the Italian boss took pity on me and offered me work as a hostess instead. For an hourly rate of eight dollars, I tried to smile at people rushing towards me through the thick sheets of water. 'Would you like to look at the menu?' I mumbled, blushing faintly. Still the old Italian wouldn't fire me. It was I who resigned a week later. J, who kept shepherding me from afar, found me a job in a burger shop that belonged to an acquaintance of his. I was paid ten dollars an hour now.

J framed my move to Natasha's as a sound, yet temporary, solution, since at home the toilet and bathroom, like the kitchen, had gone in the cloud of dust. J thought a hotel stay during the renovation a waste of money; he camped in the living room in a sleeping bag. 'A princess like you wouldn't manage in such conditions. It's better, *neshama*, you stay with your friend until I fix the place,' he'd said the night after I left, as if my leaving was his idea. He'd waited for me by Natasha's building. He wanted to talk, he said, but refused to listen to what I had to say.

A princess wouldn't manage, but a Swedish tourist and her little daughter did. In our later meetings near Natasha's building, J informed me they'd brought their sleeping bags into *our* apartment, blaming me for this new entanglement. If only I'd stayed … Natasha blamed me too, for taking J's phone calls. For meeting him. I was spineless, she said. The work permit, which was due any day now, still wouldn't come. The *raskladushka* kept sinking under my spineless back. During one work shift, I placed a dish wrapped in foil in the microwave and killed the appliance. There were a few hundred dollars, which I didn't have, to pay to the owner. There were utility bills to share with Natasha. My newly found freedom by now felt like a prison. The next time J called, he told me the Swedish tourist was gone and so was the dust. The renovations were over. He'd tiled the bathroom in charcoal marble and painted the walls green and purple, according to my wishes. I packed my suitcase, left whatever money I had for Natasha and went downstairs.

We were settled again, in a freshly renovated apartment. To please me further, J purchased another new piece of furniture (of course, bought on special): a large couch on which we could just fit beside our bear. Lured by these domestic comforts, I baked potato bread and re-scattered my art books over our hideous coffee table. We spent the nights quietly now, drinking wine and watching Tarantino movies. I was kind of okay, playing at having a home more than at having love, but J thought this was happiness. To demonstrate his commitment to art and to me, he bought Chagall's print depicting the dangerous bride. I chose the painting in a print shop in Carlton; it appealed to me how alone and in control the naked woman seemed. That night, after J fell asleep, I wrote in my diary: 'I'm so miserable and still my email password is happiness. What will become of me?' Soon after, my work permit arrived.

Within a week, I'd found my first proper job in Australia—managing a fundraising campaign for environmental work in Israel and Australia. The salary was modest, but at the time it struck me as a fortune. I could finally get a credit card and a mobile phone, and resume existing in my own right. I even had a little office now, the first space I'd been able to call my own since I'd come to Australia. I stayed there until late, planning the campaign, restoring myself.

Most of the volunteers I inherited with the job were Holocaust survivors who had done well in Australia and lived with vitality. They preferred to talk to me about their grandchildren than about their past, but still it lurked in their agile, furrowed faces and in the songs they'd often hum in languages I didn't understand. I related to them more than to their offspring, who would occasionally race through our office, laden with jewellery and daily hassles, dropping donations or wheeling their parents away in their four-wheel drives. But the grandchildren, whom I chased for more help and who eventually also began arriving in merry, gaudy flocks, were charmers like their *bubas* and *zeidas*. They seemed sweeter and calmer than their Israeli peers. I loved the flurry of laughter and freshness those kids brought into my office. Once we'd finished our duties, we'd talk about truly urgent matters: what was a life worth living; how low you could wear your pants before getting into trouble at school; love. The normality of my life at work stunned me. I didn't want to go home to J any longer.

Thanks to my new job, I now lived steeped in English. This language and its country were altering me. In Israel, I'd always policed my tongue, trying not to roll it with the treacherous Russian '*rrrrr*', afraid of exposing myself as a fraud while trying to pass for a local. Australia liberated me of pretence. Here, foreigners were tolerated better and, anyway, no effort would eliminate my accent when I spoke in English. For that, I was too old.

I also found English a language of dreams, fog, romance. Speaking it softened me, slowed me down. I liked myself better when I spoke English, even if I often failed at it. Now that I'd finally sent my novel off to my Israeli publisher, I began dreaming of doing what everyone told me I couldn't—writing in English. I became a member of a writers' centre and began attending a local writers' group, even though I often struggled to understand what was said there. I wrote in my diary:

> I'm learning to do what I really want. I surround myself with yellow, eat meat—even in the mornings—read what I want rather than what's supposed to be 'good' for me, try writing in English. Does this mean I'll soon find a man I really want?

J, who never fitted into any organisation anywhere, observed these developments with interest, even awe. The problem was, the changes I was making were weakening his argument that I was a dreamer who wouldn't survive in Australia without him. To help resolve this confusion, he began seeing some Israeli woman he called *a friend*. I wasn't sure whether they were fucking, but they were certainly discussing me in detail. J shared this fact with me eagerly, since the woman in question apparently shared his opinions of me. This verbal betrayal pained me more than the possibility they were having sex.

Asymmetrical non-monogamy can happen even when both lovers wish to maintain sexual freedom. I was still interested in abundant love, but no longer believed J was the man to live it out with. We had different aims. J's own non-monogamous dreaming appeared to be driven not by the desire for abundance, but by some lack. Yet I, too, began acting out of motives that had nothing to do with pleasure. Now that J had this new 'friend', I decided to have my own affair—with a young Russian man we both knew—for revenge. One night, I came home after seeing that man and wrote in my diary: 'I seem to have Nin's ability to jump from one bed to another, but now I also understand her complaints about how exhausting this can be.' Of course, where there is more purposefulness than pleasure, fatigue sets in fast. And I achieved my purpose. J was jealous. He, too, apparently, had his limits. What he wanted was comradely non-monogamy that involved strangers, like he had with Esther, nothing else.

Ironically, by becoming J's major source of misery, the depository of his anxiety, I unwittingly came to be even more indispensable to him. But for myself, I was now done with the 'badness experiment' and wanted to qualify Rimbaud's instructions for writers. Although I still believed writers need to live in order to write, I was no longer sure that they require *all* the poisons. Excessive living could sap creative energy.

J's obese French friend invited us to celebrate his just-found bride, by drinking Bloody Marys at a bar he'd purchased. Out of boredom, I laughed at all his tedious jokes. Back home, J became furious: I was a flirt. He smashed my jewellery bag. As I watched my silver rings, and pieces from the necklace my mother had given me before I left for Australia, rolling around the floor, dread cut through me. What would J break next? I locked myself in the bedroom, relieved to hear the door slam, then J's footsteps on the stairs.

My new colleagues nicknamed me *Kof*, not so much because of my surname as because of my now-perpetual cough. These days, I was constantly having arguments with J in my head and, at least, there I always had the upper hand. I began looking for a room to rent, since, with my new salary, I could afford something very modest. Still scared of driving on the left side of the road, after work I'd ride trams to inspect places with musty carpets and similarly musty prospective housemates. This wandering went on and on. I couldn't bring myself to make the final move and not just because the places I saw depressed me. Not knowing how to be alone, particularly in this country, somewhere, deep down, I still tried to believe there was a happy ending in store for us. I told J that, for our sake, he had to see a therapist. Reluctantly, he did. The therapist, a groomed middle-aged woman, told J on their second meeting to bring me along the next time. She looked at us doubtfully, as I cried so much in her office that I couldn't talk, then suggested we consider whether we should stay together. After that, J refused to see her again.

'*You* fix me,' he said, once again appealing to my fantasy of metamorphosis. Then, keen as ever to call on Eastern divinities for help, J attended some chanting classes. But no chunky Buddhas could stop Noah, my paradoxical knight with pacifist convictions, from coming. In fact, I invited him along.

A silver-cool evening stretched its arthritic limbs into our windows. J wanted to go to a party somebody he knew was putting on. I said I wasn't up for it. J looked at me coldly: 'What will we do at home then … fuck again?'

Words, and the hurricanes they create. The injury felt somehow pleasant, like the salty taste of a split lip. *What will we do … fuck again?* For some reason, that single phrase rendered the absurdness of my situation more vividly than any of J's actions did. The world was stirring outside, dense, bottomless. There was so much to take in and I wasn't prepared to be responsible for J's boredom any longer. I wore Esther's blue dress, hoping to borrow its boldness. I made a pledge to myself—I'd give my mobile number to the first single man I met at the party.

I walked into the backyard, which was lit by an open fire, keeping my distance from J. We weren't speaking. He went inside the house, where, ironically, his then-favourite song, 'I'm Outta Love', was booming. I stayed outside, warming myself against the flames. Noah offered me a cigarette. Several days later, he called my mobile. The ring had the sound of salvation.

One of the dangers couples who bring in a third party face is that the newcomer could overtake their intimate space. But ours wasn't a tale of misplaced focus, but of mismatched intentions. Noah was a stranger and so, at first, J didn't mind our dates, thinking I was finally following in Esther's footsteps. He stuck to his old script, trying to write Noah into *our* story. He wanted to know what we did together. How we touched. But I kept silent. It didn't take him long to realise that Noah was going to be *mine*, not ours; that Noah was my final proof I wasn't Esther.

My relationships hardly ever ended in a clear-cut way. They wouldn't simply go, but danced themselves away in tango steps, swaying forward and backward, backward and forward. J saw how well Noah fitted into my new life and pulled his strongest card. 'You know you're in a fragile position,' he said, referring to my residency, which still hadn't been finalised. 'It's enough if any suspect report reaches immigration …' He wouldn't do such a nasty thing, of course. As long as Noah was out of the picture.

Without Noah, and with my job the only constant in my life, I distracted myself by writing. I wanted my next novel to be about J and Esther. But did I really understand either of them? One morning, J woke up at dawn, looking sombre. He put on his running gear and told me it was the anniversary of Esther's death. To commemorate her, he was going to wear himself down, circling Albert Park Lake. His eyes were clouded as he spoke. 'Describe their relationship without judging, without dividing them neatly into the "victim" and "perpetrator",' I instructed myself in my notes for my novel after J left. What really happened between them in the months, and years, before Esther tripped and flew down? If I couldn't find out in real life, I could at least imagine it in fiction. But that morning, in my study, I was unable to write. My mind was already turned away from *them*, towards Noah.

J was taking another risk. Or, rather, risk was seizing him by his muscled wings, animating them into flight. He bought a ticket to Israel. It'd be a short trip, J said. To visit his parents. I didn't call Noah after J's departure. I was exhausted; I needed solitude to gather strength to take my own risk. The flat where I hurriedly subleased a room was in an art deco building. The living room overlooked a large park heaving with dogs and runners. My roommate managed a fancy hotel at night and spent his days in shopping centres. Sometimes he cooked the kind of dinners for his friends that you see on television cooking shows, with sumptuous arrangements of mussels, bean sprouts, cherry tomatoes. We seldom crossed paths and even then we'd struggle to find words to explain ourselves to each other. Despite that, we lived in a contented peace. Until J returned to his now-empty-of-me apartment.

To write about that final year I spent in J's shadow, which began with a pounding in my chest when I left my workplace one day and spotted J waiting nearby, the rage grazing his face, is as tedious as any account of a prolonged drama can be. To write about that year is to write about J's calls to Noah, Noah's smashed car, a note dropped in my letterbox that was handwritten by yet another of J's women trapped in his honey ('Go back to him. I know he loves you'). To write about that year is to write about J always lurking, calling and calling, peeping into my apartment when he thought I had a man there (which sometimes I did) and about my persistent fear of J acting on his threats; and his body in my bed, clothed because I said so, and, when I felt particularly threatened or lonely, my body in the bed that was once ours, and about how sometimes we'd pretend we were back together again, for real.

To write about that year is to write about that endless push-and-pull between us, when J would pick me up from my place, then drop me back. When he'd say he loved me, then curse me. *You bloody princess. You used me. You wanted my money. You're the best thing that happened to me. Or the worst. I won't get out of bed if you go. I'll kill myself. I have all these women, I don't need you. Go. Don't go. I want you. I don't want you. But I want you.*

I know how much J wanted not to want me. I, too, wanted him not to want me. But sometimes I wanted him to want me. Boy, I did … I confess: I also had a hard time letting him go. It is possible to understand people's life choices better when you consider what they are prepared, or not, to tolerate. I had zero tolerance for being unloved, even under-loved, but plenty for being loved, even obsessively, even by men who weren't good for me. J's love wounded me but, at the same time and for a long while, it kept me intact. Yet, what initially attracted me to J, how ripe-heavy he was with visceral, grim discontent, no longer appealed to me. From the very start of us being together, a part of me had known there would be an *after*, and that in that after, there would be no more men like J. At the time, that understanding rendered J even more desirable, until I came to see him as rotten, rather than ripe. During our last year, his smell, which once I'd loved, felt to me like a mixture of farts and fish, like all the bitterness he had inside him. I felt revolted, and would cough and cough, would stay back even later at work. Every man-free weekend I had, I'd rent a stack of art-house films and for the hours that the movies played, I'd be happy at last.

In the blur of that last year with J, one evening stands apart. He came to pick me up from work, and we were walking among the rattle of trams and schoolchildren when he said, 'I can't believe we walk like strangers now. That I don't hold your hand.' The memory of our early days, when J used to walk with his hands in his pockets, when I pined for him, hit me then. I felt J's pining, so close that it hurt, but *my* hands were now tucked firmly in my pockets, grounding me so that my step felt steadier than it had been in a long, long time.

The last time I saw J was just before he took his delayed but inevitable one-way flight to Israel. He was selling his properties and tidying up other affairs. I, by then, had left the apartment near the park and been hiding in Noah's place for six months. I still made sure I answered J's, now-less-frequent, phone calls. He knew I was living with someone, and even came to accept it, as long as he believed it wasn't Noah, the man who, in his view, had robbed him of his woman. J wouldn't let go of that account. But he let go of Australia at last. Now he asked me to come and say goodbye.

With a sense of hollow dread, I walked up the familiar flight of stairs. I mostly feared the 'goodbye business' might be a hoax. I made myself unattractive that day, wearing old sneakers and shapeless corduroy pants. Still, as always, J watched me with appreciation and I couldn't help but appreciate him back, just a little. He had lost his potbelly and was again as slim as when we had first met. His blue eyes still bubbled like champagne.

'Why are you going?' I asked, perched on a bar stool in the living room, which was now empty but for some paintings still hanging on the wall. J shrugged his shoulders, saying that now I was gone, there was nothing for him here in Australia.

'But the business?'

He'd do just as well in Israel. The country was booming again, J said, with what seemed to me wishful thinking. We tried some more talk that wasn't about *us*. As always with J, there was some woman around, and she was going back with him. Apparently, he struggled to fall asleep beside her but, at least, unlike me, she was right into business. And I? Was I happy? I tried to look unhappy, which—being at J's—wasn't difficult.

'We had some good times together, didn't we?' J forced a smile. I stared down at my ugly sneakers, dying to get away. But I could see he still wanted to talk.

'Listen,' he finally pushed the words through—language never came easily to J, unless it added up to jokes, business talk or sex talk. 'I did learn my lesson with you.' He'd never let his women be with other men again. 'It never ends well,' he said, staring at me tensely.

It was my turn to shrug. I was uncertain how I felt about what he'd just said. I'd never wanted to 'normalise' him, just make him bearable. The only thing I was certain about now was that I wanted to get out of there as soon as possible. I said I'd better go.

'Hey, Lubochka,' J said, even more hesitantly, when I was at the door. 'You like this painting, don't you?' At that, J, who hated giving anything away if there were nothing to gain in return, seemed very uncomfortable. He handed me Chagall's picture of the dangerous bride.

Shocked by this final gesture, I pecked J's cheek awkwardly, as if we'd never been lovers. Then, with the weighty painting in my hands, I flew down the stairs.

I never told Noah where the dangerous bride came from.

Israel didn't prove kind to J. Business problems had awaited him there, or so I heard in the years to come. Perhaps, eventually, he found a happy ending, I don't know. Anyhow, my interest lay more in J's past than his present. For years, I kept working on, and failing at, that novel. I made more notes: 'J the OCD sufferer, the angry lover, the self-destructive man who was always heading towards the abyss—like the Indian birds.'

Such notes, though, ended up being more plentiful than my fictional attempts to capture his story. I wrote them in the early years after J's return to Israel, when I was still gripped by occasional fury. Sometime before I gave up on the novel and went to Perth, I rethought my account of J. I recalled his father, who visited us once and couldn't talk about much except for money. And J's mother, who came here too, terrifying us both. And even how, when we watched movies, J would sympathise equally with the bad and good guys. I recalled our country travels too, and that J often ruffled my hair and talked sweetly, heartily, about his love for me. I revised my notes: 'This is a story of a deeply troubled man, a grief-and-guilt-stricken man who cannot handle his own company, who had forgotten, or maybe never knew, where he belongs.' I felt proud of my newfound compassion, yet no novel ever came from it.

And now, here, I must give J his due. After all, he *was* indispensable to me. The truth is, J was a comet that has crossed the landscape of my life, leaving in it the deep tracks where the art dwells. Eventually, his fire did write itself into my short fiction. Then into here. Oh, J, I thought it was your woman I was after, but it was you who was my real muse.

12

A Tale of Porous Couples

'Don't make love with anybody, if you can help it. Only if you find a real F.W. (Fucking Wonder), but don't love her.'
Frida Kahlo's letter to her lover Nickolas Muray

While my marriage was unravelling, so was Melbourne. That summer, interest and rental rates soared and hung, suspended, above our cityscape, like menacing hot air balloons. Vacancies diminished. Families were losing their houses, students went homeless. Real estate agents grew more royally dignified and unapproachable by the day. Newspapers told the story of two friends who refused to dispose of their dogs to improve their chances of renting a home, and were now living in their car. Next to all that misery, I felt unentitled to self-pity. I kept scanning *Domain.com* and driving through a Melbourne that was blazing with summer. My car door wouldn't close, the air conditioner didn't work and I no longer had a husband to help me with such things. The property inspections were filled with dozens of other sweaty, dazed people, pushing through each other like dancers at rave parties.

My rental applications were rejected. Night after night, I came home and snuck into the bedroom past Noah, who, in a furious silence occasionally punctuated by shouting, watched television on the couch, where he also now slept. His pain coupled with mine and, once the bedroom door was shut, I'd cry myself to sleep. I began to believe I'd never leave, that my life would become a succession of days spent in futile property inspections and nights spent in mourning. To lift the curse, I started packing—just in case. I collected greasy boxes from grocery shops, stuffing them with my new underwear, books, and all those other things I'd always accumulated when I felt happy. There were also the bookcases to take and the large writing desk; those objects that had once liberated my mind but now imprisoned Noah and me together. I hoped to find a place to accommodate all this stuff, so as to preserve some remnants of the life I was leaving. I was a pawn, after all. I couldn't go backward. But the boxes kept falling apart and I kept repacking them.

I emailed a friend:

> Tomorrow I'm giving a writing workshop on my favourite topic, the writer's voice, and I haven't even finished preparing. And I'm writing to you sitting amongst half-packed boxes. And I don't even know where I'll be going ... If I'll be going ...

But in that workshop, in the company of people who also needed an oasis made of words, I forgot the husband I was letting down, the boxes, the inspections. I forsook my dishevelled self to speak of the shamanic beat in the sentences of Marguerite Duras. I urged everyone to write about the world as they saw it, rather than how it was supposed to be. After all, the sun wasn't always yellow, children innocent, the sky blue. After the workshop, my step felt lighter; my face was hot, cleansed. Sometimes writing felt like religion. Sometimes I thought I wasn't that different from my parents.

I couldn't face going home yet and went to my local café. Near my table, a young woman with luxurious, long honey-coloured hair, and glasses framed in red plastic, spoke loud Hebrew to a blonde man who was handsome in that wholesome Aryan way. She must have thought no one else could understand her, as her teary voice soared up and up: 'My life is so rich, so many things happen to me, but I can't share anything with you. I feel alone ...'

The young woman's companion sat very still, clasping his hands until their knuckles turned white while she kept on with her monologue or, rather, an ancient female lament meant for any man anywhere: 'You don't know what's going on in my head, you don't understand me.' Tears were rolling down her skinny face, against the man's silence. Perhaps she hoped that the mere sound of her voice would bridge the gap between them. Perhaps, I thought as I walked home, this business of leaving, then again becoming a newcomer into what was just another country of love, was a futile enterprise that always brought you to the same end point. Perhaps the happy ending I kept seeking didn't exist for couples. The only happiness I'd glimpsed so far belonged to the polyamorists.

Noah took pity on me and brought home boxes, neat and carefully folded, from his workplace. In many ways, he was better than I was at loving. I saw this gesture also as an indication that he, too, was feeling we were no longer good for each other. Still, as I kept packing, he'd come in sometimes, furrowing his thick eyebrows as he always did when he was angry, to remind me how I didn't try hard enough. He went away and came back and went away again, with doors opening and slamming shut.

And maybe I'd been a lazy wife, hadn't tried enough. These doubts broke some internal dam where rivers of guilt were stored, darker even than loneliness. The possibility that I hadn't done something that would have helped us stay together was unbearable. Tears now flowed out of me continuously as I kept searching for apartments I didn't get, borrowed books on bodies and selves for the PhD I couldn't focus on, and planned classes I was too distressed to teach.

Luckily, life kept intruding, parting the Red Sea of my misery and creating small passages of sanity. Poetry performances were scheduled, work contracts signed. I had to do a mock teaching session to secure another university job and my set topic was the social construction of death. In preparation, I re-read the brave new theorists who pulled their noses in dismay at how removed from the everyday, and tucked away into hospitals, death had become. They all thought India, where corpses lay in public view, was exemplary in this regard, suggesting life there was more honest and therefore better. Seeing death was supposed to help people to stay connected. But to what exactly and for what purpose? And didn't we all rely on some degree of denial to deal with our mortality, be this belief in gods, or excessive academic workloads that didn't leave the scholars of death any time to imagine the terror of nothingness?

I wondered what these academics would have made of the Soviet hospitals, where death was laid bare even in children's wards. I recalled the rooms I was in, each holding ten or so beds. The turnover was high and—in our cardiology ward, at least—the discharge was as frequently to a cemetery as to home. As an eight-year-old, I was already clear on how easily my bed could become the next empty one. I don't think that experience made me a better person. Rather, the dread of annihilation had never really deserted me. As an adult, I atempted to cope with it through love (or what I fancied to be love), trying to save myself in another's warm body. Now that I'd lost that panacea, I felt myself drifting back into Dylan Thomas's raging against the dying of the light. Yet, desperate for work, I waved my finger sternly at Western attitudes to death during the teaching session. I must have been convincing, because I got the job.

Valentine's Day was advancing, with its artillery of heart-shaped cushions and roses wrapped in plastic, along with the day's usual troops of allies and critics. Despite the obscene commercialisation, I've always sided with the allies. A holiday that, instead of gods, queens or horses, took on the so-often-bad-mouthed romantic love was just my kind of celebration. But this year, the festive spirit bypassed me as I kept moving through Melbourne, searching for a place to rent. Finally, a real estate agent judged me worthy of a barely affordable one-bedroom unit in Cheltenham. The little place, nestled among fruit trees, seemed to be a luxury, particularly as I'd never lived without a partner or at least a housemate. But, rather than feeling relieved, I kept weeping as I drove to the office to sign the lease.

I signed the paperwork that the agent, a large woman, handed to me, and pulled out a bundle of cash, then put it back in my handbag. The agent kept fiddling with her computer, her face clouded with curls. 'I'm so sorry …' I croaked. 'I've changed my mind.'

The woman tore up the lease. 'So why did you come, to waste my time?' I had no satisfactory answer for her, or for myself, particularly given that I felt no relief after I left the office. I asked Noah to meet me near his workplace, in a shopping centre full of people buying presents for their beloveds. I told him I wanted to stay. But even as we embraced at my news, we did so tentatively. Noah's body felt tense.

The next day, as I began unpacking the boxes, I found a copy of my wedding speech. I re-read it, shocked to discover that J was there, written all over my marriage.

> I first met Noah at a party where neither of us wanted to be. In my case, it was my then-partner who had insisted we go. I was so angry at him that I swore to give my phone number to the first man I'd meet. As I stood outside by the fire, a stranger offered me a cigarette. We started talking about the Margaret Atwood novel I was then reading. Afraid that my partner might walk in anytime, I soon offered the man my phone number. The stranger, who of course was Noah, seemed quite overwhelmed by my initiative. I guess he related this to our cultural differences, or—less politely—to that famous Israeli *chutzpah*. Still, he called me and a week later I received a gift from him—not flowers or chocolates, but Atwood's latest novel. I knew then I'd met

my man. But, as you'd know, our love didn't proceed that smoothly all the way through. We had two weeks of some peace together before the troubles with my then-partner began. On this happy day I'm not going to give the entire account of what happened. I just want everyone to know what a man I'm marrying. It is not accident he is dressed as a medieval knight today. I made a list of events from the first eighteen months of our courtship, but it sounds more like a second-rate Hollywood scenario. I'm not sure how many men would have stuck through such times. Among all else we had:
three break-ups
one car chase
one year apart
several love letters
six months of living together in secret.

But as the old Israeli saying goes—*if the end is good, then all is good …*

I put down the speech, my face burning at my own stupidity. I had thought I was writing our happy ever after, failing to notice that the end of us was already imprinted in our beginning …

Outside, a grand windstorm was brewing. The few pedestrians shook too, their hair flowing, their leashed dogs unsteady on their paws. Even the cars swayed as they drove past. The large tree under our windows looked, with its branches all moving in opposite directions, like a many-headed Hydra affected by Parkinson's disease. Only the city buildings stood still, outlined clearly against the sky. I thought how at different times of my life, I'd wanted to be either a city building or a swaying tree. I thought our marriage had been a good marriage, really. Perhaps it wasn't sexual because it wasn't meant to be. Perhaps our tale was not that of lovers, but of the saviour and the saved. And perhaps we needed to become each other's extended childhood.

No wonder I often spoke to Noah like he was a child and was demanding like a child, curling against his body as if I were a little girl. No wonder I took to calling him all those cute names. He had seemed to like that, although lately—when the cuteness had taken over almost everything else between us—he'd sometimes wanted to stop all that. Still, Noah kept pursing his lips at me like a boy and I kept curling against him.

In our good times, we'd played to our heart's content, helping each other to avoid the sin of earnestness. But now I'd gone as far as I could go with Noah, and maybe he had too. This time, when I said I'd continue looking for my own place, Noah seemed more sad than angry. He returned to the couch, and the tears and the silences returned, along with some shouts. But even they felt quieter now. I kept trudging through inspections, heavy with pockets of guilt under my skin.

Since I'd begun talking about my book to everyone, finding people to interview had become a little easier. Apparently, underneath the conservative veneer of Coupledom, desire was bubbling. I told myself I'd keep doing interviews just for the distraction, to get away from home and wait out the few weeks before the teaching semester started, but maybe some hope was still burning inside me. I was always a mad hoper.

'We threw out our contract,' David told me, his cleanly shaved head gleaming under a bare bulb in his recently bought double-storey old house, and my heart skipped a beat.

The unbearable irony of being kept diligently following me around ... It was in Caulfield—the suburb of family dinners and synagogues, the place I prided myself on escaping after quitting the fundraising job, and amid diapers, school satchels, renovation plans and silver Shabbat candlesticks—that I finally came closest to that elusive thing I'd been yearning for since I was seventeen: my own version of *Henry & June*.

I had felt surprised when Lora, David's wife, offered to help with the book. I'd known them both for years and would have never imagined them as fit subjects. We'd met when I was still working in Caulfield, and making my way through the tangle of J and Noah. Two years younger than me, Lora and David already had one child, a son. On the surface, they were my only friends who could be described as a 'good Jewish couple'. They'd met in a private school where they were both straight-A students, and had married at twenty, when no one else did. Now, between the two of them, they had several degrees, three children and two solid incomes. David worked as an accountant and Lora did something similarly obscure (from my point of view) in commerce.

Yet, under their tidy veneer, my friends were prone to abundance. The commitments of careers and parenthood didn't defeat or sedate them. They retained a youthful greed for self-reinvention, living through a series of metamorphoses. For a while, David ran a popular debate club and Lora worked in fashion. Later, they turned to God for self-expression. David wore a yarmulke on his bald head and Lora covered her dark wavy hair with a headscarf; they mastered Hebrew and Kabbalah. Once they found God's charm to have expired, Lora went back to wearing tight slacks that closely fitted her long, slim legs and David turned vegetarian. Most recently, Lora had become interested in Eastern divinities. She now spoke of auras in the same way she'd once spoken of the tree of life. David was planning to open a nightclub. Still, I'd never suspected they'd extend their experimentation to the area of love.

I'd arrived just after nine pm, when the children were supposed to be asleep. In reality, David was pacing around the room with their one-year-old beauty wrapped in some pink fluff, rocking her to sleep. The older boys were also around. 'Where is my dummy?' David asked Lora.

'I know where *my* dummy is, but not *yours*,' she fired back while sweeping the floor. Their boys, cringing at the parental joke, found the dummy and the baby dozed off. Once the children were settled in their bedrooms upstairs, the three of us sat around the dining table in awkward silence. Although we were friends, ours was a rather action-based friendship, made up of parties and outings together. David and I, particularly, weren't in the habit of sharing confidences. Now he hid behind his collection of flat-screened things with buttons I never understood. Lora sat stiff, her arms crossed. I noticed a bouquet of yellow roses on the table and, to break the silence, said it was beautiful.

'It's from David,' Lora stretched her lanky body coquettishly. 'We've just had our twelfth wedding anniversary.'

'That's a long time!' I said, stating the obvious.

David stopped fiddling with his electronic gadgets. 'We were kids when we met. Our idea of marriage was very different than it is now. Our marriage always continues to change. How is that, for a start?' He smiled, wrinkling his bright green eyes.

All I knew about those changes was that, three years before, David had moved out for several months, then again, more recently, when Lora was eight months pregnant with their daughter. Both times, he remained living close by and took care of the children.

Lora said: 'The first time we separated was when I started feeling we weren't developing any further as a couple. I felt like I was too dependent on David: on his interests, friends, his ideas about life. I was losing my identity. I never had female friends, because, since we'd been at school, we'd always been together. David also got dependent on me and my approval. I told him I needed to become more self-sufficient. He took it …'

'As a betrayal,' David said.

'He wanted a submissive wife who cooks and cleans. But I work as much as he does, and earn as much. So I said "Fuck it," and he decided that ... I don't love him anymore?' Lora looked at David, who said quietly, 'Fair enough.' That was when he decided to leave.

'As soon as I moved out,' David said, 'everything in our relationship got better.'

'Including the sex,' Lora interrupted and we laughed.

'We respected each other more, we loved each other more. But the fact that things were better once we separated felt to me like a sign that our relationship was wrong, like we couldn't live together. But, as they say, if it doesn't break you, it makes you stronger ...'

I suggested that perhaps their two separations fitted into their overall continuous search for better models of living, and they agreed with me. But for David especially, they were also about sexual inexperience: 'I was too young when I got married to be entering a monogamous relationship. But I was in love with Lora. I don't regret anything, but fifteen years later, I felt like I was missing out.'

When David moved out the first time, he leaped into the world of singledom with the same fervour he'd once had for God. But, like me, he was too romantic to seek pure pleasure. He needed sex to be bound up with an emotional connection. So the second time he left, instead of going for bar hook-ups, David opened profiles on dating websites.

'So while I was here, after having had a caesarean,' Lora said with great emphasis, 'David was dating other women ...'

For many couples, this would have been the end of their marriage, or the entry point to so much bitterness that if they stayed together, their relationship would be defined by it. But Lora and David were accustomed to complexity. Perhaps even more importantly, their shared sense of humour protected them.

'But I also looked after the boys fifty per cent of the time.' David put a hand on his wife's shoulder. 'And I even learned to cook!'

Lora smiled at him. 'The best thing was when I went to his place, he looked after me. I felt he really loved me, because instead of asking me, "Cook this, clean that," he was doing everything himself. He was caring.'

'What changed?' I asked David.

'Ah ... I was able to compare Lora with other women and she compared well.' He laughed in his lively way. 'Other women didn't satisfy me—sexually, emotionally.'

It seemed that for David and Lora, getting involved with others actually strengthened their relationship. At least Lora thought so: 'I'm grateful to my husband that he made the decision to marry me so early. I feel special because of that. And he has been a very good husband all these years. But because we met so early, I felt David didn't appreciate me as a woman.'

David needed the comparison. But was this all about his needs? During their separations, Lora still wanted to be David's part-time lover, as she put it, but without the wifely commitments: 'I'd go out with other men, but then sleep with him.'

I wasn't sure I believed her: 'You didn't have other lovers?'

David raised his eyebrows while Lora laughed joyfully. 'I'm not saying!'

The second time David moved out, it took them only months to figure out that their problem wasn't that they had fallen out of love with each other, but that their old ideas about what marriage was had changed. This was when, David told me, they threw out the contract: 'A friend said to me, "Go back to your marriage and rewrite the contract." And I thought, "Yeah!" But then I found out Lora had already taken the contract and thrown it in the bin ... Here I was, rewriting the contract, but for her there wasn't one!'

'I don't think people belong to each other,' Lora said. 'And it's normal to like other people. Otherwise you're too dependent on each other. But does it have to be sexual?' She asked this in the manner of a Talmud scholar, or—more appropriately for her nowadays—a Zen sage. 'Maybe ... for me, it's more about the purpose of the connection. If there is a purpose, it can be a sexual connection too.'

'I'm not actively looking for a relationship with another woman,' David said. 'But I'm not crossing out the idea. Non-monogamy is not out of need for me. It's out of want.'

I liked that distinction. This was how I had once felt, in the fetish club—the fun of want, before it turned into a need. 'Sometimes just knowing that you're permitted to do what you want can be enough ...' I said wistfully.

David liked the idea of 'permission': 'That's the main thing that changed for me. I had a duty, I felt, to avoid other relationships, and there were a few I regret I didn't act on. The idea that if now someone interesting came along I could do something makes me feel comfortable.'

'And how do *you* feel about it, Lora?'

'I feel all right. But if David had had relationships when he first wanted to, I probably wouldn't have been able to handle it. Now I can and this is the difference.' She yawned. I didn't want to go home but asked if I should. They wanted to continue talking.

'You wouldn't be jealous now?'

'No. When David moved out, I worried I may lose the person I love and the father to my kids, because I might do something wrong. But I wasn't jealous then, and not now, about him seeing other women. I'm confident in myself. I know I'll never lose him because of other women. *He* was always jealous and controlling.' Lora pointed a manicured finger at her now-embarrassed husband.

'I think jealousy is a natural self-defence mechanism,' David said in self-defence. 'It's an evolutionary device, like a warning to the system. It tells you there is a risk of losing someone. You can't have love without jealousy.'

'I disagree. I don't think if you love somebody, you need to be jealous. It's like, will I be jealous if someone else has a better house?' Lora said, positing a koan.

'It's different. Different consequences,' David said and Lora disagreed again. I could see this was a longstanding argument between them, but an invigorating one too.

'For some people, jealousy can be a visceral response …' I interjected. For a while now, the interview format had loosened up, slipping into the kind of friendly debate we'd often have. 'So how do you deal with jealousy now?' I asked David.

'There is always the risk when you don't have a contract,' David said. 'But I think most interesting things in life happen only when you take risks. And that's what monogamous relationships lack—the risk that keeps life interesting. Yes, we have something fantastic together and a great family we both want to preserve, but, at the same time, we have our individual lives and occasionally we want to take risks.'

'Do you give Lora permission to take risk if she wants?'

'It's not up to me to give her permission; that's what changed. It's her decision. I'd be jealous to know Lora is with someone else. But it's the sort of pain I'm now prepared to live through,' David said, and I thought that this was the closest to my own heart's standpoint on jealousy I'd heard so far.

Lora said: 'See, that's why I don't tell him whether I was with other men. Not because I'm scared, but because I don't want to hurt him.'

'But I want to be hurt! If you guard yourself from everything, you don't live,' said David, who had opened and closed several businesses, who rode red motorbikes. Once, on Lora's birthday, he sent a giftwrapped car to her workplace.

'It's not his business, my relationships.' Lora refilled his cup with fresh coffee.

'As you can see, on the information-sharing bit, we disagree.' David smiled theatrically. 'Lora doesn't want to tell me and doesn't want to know.'

'I hate when people talk about things like that, full stop. A sexual act is a spiritual experience. Once it becomes a topic of discussion, it's not a spiritual experience anymore. It's *an experience*.' Lora's stance resembled Noah's. The major difference was, she and David talked openly about not talking, whereas I never knew where I stood with Noah, and, recently, neither had he with me.

'I don't like secrets,' David argued back, rather affectionately. I was getting the impression they'd attained their wish of finding some separateness in their togetherness.

'But why do you see this as a secret? A secret is when you hide something, because you're afraid of punishment. All I'm saying is, I don't want to share this information.'

'I don't need privacy.' David turned to me now. 'I'd like to experiment together.'

'Lee, I can actually see him doing this in a group. But do you see *me* being a part of it?' Lora asked rhetorically. We'd talked many times about how we were both loners.

The younger boy came in. He'd had a bad dream and we all gave him hugs. David took him back upstairs. Upon his return, he said, 'I always wanted a threesome. It was supposed to be my thirtieth birthday present, but it probably won't even be for my fortieth …' I marvelled at how easily both David and Lora kept switching from being parents to lovers, and back. 'I bet I'll get my present at eighty, when I'm impotent.' David smiled mischievously.

'Well, that's your motivation to live to eighty!' Lora bantered back, as though they were still on the subject of the dummy. I watched them greedily. Seeing couples in love always made me feel hopeful. I wanted to linger here, bask in them. Perhaps I was better suited to be a third party in a relationship than a wife.

'It's wonderful how you talk to each other,' I said, with what I hoped didn't sound like envy. I could see their marriage wasn't an easy one, but then, whose was? At least David and Lora had found the courage to enter that shadowy marital territory that struck me not as 'open', but as 'porous'. Porous materials absorb fluids, and allow their passage in and out while retaining their shape. This model—more muted and nuanced than other non-monogamous varieties I'd seen, where permission matters more than action, and where occasional rendezvous are supposed to seep through small openings in otherwise solid love—would have suited me, satisfied my old dream of love and freedom coexisting. Of course, retaining the relationship's shape is the ideal, not always the reality. As David said, risk is integral to porous relationships. But it is to impermeable love stories too; otherwise, why are divorce rates so high?

'Don't know if that's the word,' Noah emailed me, not long after I said I was leaving, 'but our views on love were polyamorous.' Yet, rather, they were, or could be, porous. In any case, it was too late for us now …

'It's taken us eighteen years to get there, and with a lot of pain …' David said. 'You establish your marriage as a separate entity and that entity doesn't change as quickly as people change. You can lose yourself in marriage. It took us a while to re-establish ourselves as individuals, then re-establish the marriage too. But, really, it's all about Lora … She is so sexy. This is what it really is!' At that, Lora wagged a finger at her husband, then held his hand.

A cuckoo clock struck a noisy eleven pm. I really didn't want to go, but Lora was still breastfeeding at night and needed sleep. My friends walked me out, entwined like lianas. I could sense the electricity running between them; it charged through me, too. That was the thing about Eros. Sometimes a mere conversation about what was possible sufficed. But it took so much skill and courage for lovers to master talking as two separate people without feeling like strangers. Noah and I had never managed that; at least, not with each other.

Two days before Valentine's Day, the removalists' truck arrived. All my love stories ended with such trucks, and the strong men with weathered, expressive faces who came along with them to carry away my books and frocks. The men would pretend not to notice my red eyes. They'd joke with me but never ask anything apart from travel directions, and would handle my stuff with care. I was always the one to move out into apartments that were always worse than the ones I left, unpacking my boxes quickly in a futile attempt to defeat the alienation I'd feel in the new places.

Now I moved among the removalists, grateful for their thoughtful silence, picking things up, cleaning up. Under my busy facade bubbled that familiar emotional cocktail of relief and of terror at the knowledge I wasn't anyone's beloved any longer. Finally, I locked the windows and walked out forever. The Chagall print of the dangerous bride—or perhaps she was really just a sad woman waiting for a groom who never arrived—I left behind. Noah had always loved that painting.

I drove to my new home, the only other rental apartment I'd managed to get. The secret of my success was that no one else wanted to live there. The building was set in the wilderness of West Footscray, crawling with vermin. I walked through the parking lot past a woman with a covered face, who was hanging flowery polyester sheets on the clothesline. Nearby, men with moustaches spoke loudly in a language I didn't understand. But I understood everything else—the empty McDonald's bags scattered outside the bins, a crookedly paved path leading to the entry of my apartment, the smell of burned oil wafting from the windows of my new neighbours. Poverty looked, smelled and felt the same, whether in Ashdod or Melbourne. As I ascended the staircase, I spotted a dead mouse.

I was un-married now. Un-done.

Interlude:
InLoveLikeACat

The name my parents gave me is 'Lyubov', which in Russian means love, and even though I have since changed my name twice, one cannot escape one's origins any more than one can escape history. Or one's parents, for that matter. Whatever I write always ends up being about love. Whatever I write ends up being about my mother too. Perhaps Freud was right and our love stories begin before we are even born. With our mothers. We love like they love, or against how they love, or to escape them, or to make them happy, or to drive them mad. In my case, all the options apply.

My love story might as well have been drafted first in the Siberia of the early nineteen seventies, when my mother dreamed one night of an older magician offering her my father, a reticent physicist whom she hardly knew at the time, as a gift from his hat. This happened, she would tell me years later, during the Jewish month of Kislev, which is known as the month of prophetic dreams. She didn't know this back then.

The next night—remember, this is a true story—in a Novosibirsk University dormitory, around a table greasy with spilled herring oil and *samogon* (home-made vodka), my mother's classmates celebrated her marriage to the awkward stranger who hadn't even proposed to her. She hadn't proposed to him either. Yet, there they were, sitting side by side that night, my young, handsome father, with fleshy lips and rotting teeth, and my mother, shyly covering her face with an azure scarf, like Rebecca did when she first met her Yitzhak. Some months later, they signed the official papers. But for my mother, the real wedding occurred in the dormitory. 'I was in love with your father at once, madly, like a cat,' she always told me. The cat was a Russian expression I didn't understand. What did the cat stand for? Was it like the English *bitch in heat*? But my mother was more romantic than that. Inlovelikeacat … whatever the words stood for, they conveyed the fierceness of her emotion.

My mother sees my father and at once she is inlovelikeacat. How could I ever compete with such a love story?

But true love didn't turn out to be a happy affair in our family or, at least, not until much later, when the last of my siblings left home, allowing our parents to be lovers again. For most of my life, I watched them struggle—against the Soviet regime, poverty, my childhood illnesses, two migrations, each other. My mother always called my father a prince, but he was an impoverished one. It became her duty to ensure his royal existence could continue, that he could keep solving his theoretical equations while fortified within the palace of his mind. My mother's hands had roughened from hard work. She acquired a labourer's habits, eating with an open mouth, picking her and our noses. My father, the prince, was revolted by these manners, even though he himself was not much in favour of showers. For that and many other reasons, my parents argued often. Still, my mother remained a romantic. 'When you fall in love, you just know it straight away, you have no doubts,' she repeated in my ear as I introduced her to my succession of men. I sneered at her, because I was weary of the superiority of her certainty and because I always had doubts. She was old-fashioned and I fancied myself fashionable. Or perhaps I was just scared of love.

At the risk of the story sounding contrived, I'll relate the events as they really happened. It is now two months since I left my marriage. I share my flat with at least two mice and countless cockroaches. My kitchen roof leaks. My neighbours party loudly and litter our shared stairwell with cigarette butts. Still, I am gloriously smug about the new woman I am becoming, a woman who, for the first time in her life, lives in a place that is hers alone. This new woman goes on a blind date, something she hardly ever did in her former life, which was mostly a chain of relationships.

My expectations are low. The sole facts I know about the man are that he is Jewish, a doctor and has a teenage son. None of these render him attractive in my eyes. Especially irritating is the thought that such a summary makes this man my mother's ideal. I go, though, on the recommendation of a friend who insists the man is somewhat left of centre. I have spoken to him briefly on the phone and I doubt what she says.

I walk into a little Israeli restaurant situated in East St Kilda. The smell of *shakshooka* hits my nostrils. Everything here is in the comfort zone that, these days, I need more than I used to. Everything, that is, except the lanky, graceful man with the youthful face, and thick curls touched by silver, who sits where we arranged to meet. He looks like a fox, I remember thinking, and then my brain takes a break. The Jewish doctor with a teenage son smiles at me and hits my heart.

He hits my heart.

Many times have I said to men 'I love you'. But I guess what I really meant was 'I want to fuck you,' or 'I love living with you,' or 'I care about you.' And always—'I love that you love me.' The thing is, when you fall in love in the way my mother meant, the words 'I love you' cease coming from the brain and become more difficult to pronounce because you feel them so fiercely.

He hasn't even spoken yet.

He hits my heart.

I am still not *madly* in love, like a cat. But very soon I will be. For the first time in my life, I'll take the leap and be the first one to fall into the love, to take the risk of loving with no return. For the first time, I will be aching with the anxiety I've always been at pains to avoid, and a part of me, deep down, already knows it. But for several months, I'll withhold the words while I'll feel them all the time—under my skin, in my bones.

My father is a shy man. He barely spoke to my mother before or during their mock wedding. But when my mother's friend, who knew about the dream and decided to arrange that wedding as another excuse for getting drunk, came to his room that evening and asked him, 'Will you come to marry Olga?', my father, who has always been chronically indecisive, simply said, 'Yes.' Much later, he'd reveal to my mother it was her splendidly warm laughter that made him do this. Once he'd heard her laugh, at the party where they first met, he was filled with an irreversible desire to follow her, like those dazed children who followed the Piper from Hamelin.

The man smiles at me. I see white teeth and something strangely familiar about his face. I follow the warmth of his smile. Perhaps our love stories begin with our fathers too.

Epilogue: A Tale of Elastic Love (2010–2012)

It is difficult to keep dismissing divinities when your own life is a web of divine serendipities. In September 2010, almost three years after I met Bianca and her cross-dressing boyfriend in Fremantle, I finally began writing her story. I was doing this in the Neverland of Sydney's Homebush, among deserted Olympic constructions. Daryl and I were staying there for a few weeks, while he spent his sabbatical at the Westmead Children's Hospital and I performed the tortured artist's role to perfection. Writing never came easily to me, but now my usual self-doubt grew worse as I kept trying, and failing, to capture the mood of that conversation and Bianca's complexity. After a week of writing that resulted in no more than two artless pages, an email appeared in my inbox and I briefly considered calling my mother to ask her what angel she'd sent my way.

This was the first time I'd heard from Bianca since the summer of our meeting. She wrote that recently she'd been thinking about my book, because her relationship with Kieran had been renegotiated. I emailed back, asking for more details. Apparently, they were still together and still living apart. Kieran had been having casual sex with men. As for Bianca, not long after our interview, the difficult African–American lover she'd had before meeting Kieran had reappeared, wanting her back. Bianca had told him this time they'd be together on her terms; he'd have to share her with Kieran. The man had reluctantly agreed. Shortly afterwards, he'd been diagnosed with cancer and Bianca had nursed him until he died.

The waves of Bianca's grief had only recently subsided. At the same time, Kieran's children had returned to Perth and he'd been busy with them. Bianca had decided that now it was her time to play. She went online and found that men lurked in abundance in the cyberspace. She had several lovers now. Hers weren't casual like Kieran's, but of the 'ongoing' variety. But her life wasn't only about men. Bianca was also busy cycling around Fremantle, swimming through the ocean's seaweed tracks, reading cyberpunk novels; she took up boxing and had even begun to write. She didn't believe in fairytales, Bianca wrote, but lately her life was going really well. And what about me?

I wrote back:

Two months after I left my marriage, I met the love of my life. We're about to get married this summer, but like you I don't believe in fairytales. As much as we love each other, it's not always easy. This book I'm writing causes a lot of heartache.

I wasn't honest in the fairytale bit; I was just trying to preserve some dignity. I'd have loved to end my email, and this book, with that tale made famous by Doris Lessing, Germaine Greer and other strong, gifted women: *a woman finds a man, a woman loses herself in a man, a woman loses a man and finds herself.* But this is not my story. Because, as much as I'd like to, I don't believe in the afterlife, or in living the only life I have alone. Because, at heart, I am a princess and so I've always expected to meet the prince. But neither is mine a traditional fairytale of the *happily ever after* variety. There were times when writing this book has almost cost me my love, which is why I sat down to write Bianca's story three years down the track and kept struggling to write it.

Since meeting Daryl, I've committed myself to monogamy. My man, who is everything to me now, has no interest in abundance. Even buffet dinners are too much for him. This is not because he shies away from complexity; rather, he likes focusing on one complexity at a time, in depth, and, according to him, I, with my multitude of complexities, already confuse him. Clearly, a non-monogamous model wouldn't work in these circumstances.

So, I gave up my *Henry & June* dream and it actually hasn't been difficult so far. But it would be simplistic to conclude that love alone has solved the problem of my greed, that my past appetites were merely restlessness induced by unsuitable relationships. True love certainly makes fidelity easier. But I believe that if I hadn't lived messily before I met Daryl, hadn't wrestled with that mess, I'd most likely not have managed to preserve our love. And although I never found what I wanted in non-monogamy, the search itself satisfied some of my need. Monogamy now feels like a choice I've made, rather than an imperative.

Yet, my old romantic dream or, rather, what it stands for—risk, independence, lack of convention, havoc, adventure, curiosity, the sleaze of 'Relax', havoc again—has crept into our marriage in other ways. Writing this book has become a sublimation of sorts. The excitement of the unknown, the expression of my flirty, reckless side, even my attempts at beating mortality, have all been integral to the writing process. So, it's no wonder the book came to hang above us like a sword of Damocles.

I understand well Daryl's discomfort with all that writing time I've spent with the ghosts of my past. I am greedy for him too and whenever I feel I'm not at the centre of his attention, I suffer. But I didn't stop writing, and he didn't ask me to stop. The compromise we reached was porous in nature—I could write this story but not talk about it. Of course, practice always defeats theory. No matter how much we avoided the subject, every few months it would scrape us. Still, we'd come together again, for the beauty and urgency of us. Because my husband, at heart, is a prince, even if he doesn't like me to say so. He needs poetry, wine, roses and kisses the way I do. He is a romantic. When we are good, he is my *Henry & June*.

During the summer of my wedding, the emails between Bianca and me kept flying. I felt inspired again, because her personality—at once reckless and thoughtful, hard-edged and poetic—shone through her emails. Her story kept gaining shape. I noticed she was writing less and less about Kieran, and more about the dead man and her new, living, lovers. Some months after we began our correspondence, Bianca wrote that she'd left Kieran. In response, and with trepidation, I sent her the excerpt from my book where I'd expressed doubts about their relationship. Bianca wrote back: 'I think you got it about right.' Apparently, Kieran's lack of emotional expression always disturbed her. Now she had to rush off, she added, to see a man who was in the habit of giving her sudden bites on her nose while telling her he loved her to bits, just like her difficult, now dead, lover used to …

Contrary to the tragedy discourse, non-monogamous relationships don't necessarily end for reasons to do with (in)fidelity. Now that I've written this book, I can see more clearly that my relationships with J and Noah weren't ruined by our affairs. For me, it was, if anything, the lure of freedom these men offered me, each in his own way, that prolonged our time together.

Non-monogamous relationships don't necessarily end full stop, with research showing their survival rates are similar to those of monogamous ones. The stories of people I met seem to fit these findings. In the summer of 2012, I was invited to read from this book at a literary event with a theme of bisexuality and polyamory. In the audience, I spotted Anne, looking as pretty as she had four years before, when I first met her. She told me she and Peter were nearing two decades together. Recently, Nuo had been seriously ill, and Anne had spent a great deal of time on the coast, helping Peter to tend to her. I've lost touch with Karen, but David and Lora are together as they've always been, and still without a contract. Brad's monogamous relationship fell apart and, the last I heard from Ophelia, he was having a liaison with a married couple. Ronit is still alone. And Nina … Oh, Nina.

I still send her occasional emails to which she never responds. Perhaps some confessions should remain between strangers, even if one of them is a writer.

Non-monogamy still appears to be taboo, but I keep spotting signs that the zeitgeist is, slowly, subtly, shifting. Exceptions to the rule are becoming more common. The importance, and nature, of fidelity is being rethought by some—still in the minority, but notable—public thinkers. American author Susan Squire, for example, argues in her book about the history of marriage, *I Don't*, that a lasting, supportive union might be more valuable than a faithful one. In an interview for *New York Magazine*, she asks (reasonably, I think):

> Why does society consider it more moral [than being non-monogamous] for you to break up a marriage, go through a divorce, disrupt your children's lives … just to be able to fuck someone with whom the fucking is going to get just as boring as it was with the first person before long?

The renowned English editor Diana Athill, who has worked with the likes of Philip Roth, expresses a similar attitude in her memoir *Somewhere Towards the End*, suggesting we should broaden the concept of fidelity beyond its sexual meaning:

> Where spouses are concerned, it seems to me that kindness and consideration should be the key words … and sexual infidelity does not necessarily wipe them out. Fidelity in the sense of keeping one's word I respect, but I think it tiresome that it is tied so tightly in people's minds to the idea of sex …

Athill is writing from personal experience of having had happy relationships that accommodated other lovers. In Australia, the academic Liz Conor publicly critiques the idea of lifelong monogamy as the only relationship paradigm.

Artistic imagination, too, occasionally breaks away from tragic clichés in favour of a more complex exploration of non-monogamy. The French film *Happy Few* (later renamed *Four Lovers*), nominated in 2010 for the Golden Lion at the Venice Film Festival, tells the story of an involvement between two couples. Although the film's message seems to be that such relationships cannot be sustained for long, its protagonists are depicted sympathetically, as intelligent, decent people who love their children and spouses in a familiarly fierce and flawed way. There is nothing sinister or perverse about them and when, after much joy and heartbreak, the couples return to monogamy, it is unclear whether they're going to be happier this way.

The German film *Three*, which collected several awards and nominations, offers a truly striking take on non-monogamy. In it, such a relationship is the happy ending for two of our era's typical intimate models—a faithful couple and a promiscuous single man. Only after forming a triad relationship do they find happiness. Even more daringly, the filmmakers show the couple's years-long struggle to conceive ending successfully once the triad is formed and—in a clever filmmaking choice—the father's identity remains unclear. I was particularly excited to see it receive a spontaneous standing ovation at the sold-out screening at the Melbourne International Film Festival I attended.

Novelists are also reimagining non-monogamous love. The English writer Hanif Kureishi's *Something to Tell You* echoes the pagan belief in the restorative potential of group sex. There, a self-pitying theatre director rediscovers his joie de vivre upon meeting his beloved, who initiates him into orgies. Some Australian writers, too, have written positively about non-monogamy. Andrea Goldsmith, in *Reunion*, portrays non-judgementally a rather porous marriage; and Maria Pallotta-Chiarolli published a young adult novel, *Love You Two*, in which a teenage heroine comes to terms with the polyamorous marriage of her parents.

In the media, stories about non-monogamy are increasingly being featured. Popular American relationship columnist Dan Savage keeps urging his heterosexual readers to learn from gay men's relationships, which range widely on the spectrum between monogamy and rampant promiscuity. Some celebrities, Will Smith, Tilda Swinton, Monica Bellucci and Mo'Nique among them, have spoken publicly about their unconventional arrangements. And polyamorists are so inundated by interview requests that they recently established an international media training organisation, and, according to Australian academic Niko Antalffy, who analysed media representations of polyamory between 2006 and 2011, the coverage is becoming increasingly sympathetic. Generally, academic research on non-mongamy has been increasing over the last decade. *Understanding Non-monogamies*, by Meg Barker and Darren Langdridge, the first book to bring together such scholarship, was published at the end of 2009, followed in 2010 by Maria Pallotta-Chiarolli's study of polyamorous families, *Border Sexualities, Border Families in Schools*.

Australian polyamorous organisations are thriving, with more and more people showing up at their events. In 2011, for the first time, a polyamorous float joined the flotilla in Sydney's Gay and Lesbian Mardi Gras. The next item on the polyamorous agenda might be to follow the gay community in their fight for marriage rights, by lobbying for group marriage. In the long term, they'll probably succeed—already there have been legal advances. In 2011, in a milestone case in Canada, polyamorists successfully challenged anti-polygamy laws that potentially could criminalise their activities. In the same year, Australian magistrate Philip Burchardt refused to remove children from a triad household, noting he didn't regard the relationship as damaging to the children. In California, a foursome signed documents showing them to be legal spouses, whereas Barack Obama has appointed Chai Feldblum, known for her support for legal rights for polyamorous families, to the US Equal Employment Opportunity Commission.

In the therapy sector, so-called polyamory-friendly practitioners have emerged, and, in 2010, American psychologist Christopher Ryan and his psychiatrist wife Cacilda Jethá joined ranks with Esther Perel, suggesting in their study of human sexuality, *Sex at Dawn*, that non-monogamous relationships are a viable option.

The zeitgest might also be changing in the private sphere. In 2008, the UK ICM Poll revealed that one in five young Britons considered monogamy 'undesirable'. How representative these figures are is difficult to know, but curiosity about alternatives to monogamy seems to be high. Perel's *Mating in Captivity* has become an international bestseller, and there is a considerable market for books advising on polyamory (for example, *The Ethical Slut* has sold more than 100,000 copies in the US alone since its publication in 1997). When, in 2011, the comedian Sue-Ann Post and I spoke about non-monogamy at Brisbane's Ideas Festival, our session sold out fast.

The prevalence of non-monogamous arrangements is difficult to estimate, but people seem to be practising its various forms more than we might think. In a survey of 14,000 respondents on Oprah.com, conducted in 2007, twenty-one per cent said they were in some form of an 'open marriage'. And the historian Pamela Haag, who conducted an extensive study of modern marriage that she presented in her book *Marriage Confidential*, published in 2011, thinks that what she calls 'affair-tolerant' relationships are on the increase. She speculates that:

> Marital non-monogamy may be to the 21st century what premarital sex was to the 20th: a behaviour that shifts

gradually from proscribed and limited, to tolerated and increasingly common.

This suggestion makes sense especially in light of the existence of the internet, which has made it easier for people interested in swinging, polyamory, 'closed loops' (relationships where bisexual people have a straight spouse and a lover of their own gender), or other non-monogamous models, to connect.

I, too, over recent years, have found it easier to meet non-monogamous people. Once I'd given up on my wish to find the 'right' interviewees, I talked to students, engineers, psychologists, poets, disability workers, a bricklayer; and, from what I've seen, twenty-first-century non-monogamists lack the evangelism of the sexual revolution (although the occasional few, mostly the younger ones, can sound like critical theory textbooks). Most told me their stories without generalising from their experiences. But *I* have tried to make some generalisations—about what may, or may not, work in such relationships.

My impression now is that any style of non-monogamy—whether practised jointly or separately, in a group or alone, focused on love or pleasure, bound up with voyeurism or exhibitionism, open or porous—can work without destroying relationships. What matters is not the shape the relationship takes, but whether it springs from a secure base. Still, that factor alone doesn't suffice. There has to be some fit, or at least a sound compromise, between the spouses' expectations. It also helps if both can tolerate ambiguity and navigate grey areas, and be open to ongoing change.

John Bayley wrote in his memoir *Iris* that Murdoch eased his jealousy 'just by being the self she always was with me, which I knew to be wholly and entirely different from any way she was with other people'. The happiest stories I heard were from couples who cultivated their intimate space above all else, making each other feel special. For example, Catherine, an

Indigenous teacher in her early sixties who I spoke to, thought her husband wasn't jealous of her affairs because she ensured he knew he always came first for her; that he wasn't losing anything because of her other relationships. But it wasn't always that straightforward between them: for over thirty years, their love story had ebbed and flowed with as much heartbreak as passion. Only in the last decade had Catherine and her husband settled down together, still freely but more peacefully.

In fact, in most narratives I heard, exhilaration and heartache were inseparable. But then, what relationship is not complicated? It seems to me that both non-monogamous and monogamous happiness are possible but hard to come by. Yet, happiness in non-monogamy might even feel more vital because—as Anne, and Nin and Rimbaud have all suggested—once you break rules in love, you're more likely to live adventurously in other areas of your life too. The questioning of the 'truths' of modern intimacy can be illuminating in thinking generally about how to live on better, richer terms.

Of course, I am not suggesting that risk and adventure enter relationships only in the shape of lovers. American psychologist Arthur Aron coined the concept of 'self-expansion' which measures the degree to which our spouses provide us with exciting experiences that expand our horizons. In Aron's view, self-expansion is the key factor in relationship happiness: the more couples venture into new territories, the happier they are. Non-monogamy can be seen as one variation on such explorations.

The popularity of internet-based flirtations among married people supports the view of some researchers and therapists that adultery is changing its shape and that modern 'cheaters' seek emotional connection as much, if not more, than they do sex. This trend, alongside current unprecedented longevity that means we can expect to spend fifty or so years with our spouses, furthers the budding debate about the distinction between sexual and emotional fidelity. It begins to make sense that some permissiveness in relationships can actually invigorate and preserve, rather than end, them.

A small but vocal minority of modern prophets—polyamorous authors Deborah Anapol and Ryam Nearing, and the authors of *Sex at Dawn* among them—goes so far as to suggest that monogamy is dying out. But I cannot (and don't want to) see polyamory, or other non-monogamous varieties, ever become the 'new monogamy'. Such a development would be at odds with the twenty-first-century zeitgeist of shifting between different ways of being, rather than following one pathway. The younger generations appear to be more at ease with ambiguity. It seems, nowadays, *multitudes* are the new black. They lurk everywhere: in the current fascination with bodily transformation through piercing, tattooing and cosmetic surgery; our increasingly patchworked work histories; our now-habitual navigation of the globe. The once academic language of hybridity has become common speak. We sample spiritual traditions, often picking and choosing from them to create our own belief systems. Our cooking scans the globe, sometimes fusing several cuisines in one meal. Our marriages scan the globe too and some of us— due to our mixed origins or migrations—embody several cultures, each with its own internal paradoxes and multitudes. Sociologist Harvie Ferguson calls this mode of living 'ontological playfulness', arguing this is one of the dominant moods of our era. So, it is possible we're becoming more playful in love too.

'We're currently NPNM,' Emilie, a lanky blonde of twenty-five, told me. We were sitting, among chickens and tomato plants, in the backyard of the house she shared with friends. I knew she wouldn't be here for long: she and Deborah, her partner, were in the process of buying a house together. Their next plan, once Emilie completed her law degree, was to have children.

Always baffled by English acronyms, I stared blankly at Emilie. 'Non-Practicing-Non-Monogamists.' She smiled at the pomposity of an expression I'd never heard of, but that her generation apparently had. 'The non-monogamous aspect of our relationship is sometimes more, and sometimes less, important. We have phases when we don't sleep with anyone else and sometimes I feel really relieved then, because nothing is complicating our life. But non-monogamy is really good sexually: you don't fall into routine. When I sleep with someone else, I actually want to sleep with Deborah more. It's not perfect, but I think it's better to live like that.'

The elasticity of their relationship makes sense to me. If we are moving towards a choice around fidelity, then it is only natural that some couples will continue to shuffle back and forth between monogamy and its alternatives, to nut out what works best, or to match shifting needs. After all, while for some, monogamy or non-monogamy are natural modes, our needs can also change throughout our lifespans. Love and desire are already elastic on so many counts. On my last visit to New York, to introduce Daryl to my parents, I saw my father pat my mother's shoulder, saw him snatch her hand on the street. He still, of course, tells her to eat with her mouth closed. She still nags him to wash more often. But she showed me a red nightgown trimmed with lace she bought for Tu Be-av, the Jewish holiday of love, and I heard my father call her Olyusha, the affectionate diminutive of her name, as he did in their youth.

Oh, the elastic business of love. I'd thought, after meeting Daryl, that if I let the idea of sexual freedom go, I'd at least get a taste of that renowned monogamous peace. But, as I write these final lines, it is raining heavily outside, just as it did in the autumn, when we first met, when the rain would keep sluicing Melbourne with streaming silver. I would drive my car aimlessly, listening to all the stupid pop played on the radio and get the lyrics completely, viscerally. I would drive and drive, with the rain belting my window screen, through the flowing, glistening city I've loved from the first time I laid eyes upon it, and cry. I would return to my apartment in Footscray, from our long, long dates, when we would wander through the dark fog between cafés and bars, lingering in each place until the chairs would go up on the tables, until the tired waiters would finally ask us to leave, and cry. And cry. My face would rain like the city. I was so scared, so terribly scared then of that thing called true love that had finally descended upon me for the first time at the ripe age of thirty-four.

I am still scared.

BIBLIOGRAPHY

Many times in the text of this book, it has not been possible to attribute sources by name or to quote them at any great length. All of these sources, and also several works that implicitly inform the thinking behind this book, are acknowledged in full below. Quotations from the sources published in Russian rely on my own translations. Any imperfections or infelicities in them are my own responsibility.

Anapol, Debora M., 2012, *Polyamory in the 21st Century*, Rowman & Littlefield
Anderson, Eric, 2012, *The Monogamy Gap*, Oxford University Press
—, 2012 (May 19), 'Is cheating a rational choice?', *Huffington Post*, www.huffingtonpost.com/eric-anderson-phd/cheating_b_1528890.html
Antalffy, Niko, 2011, 'Polyamory in the media', *SCAN*, vol. 8, no. 1
Aron, Arthur, and Aron, Elaine N., 1986, *Love and the Expansion of Self*, Hemisphere
Athill, Diana, 2009, *Somewhere Towards the End*, Granta
Bair, Deirdre, 1996, *Anais Nin*, Bloomsbury
Barker, Meg, 2005, 'This is my partner, and this is my… partner's partner: constructing a polyamorous identity in a monogamous world', *Journal of Constructivist Psychology*, vol. 18, no. 1, pp. 75–88
Barker, Meg, and Langdridge, Darren, 2009, *Understanding Non-monogamies*, Routledge
—, 2010, 'Whatever happened to non-monogamies? Critical reflections on recent research and theory', *Sexualities*, vol. 13, no. 6, pp. 748–72

Bayley, John, 1998, *Iris*, Abacus

Bearup, Greg, 2011 (January 29), 'Cheating hearts', *Good Weekend*

Bennett, Jessica, 2009 (July 29), 'Only you. And you. And you.' *Newsweek*, www.newsweek.com/id/209164

Bergner, Daniel, 2009 (January 22), 'What do women want?', *The New York Times*

Bergstrand, Curtis, and Blevins Williams, Jennifer, 2000, 'Today's alternative marriage styles: the case of swingers', *Electronic Journal of Human Sexuality*, vol. 3, pp. 1–11

Black, Sierra, 2012 (January 21), 'Our successful open marriage', Salon.com

Blum, Deborah, 1998, *Sex on the Brain*, Penguin

Bonello, Kristoff, and Cross, Malcolm, 2010, 'Gay monogamy: I love you but I can't have sex with only you', *Journal of Homosexuality*, vol. 57, no. 1, pp. 117–39

Calligeros, Marissa, 2010 (January 12), 'Australian swingers resort boss plans book', *Brisbane Times*

Caplan, Jeremy, 2009 (July 27), 'Adultery 2.0', *Time*

Conor, Liz, 2011 (November 1), 'The disaster of monogamy— we should acknowledge that it rarely works', *The Age*

Conradi, Peter J., 2001, *Iris Murdoch*, W.W. Norton & Company

Dalí, Savador, 2000, *The Secret Life of Salvador Dalí*, Dial Press, translated by Haakon M Chevalier

Daum, Meghan, 2001, *My Misspent Youth*, Open City Books

De Salvo, Louise, 1999, *Adultery*, Beacon Press

Donaldson James, Susan, 2011 (December 8), 'Polyamory on rise among divorce-disgusted Americans', abcnews.go.com

Druckerman, Pamela, 2007, *Lust in Translation*, Penguin

Easton, Dossie, and Hardy, Janet W., 2009, *The Ethical Slut*, Greenery Press

Elliott, Geoff, 2007 (November 3), 'Searching for our lost libido', *The Australian*

Elton, Catherine, 2010 (May 23), 'Finding the D spot', *The Age*
Feigel, Lara, 2008 (January 13), 'The end is in sight', *Guardian*
Ferguson, H., 2009, *Self-identity and Everyday Life*, Routledge
Fernandes, Edward M., 2009 (January 23), 'The swinging paradigm: An evaluation of the marital and sexual satisfaction of swingers', *Electronic Journal of Human Sexuality*, vol.12
Figes, Kate, 2012, *Couples*, Virago
Foster, Barbara M., Foster, Michael, and Hadady, Letha, 1997, *Three in Love*, Harper One
Franck, Dan, 2002, *The Bohemians*, Phoenix, translated by Cynthia Hope Liebow
Garner, Helen, 1996, *Monkey Grip*, Penguin
Goldsmith, Andrea, 2010, *Reunion*, Fourth Estate
Gould, Terry, 1999, *The Lifestyle*, Random House
Griffin, Michelle, 2011 (April 26), 'Prime mate norm bucks animal urges', *The Age*
—, 2011 (October 3), 'Author slags off convention to cast word in a new light', *The Age*
Grossman, Yakov, and Gens, Inna (eds), 2011, *Lilya Brick— Passionate Tales*, Dekom, in Russian
Gubby, Rachel, and Halliday, Claire, 2010 (February 28), 'Secrets and lives', *The Age*
Haag, Pamela, 2011, *Marriage Confidential*, HarperCollins
Halliday, Claire, 2004 (April 25), 'A bit on the side', *The Age*
—, 2006 (October 2), 'Flirting with danger', *The Age*
—, 2009, *Do You Want Sex with This?*, Viking
—, 2010 (February 28), 'All dressed up with somewhere to go', *The Age*
Harris, Paul, 2005 (November 13), 'Forget monogamy and swinging. We're seriously polyamorous', *The Observer*
Hawkes, John, 1970, *The Blood Oranges*, New Directions Publishing Corporation
Herrera, Hayden, 1998, *Frida*, Bloomsbury

Herzog, Dagmar, 2008, *Sex in Crisis*, Basic Books
Higgins, Ean, 2011 (December 10), 'Three in marriage bed more of a good thing', *The Australian*
Hrdy, Sara Blaffer, 1999, *Mother Nature*, Pantheon Books
Jenks, Richard, 1985, 'Swinging: A test of two theories and a proposed new model', *Archives of Sexual Behaviour*, vol. 14, no. 6, pp. 517–27
—, 1998, 'Swinging: A review of the literature', *Archives of Sexual Behaviour*, vol. 27, no. 5, pp. 507–21
Kerouac, Jack, 2004, *On the Road*, Penguin Classics
Klesse, Christian, 2006, 'Polyamory and its "Others": Contesting the terms of non-monogamy', *Sexualities*, no. 9, pp. 565–83
Kureishi, Hanif, 2008, *Something to Tell You*, Faber & Faber
Lawrence, D. H., 2003, *Kangaroo*, Fredonia Books
Llewellyn Smith, Julia, 2011 (January 2), 'Unfaithfully yours', *The Age*
Mandelstam, Osip, 1928, *On Poetry*, Academia, in Russian
Marshall, Andrew G., 2011, *How Can I Ever Trust You Again?*, Bloomsbury
Mayakovsky, Vladimir, 1961, *Collected Works*, State Publisher of Literature, in Russian
McEwan, Ian, 2001, *The Comfort of Strangers*, Vintage
Millet, Catherine, 2003, *The Sexual Life of Catherine M*, Grove Press, translated by Adriana Hunter
—, 2009, *Jealousy*, Serpent's Tail, translated by Helen Stevenson
Moody, Rick, 2002, *The Ice Storm*, Back Bay Books
Munro, Ian, 2010 (February 1), 'Rockfeller "not known" on swingers party scene', *The Age*
Nabokov, Vladimir, 2002, *Lectures on Literature*, Mariner Books
Nearing, Ryam, 1992, *Loving More*, Polyfidelitous Educational
Nietzsche, Friedrich, 2008, *The Complete Works of Friedrich Nietzsche*, Gadow Press, translated by Marion Faber and Stephen Lehmann

Oppenheimer, Mark, 2011 (June 30), 'Married with infidelities', *New York Times*
Paglia, Camille, 1991, *Sexual Persona*, Vintage Books
Pallotta-Chiarolli, Maria, 2009, *Love You Two*, Random House
—, 2010, *Border Sexualities, Border Families in Schools*, Rowman & Littlefield Publishers
Parker-Pope, Tara, 2008 (October 28), 'Love, sex and the changing landscape of infidelity', *The New York Times*
—, 2010 (June 10), 'The science of a happy marriage', *The New York Times*
Perel, Esther, 2006, *Mating in Captivity*, HarperCollins
Phillips, Adam, 1996, *Monogamy*, Faber & Faber
Potter, Alicia, 1998 (October 15–22), 'Free love grows up', *The Boston Phoenix*
Powell, Julie, 2010 (April 24), 'Dish on the side', *Good Weekend*
Prose, Francine, 2002, *The Lives of the Muses*, HarperCollins
Rilke, Rainer Maria, 2008, *Letters to a Young Poet*, BN Publishing, translated by R. S.
Rimbaud, Arthur, 1966, *Complete Works, Selected Letters*, University of Chicago Press, translated by Wallace Fowlie
Roiphe, Kathy, 2009, *Uncommon Arrangements*, Virago Press
Rose, David, 2010 (June 24), 'Sex study uncovers the hidden dangers from oldest swingers in town', *The Times*
Roth Pierpont, Claudia, 2000, *Passionate Minds*, Scribe
Rubin, Roger, 2001, 'Alternative lifestyles revisited, or whatever happened to swingers, group marriages and communes?', *Journal of Family Issues*, vol. 22, no. 6, pp. 11–26
Russell, Bertrand, 1996, *The Conquest of Happiness*, Liveright
Ryan, Christopher, and Jethá, Cacilda, 2010, *Sex at Dawn*, Scribe
Schnarch, David, 2003, *Passionate Marriage*, Scribe
Schweitzer, Viktoria, 1992, *Tsvetaeva*, Farrar, Strays & Giroux
Scrimgeour, Heidi, 2009 (November 21), 'Adultery, she wrote', *Good Weekend*

Shaw, Bernard, 2006, *Man and Superman*, Echo Library
Shef, Elisabeth, 2005, 'Polyamorous women, sexual subjectivity and power', *Journal of Contemporary Ethnography*, no. 34, pp. 251–83
Sims, Karen E., and Meana, Marta, 2010, 'Why did passion wane? A qualitative study of married women's attributions for declines in sexual desire', *Journal of Sex and Marital Therapy*, no. 36, pp. 360–80
Squire, Susan, 2008, *I Don't*, Bloomsbury
Talese, Gay, 2009, *Thy Neighbor's Wife*, Harper Perennial
Tsvetayeva, Marina, 1995, *Collected Works*, Ellis Luck, in Russian
—, 2002, *Notebooks*, Zaharov, in Russian
Tyrrell, Rebecca, 2002 (May 31), 'Memoirs of a sexual predator', *The Telegraph*
Unauthored, 2008 (October 27), 'Promiscuous Poms reject monogamy', *The Age*
Unauthored, 2010 (July), 'Mayakovsky', *Biographia*, in Russian
Vernon, Polly, 2010 (March 7), 'Is anyone faithful anymore? Infidelity in the 21st century', *The Observer*
Wagner, Brooke, 2009, 'Becoming a sexual being: Overcoming constraints on female sexuality', *Sexualities*, vol. 12, no. 3, pp. 289–311
Weiner-Davis, Michele, 2001, *Sex-starved Marriage*, Simon & Schuster
Weiss, Phillip, 2008 (May 18), 'The affairs of men: The trouble with sex & marriage', *New York Magazine*
Wells, H. G., 1984, *Experiment in Autobiography*, Little Brown & Co
Whiting, Charles G., 1968 (February), 'Eluard's poems for Gala', *The French Review*, vol. 41, no. 4, pp. 505–17
Zwartz, Barney, 2010 (July 25), 'Sex: The Bible says go for it', *The Age*

ACKNOWLEDGEMENTS

First, I want to thank all those wonderful people who shared with me the unorthodox love stories included in this book—the kinds of stories that are not easily told in our culture. I am humbled by their kindness and honesty. Most have chosen, for obvious reasons, to remain anonymous—and you know who you are—but to Anne Hunter and Peter Haydon, with their permission, I extend a public thank you. I also want to thank all the other people who appear in this book, particularly 'Noah'.

This is my fourth book and the one I found the hardest to write. Moreover, I didn't even *want* to write it and, on many occasions, hoped it'd somehow go away; leave me alone. But the book persevered, hanging nearby in dark corners, shadowing me, visiting me at night-time, like an apparition. Still, in the course of the five years of writing it, there were many times I came close to giving up, and would have done so, if not for the help of some very dear people and those precious institutions that support writers.

The Katharine Susannah Prichard Writers' Centre generously gave me the residency space to begin this book and also—albeit unwittingly—the space for my transgression without which this book would have been poorer. I am grateful for the kindness of the people I met there.

Over the years, through its various fellowships, Varuna, the Writers' House, has consistently provided me with its magical environment to write, reflect and daydream. I am particularly thankful to its former director Peter Bishop, who has become a dear friend, and whose support, encouragement and book recommendations were invaluable. Throughout the entire process of writing this book, Peter kept reading my confused drafts and helping me to deepen the work. Our lengthy conversations about what I was doing would leave me dazed and exalted.

I am also grateful to the Australian Society of Authors for its assistance, through its Mentorship Program that provided me with the wise guidance of Judith Lukin-Amundsen in the later stages of the book's development. Judith saw the big picture of my work more clearly than I did and, like Peter, made me feel understood while she delivered her insights. Both Peter and Judith taught me the virtue of digression and the vice of pontification.

Where would I be without my friends and family? Leah Kaminsky, Nadine Davidoff, Bradley Dawson, Virginia Peters, Perle Besserman and Sydney Smith consistently provided me, throughout the years of writing this book, with incredible amounts of support and practical assistance. Their critical input into *The Dangerous Bride* and their ongoing belief in it were invaluable. Kate Goldsworthy read the almost final draft of this book, and her astute counsel helped me to fix some critical issues at the last moment. Nicola Shafer, Robin Hemley, Josianne Smith, Belinda Johnson, Clara Kugel, Joanna Kujawa, Karla Dondio, Linda West, and Riva and Ilya Furman gave me generous support on many occasions. Maria Tumarkin offered to put me in touch with Sally Heath from Melbourne University Press and, thanks to her, the unpublished manuscript metamorphosed into a book. Simon Klimowitsky helped with my (very personal) engagement with Russian poets, including obtaining some rare books I couldn't possibly have found myself. My mother-in-law Barbara Efron provided me with the sanctuary of her apartment so that I could hide from the world to write. My stepson Gene Efron, too, deserves a big thank you for so graciously putting up with all my distracted moods during that time. And, of course, I thank my parents profusely for being so wonderful at tolerating my writing, which consistently includes the kind of stories parents don't want to hear about their children, and in which they often feature.

At MUP, I had the privilege of working with Sally Heath—the best editor one could wish for. I am thankful to her for believing in my book and for sharing my vision for it. I have felt supported by Sally, and her sensitive and wise guidance has greatly benefited this book. Sarina Rowell, the copyeditor, performed pure magic with words; her careful and insightful work made this book so much better. I am also deeply grateful to Cathy Smith, editorial project manager, and Terri Anne King, the marketing and publicity manager, for their wonderful encouragement and responsiveness.

Finally, I thank Daryl—my husband, the father of my baby, the love of my life—for eventually understanding my need to write this book, and for letting me be the kind of writer I want to be—someone who ventures into uncomfortable spaces. I feel blessed to have met you.